THE PRESIDENTS

★ ★ ★ ★

THE PRESIDENTS

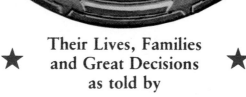

Their Lives, Families
★ and Great Decisions ★
as told by

THE SATURDAY EVENING POST

THE CURTIS PUBLISHING COMPANY ★ INDIANAPOLIS, INDIANA

THE CURTIS PUBLISHING COMPANY

The Presidents

President, The Curtis Book Division: Jack Merritt
Managing Editor: Jacquelyn S. Sibert
Assistant Editor: Cathy L. Bergner
Senior Designer: Jinny Sauer Hoffman
Art Editor and Designer: Caroline M. Capehart
Design and Production: Pamela G. Starkey
Technical Director: Greg Vanzo
Copy Staff: Jean White, Melinda Dunlevy, Jenine Howard
Production Staff: Patricia Stricker, Paula Matlock, Kathy Simpson

★ ★ ★ ★ ★

Contents

★ ★ ★ ★ ★

the **POST**
s **Proud**
o **Announce**

During the coming years former
esident Dwight D. Eisenhower plans
write occasional magazine articles
topics of national interest.

ese articles will be published in
e *Saturday Evening Post*.

General Eisenhower's first article, tit
w That I Am a Private Citizen
l appear in next week's *Post*.

s a warmly human, readable
ument in which the ex-President

THE SATURD.
EVENING PO

An Illustra   Magazine
Founded A   aj. Frankli

CTOBER 31, 1908   5cts THE COPY

WHICH?

HE CURTIS PUBLISHING COMPANY, PHILADELPHIA

A "POWWOW" AT THE WHITE HOUSE.—FROM A SKETCH BY W. M. ROURKE.—[SEE PAGE 55.]

July 10, 1776

The PENNSYLVANIA GAZETTE

Containing the Freßeß Ad-   vices, *Foreign and Domeßic.*

Photos courtesy Library of Congress, Ollie Atkins, the Estate of Homer E. Capehart, the *Post*.

★ ★ ★ ★ ★

Introduction

★ ★ ★ ★ ★

Though he might have been called "His Highness, the President of the United States of America and the Protector of the same," we call him simply "Mr. President." But the men who have held this title were not simple men. The office of President of the United States is the most powerful, dignified and demanding political position in the world, and so must be the man who fills the position.

"Unlike Congress," Albert Atwood said of the office of the presidency in the June 3, 1933, *Post*, "he is always in session. His is the incalculable strain of both ultimate leadership and final responsibility. He has no alibi. When all the experts and advisers have gone, he must fall back upon his own wisdom."

The public opinion of the men who have "fallen back upon their own wisdom" and made the final decisions is largely influenced by what is printed about them. *The Saturday Evening Post*, known as the *Pennsylvania Gazette* in 1729, has, since its conception, printed their stories— their hopes, fears, frustrations and victories.

Benjamin Franklin's *Gazette* was not quite 50 years old when the Declaration of Independence was printed on the front page. This, the first concrete sign of a free American government, set the stage for over 200 years of history-writing by the free exchange of ideas.

So, in keeping with tradition it occurred to the present-day editors to go a step farther and sort through the myriad of articles which have appeared in the *Post* during that time and to assemble them in some logical order so as to comprise a lasting treasury—*The Saturday Evening Post*'s tribute to the presidents.

Since the vast reserves of *The Saturday Evening Post* archives safely house nearly every page of the *Post*, from the yellowing parchment of Franklin's *Gazette* to the crisp, white pages of today's *Post*, and since the presidential campaign—that quadrennial event described by the *Post* in 1840 as "the business of President-making"—is just around the corner, now seems a fitting time for the task.

And what better place to start than where the candidates did . . . with the election campaigns. Early trips to the archives revealed some uniquely American campaign techniques: Buchanan and Harding held "front-porch" campaigns, Truman conducted the "whistle-stop" campaign and one man, Gerald Ford, became both a vice-president and a president without even conducting a campaign.

Further research found the *Post*, a weekly newspaper at the time, describing itself at the close of the 1840 presidential campaign (when William Henry Harrison was

Warren Gamaliel Harding.

Library of Congress

William Howard Taft.

elected) as "a neutral paper," "glad the matter is settled" and "relieved" that its public journalists could once again "pursue a quiet life." It went on to characterize campaigns in general as "keeping the whole community in a tumult for at least three out of every four years," saying they "tear the business interests of the country to pieces, invade all the courtesies and honest charities of life, render men suspicious of their best friends and rouse the very worst of passions."

Conversely, Samuel Blythe, following the 1912 election of Woodrow Wilson, saw the chaos created by presidential campaigns as purely temporary, culminating in a nationally unifying experience. Said Blythe: "The great bulk of American citizens, no matter how widely they may have been separated in a presidential campaign, get together after the result is known and stand ready to support the winner."

But the articles and editorials which have appeared in the *Post* through the years were not always written from an author's or editor's point of view. Many were written for the *Post* by the presidents themselves. In fact, every man who has been president since Benjamin Harrison, excluding Warren G. Harding, has written for the *Post* at some time or other. Grover Cleveland authored a record 18 *Post* articles between the years 1901 and 1906. Eisenhower and Hoover were close behind with 14 and 11, respectively.

Even "Silent Cal" (as Coolidge was known) managed to contribute five articles to the *Post*, despite reports immediately following his nomination which spoke of "a considerable determination on his part to say nothing." (The articles were, incidentally, submitted after his term of office had been completed.) Franklin Roosevelt, Wilson and Nixon each contributed four; John F. Kennedy, Lyndon Johnson and Teddy Roosevelt, two; and Benjamin Harrison, McKinley, Truman, Ford and Car-

(Below, l to r) Post *covers commemorate John F. Kennedy, Grover Cleveland, and Ben Franklin, founder of the* Pennsylvania Gazette, *forerunner to the* Post.

From Post covers: Teddy Roosevelt (above), Jerry Ford and LBJ (right).

ter one each—the latter carrying to the present day the tradition which was started by former President Benjamin Harrison in 1898.

Ollie Atkins wrote in the Fall, 1972, *Post* that " . . . all men are different, just as all presidents are men." As varied as the men who wrote them, these articles by the presidents deal with topics ranging from the role of the Vice-President, the subject of articles by both Franklin Roosevelt and Richard Nixon, and World War I food drafts by Herbert Hoover, to women's suffrage by Taft and the question of taxes by Coolidge, to fishing pointers from Grover Cleveland.

A sampling of each has been reprinted here in the same style in which they appeared in the *Post*. For this reason, some spelling and punctuation may appear inconsistent within a given president's chapter. One good example is James Madison's father, John Maddison. The spelling of the last name, as happened with many names, was shortened after a time, but John Maddison retained the old spelling.

The photographs and paintings which are reproduced throughout the book were taken, again, from the pages of *The Saturday Evening Post*. Many, however, were acquired through a fast trip to Washington, D.C. and a mad dash through the vast photo resources of the Library of Congress; and still others, through extensive correspondence with numerous cooperative and effi-

cient presidential libraries, federal government agencies and memorial sites.

The articles published by the *Post* which were written about a president by an author or editor are also plentiful and varied. Reprinted here as they appeared in the *Post*, they are written by the likes of Stewart Alsop and Samuel Blythe, *Post* editors based in Washington, D.C.; Irwin H. (Ike) Hoover, White House usher under nine presidents; and Henry Watterson, 19th-century U.S. journalist and newspaper editor. Some serve to entertain the reader with personal anecdotes, others, to inform or provoke thought. All concern the men who have called the White House home.

After the campaign, it matters not who the candidates were nor what the year. It matters only who has won, as the winner is President, and, as a quote from a 1931 *Post* states, "It is the President, and the President alone who speaks for the nation, and speak he must if the nation is to be served." Herein they speak.

George Washington

★ ★ ★ ★ ★

1st President of the United States

Born: February 22, 1732, Westmoreland County,
  Virginia.
Occupation: Planter, soldier.
Wife: Martha Custis. *Children:* Two step, two
  adopted.
President: 1789-1797. Federalist.
Vice-President: John Adams.
Died: December 14, 1799. *Buried:* Mount Vernon,
  Virginia.

★ ★ ★ ★ ★

George Washington is known as "the Father of His Country." He was our first president and as such set the tone of the office.

The Saturday Evening Post in 1931 published this remark on the problems involved in addressing the first President of the United States:

> The very name by which George Washington should be addressed incited bitter dispute. "His Highness, the President of the United States of America and the Protector of the same" was selected by a Senate committee, but since the House committee refused to consent to this title, reminiscent of the mother country, "Mr. President" was established once and for all as the correct form.

Washington's love for the out-of-doors as a child led him to become a surveyor as a young man and also accounts for his excellent horsemanship.

In 1775, the American Revolution began, and Washington was named Commander-in-Chief of the American Army.

Today it is thought that he was a good general but not a great one. He lost many battles, but he was always able to keep an army in the field. In spite of the many hardships—hunger, cold, lack of money for guns and ammunition—George Washington was able to inspire his men, and they felt that because he was leading them, they could not lose.

After the war was over, it soon became evident that the newly formed states could not survive as independent entities. Men from the various states met and drew up a plan for governing. The plan was the Constitution of the United States which called for a strong central government and a president to represent all the people.

Washington is inaugurated as first President of the United States in 1789 at the Old City Hall in New York, the nation's first capitol.

George Gibbs' February 14, 1902, Post cover depicts George Washington and his Cabinet (an "official council" selected by the President)—Thomas Jefferson (Secretary of State), Edmund Randolph (Attorney General), Alexander Hamilton (Secretary of Treasury) and Henry Knox (Secretary of War).

Washington was elected to this office. He picked a cabinet of qualified men, and he weighed all his decisions carefully. He knew that to be strong, a government must be able to enforce the laws, and at one time he sent troops into Pennsylvania to stop a rebellion.

Washington served two terms as president. He was asked to serve a third, but refused, believing that two terms was as long as any one person should serve as president. This decision—to serve only two terms—set a precedent for successive presidents that was not broken until 1940, when Franklin D. Roosevelt was elected for a third term.

1732—George Washington—1932

Six years ago a forehanded Congress, by joint resolution, set up a commission charged with the fitting celebration of the two-hundredth anniversary of the birth of George Washington, which will fall on the twenty-second of February, 1932.

This body has not been idle. It was given a big job,

and it has undertaken it in a big way. It has supplemented its own ideas with the advice and assistance of many experts. It has canvassed every practicality, from the participation of school children to the completion of ambitious public works designed as enduring memorials of the character and services of the Father of His Country.

The success of the commission's undertaking is, to a certain degree, already assured, but if its largest possibilities are to be realized, it must have the cooperation of every state, town and village, of all public institutions, of churches, universities, schools, women's clubs and social organizations throughout the land.

The commission will endeavor, through the daily press, the movies, radio broadcasting and other channels of nation-wide publicity, to keep the public informed as to its activities. In the meantime, the executive offices of the Commission for the Celebration of the Two Hundredth Anniversary of the Birth of George Washington, in the Washington Building, Washington, D.C., may be addressed by those who desire its literature or seek information more specific and extended than that found in its printed matter. The sympathetic collaboration of the commission may be counted upon by those who are trying to further its aims. One of its brochures contains patriotic and historical societies, for churches, women's clubs and mercantile houses. Other plans involve making all the national holidays which will occur in 1932 contributory to the importance of the Bicentenary Celebration.

Congress has already appropriated fifty thousand dollars for the rehabilitation of Washington's birthplace, in Virginia. Another Federal project now under way is the construction of the boulevard from our first President's home at Mt. Vernon to Washington, twelve miles away. Provision has already been made for the preservation, as a parkway, of a strip of charming country stretching from Mt. Vernon to the capital city. The United States Mint will strike off a commemorative medal. A definitive edition of Washington's writings is in preparation, and a dozen other appropriate undertakings will round out the list.

History affords no more satisfying national hero than George Washington. The more his life and achievements are studied, the more apparent become the many-sided nature of his genius and the spaciousness of his character. These hard and trying times are meet for such studies. A people habituated to living on the fat of the world, we are feeling the pinch of poverty. We are passing through the doldrums of stagnant business, accentuated by unemployment and

A photograph of George Washington commanding the untrained Continental Army might contrast sharply with J.C. Leyendecker's romantic representation of Washington, the General, above.

agricultural depression. In addition to the hardship everywhere apparent about us is the invisible toll that has been exacted from us in worry, apprehension and impairment of our personal well-being. Our nervous reaction, if we are to believe some of the specialists, is more grave and more widespread than that which we experienced in 1893.

In such dour circumstances Washington would have shown the temper of his steel. His biographers are agreed that he was never more truly at his best than in situations which were seemingly hopeless. Whether in the wilderness or on the battlefield, in the council chamber or in the halls of Congress, whether in jeopardy of armed foe or of treacherous colleagues, the more overwhelming the odds against him, the higher rose his courage, the more inflexible became his will, the more complete became his mastery over himself and those about him. Adversity only stiffened his resolution. Danger only increased his coolness or heightened his resourcefulness, and the joy of battle gave strength and steadiness to his performance.

His whole career bristles with examples of his personal courage, his contempt of danger and hardship, and his unacquaintance with fear. If at Yorktown he was the beau ideal of the military hero, at Valley Forge he was the demigod.

A substantial blessing, easily acquired, is a fuller and more intimate acquaintance with the character of Washington. Neither young nor old can acquire this knowledge, with alert and imaginative minds, without thereby becoming wiser and better. There is no reason why such studies should be deferred for another year.

—reprinted from the June 20, 1931, issue
of The Saturday Evening Post.

General Washington's Appointment

The following account of the appointment of General Washington to the supreme command of the continental army, June 16th, 1775, is an extract from a private journal, narrating a conversation with John Adams, Senior. *Lest we should, in any way, affect the anecdote, we give it in the very words of the narrator.—Eds. Post. [12/4/1841]*

The army was assembled at Cambridge, Mass. under General Ward, and Congress was sitting at Philadelphia. The country were urgent that Congress should legalize the raising of the army; for until they had, it was in a law considered to be only a mob, a mere band of armed rebels and untrained riffraff.

The great trial now seemed to be in this question,—Who should be Commander in Chief? The Southern and Middle States, were jealous of New England, because they felt that the real physical force was here. All New England adored Gen. Ward; he had been in the French war; and went out laden with laurels. Every qualification seemed to cluster in him; and it was confidently believed that the army could not

consider or receive any Commander over him.

What, then, was to be done? Without union all was lost. The country and the whole country must come in. One pulsation must beat through all hearts. The cause was one and the arm must be one. The members had talked, debated, considered, and guessed, and yet the decisive step had not been taken At length Mr. Adams came to his

Valley Forge

Invitation to the White House

As First Lady, Mrs. Washington entertained once a week. Washington recorded in his diary the response to his wife's hospitality. "The Levee [reception] today was thin," he wrote, but speaks of bad weather as a probable reason. "The visiters this evening to Mrs. Washington were respectable, both of gentlemen and ladies." But the phrase which expressed, from his standpoint, the most satisfactory entertainment was: "The visiters this evening were numerous and respectable."

He also listed their various guests; one entry shows how the social power of the President has increased: "The following Gentlemen and Ladies dined here today—the Secretary of State and his Lady, General Schuyler and Mrs. Izard were also invited, but were otherwise engaged."

One wonders if he would not have been surprised could he have foreseen that eventually an invitation from the President would be regarded not as a request but as a command.

—an excerpt from a January 3, 1931,
Post *article by Maude Parker.*

conclusion: He was walking one morning before Congress Hall, apparently in deep thought, when his cousin Samuel Adams came up to him and said, "What is the topic with you this morning?"

"Oh the army, the army," he replied, "I am determined what to do about the army at Cambridge, I am determined to go into the hall this morning, and enter on a full detail of the state of the Colonies, in order to show the absolute need of taking some decisive steps. My whole aim will be to induce Congress to appoint a day for adopting the army as the legal army of these United Colonies of North America; and then to hint at my election of a Commander-in-Chief."

"Well," said Samuel Adams, "I like that, cousin John, but on whom have you fixed as this Commander?"

"I will tell you—George Washington, of Virginia, a member of this House."

"Oh," replied Samuel Adams quickly, "that will never do, never, never."

"It must do, it shall do," said John, "and for these reasons; the Southern and Middle States are both to enter heartily into the cause, and their arguments are potent; they see that New England holds the physical power in her hands, and they fear the result. A New England army, a New England Commander, with New England perseverance all united, appal them. For this cause they hang back. Now, the only course is, to allay their fears, and give them nothing to complain of; and this can be done in no other way but by appointing a

Washington married Martha Custis (above), a widow, in 1759. General Lafayette (right), visiting his close friend, Washington, at Mount Vernon, holds a copy of Franklin's Pennsylvania Gazette, *forerunner to the* Post.

After two terms as president, Washington retired to Mount Vernon where he spent much of his time on horseback, supervising his many properties.

"The New Tavern Sign" (above) by Norman Rockwell, appeared as a story illustration in the February 22, 1936, issue of the Post.

Southern Chief over this force; then all will feel secure, then all will rush to the standard. This policy will blend us in one mass, and that mass will be resistless."

At this, Samuel Adams seemed greatly moved. They talked over the preliminary circumstances, and John asked his cousin to second his motion. Mr. Adams went in, took the floor and put forth all his strength in the delineations he had prepared, all aiming at the adoption of the army. He was ready to own the army, appoint a Commander, vote supplies, and proceed to business. After his speech had been finished, some doubted, some objected, and some feared. His warmth increased with the occasion, and to all these doubts he replied,

"Gentlemen, if this Congress will not adopt this army before ten moons have set, New England will adopt it, and she, she will undertake the struggle alone—yes, with a strong arm and a clear conscience she will front the foe single-handed."

This had the desired effect. They saw New England was neither playing nor to be played with; they agreed to appoint a day—the day was fixed. It came, Mr. Adams went in, took the floor, urged the measure, and after debate it passed.

The next thing was to get a Commander for this army, with supplies, &c. All looked to Mr. Adams on this occasion; and he was ready. He took the floor, and went into a minute delineation of the character of General Ward, bestowing upon him the epithets which, then, belonged to no one else. At the end of this eulogy, he said, "but this is not the man I have chosen." He then went into a delineation of the character of a Commander-in-Chief, such as was required by the peculiar situation of the Colonies at that juncture. And after he had presented the qualification in his strongest language,

and given the reasons for the nominations he was about to make, he said—

"Gentlemen, I know these qualifications are high, but we all know they are needful at this crisis, in this Chief, does any one say they are not to be obtained in the country? I reply, they are, they reside in one of our own body, and he is the person whom I now nominate, GEORGE WASHINGTON OF VIRGINIA."

Washington, who sat on Mr. Adams' right hand, was looking him intently in the face, to watch the name he was about to announce; and not expecting it would be his own, he sprung from his seat the moment he heard it, and rushed into an adjoining room. Mr. Adams had asked his cousin Samuel to move for an adjournment as soon as the nomination was made, to give the members time to deliberate, and the result is before the world.

I asked Mr. Adams, among other questions, the following:

"Did you never doubt of the success of the conflict?"

"No, no," said he, "not for a moment, I expected to be hung and quartered, if I was caught; but no matter for that, my country would be free; I knew George the III could not forge chains long enough and strong enough to reach around these States."

John Adams

★ ★ ★ ★ ★

2nd President of the United States

Born: October 30, 1735, Quincy, Massachusetts.
Occupation: Lawyer, diplomat.
Wife: Abigail Smith. *Children:* Three boys, two girls.
President: 1797-1801. Federalist party.
Vice-President: Thomas Jefferson.
Died: July 4, 1826.
Buried: Quincy, Massachusetts.

★ ★ ★ ★ ★

Our second president, John Adams, was an honest, forthright, outspoken man. He attended Harvard College, studied law, and became interested in the independence movement. He was a delegate to the Continental Congress in 1774 and the man responsible for appointing Washington Commander-in-Chief of the Army. It was Adams who insisted that Thomas Jefferson write the draft for the Declaration of Independence and then fought the hardest to get it accepted.

After the war, he became the first minister to Great Britain and was later elected Vice-President of the United States to serve with President Washington. After Washington's two terms, Adams was elected president by a slim margin. He and Alexander Hamilton were members of the same party, but with differing viewpoints, and Adams did not compromise with Hamilton. France and England were at war, and Hamilton wanted to side with England. Adams, however, through negotiation, was able to keep the United States out of this war. Keeping the peace cost him reelection.

The Adams family was the first presidential family to live in Washington, D.C. On his second night in the President's House, John Adams wrote:

"I pray Heaven to bestow the best Blessings on this House and all that shall hereafter inhabit it. May none but honest and wise Men ever rule beneath this roof." These words can be seen on a mantel in the White House today.

John Adams died on July 4, 1826, the same day as Thomas Jefferson. The following comment on the significance of this coincidence appeared in the July 8, 1826, issue of the *Post:*

> A gentleman arrived from the Eastward, last evening, informs, that the venerable JOHN ADAMS, died at his seat at Quincy, near Boston, on the fourth of July, about five o'clock, P.M. but a few hours after the sage of Monticello!—United in the grand political concerns of life, thus in death they are not divided!

The last words of John Adams were said to have been, "Thomas Jefferson still survives . . ." not knowing that Jefferson had preceded him in death by a few hours.

A group of students at College Hill University of the District of Columbia drew up the following resolution upon the death of the John Adams:

> Having, but a few days ago, clothed ourselves in mourning, our sorrow is already accumulated by the announcement of the death of John Adams, the second President of the United States. Jefferson is gone! Another advocate of our Independence—another of Liberty's apostles—another of the surviving and immortal three—resigned his breath on the same glorious day, and stood in the presence of his Maker! John Adams is gone! A member of the first Congress, of '74—the supporter of the motion to "declare our Independence," in '76—the first Vice President of the Union, in '89—and the successor of Washington, in '96, in every station, displaying superior talents and virtue—he has, at length, bowed, full of honors, to that destiny which awaits, without distinction, all mortality.

—*July 15, 1826*, Post.

At first, Samuel Adams protested his cousin John's plan to make Washington Commander-in-Chief of the Continental Army, saying, "That will never do." Below, John Adams seconds the motion that did do. At right, Washington and John Adams, later elected his vice-president.

My Dear Sir . . .

John and Abigail (right), wed in 1764, began a family line that has reached into the present century, with each generation as distinguished as the last.

The friendship between ex-Presidents John Adams and Thomas Jefferson is one of the most interesting in our history. These two brilliant men had been friends in their younger days. The 33-year-old Jefferson, chairman of the committee to prepare a Declaration of Independence, urged Adams, seven years older than himself, to draft the document. Adams insisted that his friend Jefferson was better qualified. "You can write ten times better than I can," declared Adams. And so, in Philadelphia's summer heat, Jefferson sat down to compose the immortal document.

The two remained good friends throughout their diplomatic missions abroad during the 1780's, and in the early days of President Washington's administration, when Adams was Vice-President and Jefferson Secretary of State.

Then a sad estrangement began to develop between them. This was less the fault of the two prinicpals than of their partisan followers and of gossips who magnified casual words of irritation into vicious slanders. Thus two great men, so alike in devotion to country, became cold and hostile toward each other.

The estrangement lasted through the Presidency of Adams (1797-1801) and of Jefferson (1801-1809). It con-

tinued after they had retired from public life, Adams to Quincy, and Jefferson to Monticello in Virginia. Friends joined in trying to clear up the misunderstandings. To one of these friends, in 1811, Adams exclaimed, "I always loved Jefferson, and still love him."

When word of this reached Jefferson, he wrote to Doctor Rush, "This is enough for me. I only needed this knowledge to revive toward him (Adams) all the affections of the most cordial moments of our lives."

Then was the friendship resumed. It was refreshed, during the remainder of their lives, by a wise, lively and affectionate correspondence.

The letters of these two ex-Presidents, fortunately preserved, are still, to quote Daniel Webster, such as to "excite the thoughts of men." Once reconciled, Adams and Jefferson wrote to each other without reserve. They discussed not only government and politics but also the daily concerns of us all: health, children, education, exercise, reading, the problems of old age, life, death and the hereafter.

*—taken from a May 6, 1961,
Post article by Beverly Smith, Jr.*

The following letters were published by the Post *in 1822, by permission of the authors:*

From Mr. Jefferson to Mr. Adams

Monticello, June 1, 1822

It is very long, my dear sir, since I have written to you. My dislocated wrist is now so stiff that I write slowly and with pain; and therefore write as little as I can. Yet it is due to mutual friendship to ask once in a while how we do. The papers tell us that General Starke is off at the age of ninety-three.

*   *   *   *   *   *   *

When all our faculties have left or are leaving us one by one, sight, hearing, memory, every avenue of pleasing sensation is closed, the athymy, debility, and malaise left in their places; when the friends of youth are all gone, and a generation is risen around us whom we know not, is death an evil?

> *When one by one our ties are torn,*
> *And friend and friend is snatched forlorn;*
> *When man is left to mouth,*
>   *Oh, then, how sweet it is to die!*
>
> *When trembling limbs refuse their weight,*
> *And films slow gathering dim the sight;*
> *When clouds obscure the mental light,*
>   *'Tis nature's kindest boon to die;*

I really think so. I have ever dreaded a doting old age, and my health has been generally so good, and is now

Library of Congress

"I will give you Independence Forever!" was the toast Adams had prepared for the 50th anniversary of American Independence. He did not live to utter it.

so good, that I dread it still. The rapid decline of my strength during the winter has made me hope sometimes that I see land. During summer, I enjoy its temperature, but I shudder at the approach of winter, and wish I could sleep through it with the dormouse, and only wake with him in the spring, if ever.—They say that Starke could walk about his room. I am told you walk well and firmly. I can only reach my garden, and that with sensible fatigue. I ride, however, daily; but reading is my delight. I should wish never to put pen to paper; and the more because of the treacherous practice some people have of publishing one's letters without leave. Lord Mansfield declared it a breach of trust, and punishable at law. I think it should be a penitentiary felony; yet you will have seen they have drawn me out into the arena of the newspapers. Although I know it is too late for me to buckle on the armor of youth, yet my indignation would not permit me passively to receive the kick of an ass.

Order in the Court

Being the first President of the United States presented problems, but being the first Vice-President also had its complications.

Around two o'clock during a Senate meeting, the words "levee" [reception] and "adjourn" were repeated from sundry quarters of the House. "Adjourn?" Adams had inquired incredulously. "Here are the most important bills before us, and yet we shall throw all by for empty ceremony, for attending the levee is little more. Indeed, from these small beginnings I fear we shall follow on, nor cease till we have reached the summit of court etiquette, and all the frivolities, fopperies and expenses practiced in European governments . . . ."

—*an excerpt from a January 3, 1931,*
Post *article written by Maude Parker.*

To turn to the news of the day, it seems that the cannibals of Europe are going to eating one another again. A war between Russia and Turkey is like the battle of the kite and the snake; whichever destroys the other leaves a destroyer the less for the world. This pugnacious humor of mankind seems to be the law of his nature, one of the obstacles to too great multiplication provided in the mechanism of the Universe. The cocks of the hen yard kill one another; bears, bulls, rams do the same, and the horse, in his wild state, kills all the young males until when he's worn down with age and war, some youth kills him.

I hope we shall prove how much happier for the man the Quaker policy is; that the life of the feeder is better than that of the fighter: and it is consolation that the desolation by these maniacs of one part of the earth is the means of improving it in other parts. Let the latter be our office; let us milk the cow, while the Russian holds her by the horns, and the Turk by the tail.

God bless you and give you health, strength, good spirits, and as much life as you think worth having.

Thos. Jefferson

Mr. Adams' Reply

Monticello, June 11, 1822

Dear Sir—Half an hour ago I received, and have heard read for the third or fourth time, the best letter that was ever written by an octogenarian, dated June 1st.

* * * * * * *

I have not sprained a wrist; but both my arms and hands are so overstrained that I cannot write a line. Poor Starke remembered nothing and could talk of nothing but the battle of Bennington. ***is not quite so. I cannot mount my horse, but I can walk three miles over a rugged mountain, and have done it within a month, yet I feel, when sitting in my chair, as if I could not rise out of it; and when risen, as if I could not walk across the room; my sight is very dim, hearing pretty good, memory poor enough.

I answer your question—is death an evil? It is not an evil. It is a blessing to the individual, and to the world, yet we ought not to wish for it till life becomes insupportable. We must wait the pleasure and convenience of the "Great Teacher." Winter is as terrible to me as to you. I am almost reduced in it to the life of a bear or a torpid swallow—I cannot read, but my delight is to hear others read; and I tax all my friends almost unmercifully and tyrannically against their consent.

The ass has kicked in vain; all men say the dull animal has missed the mark.

This globe is a theater of war; its inhabitants are all heroes. The little eels in vinegar, and the animalcules in pepper water, I believe are quarrelsome. The bees are as warlike as the Romans, Russians, Britons, or Frenchmen. Ants, caterpillars, and cankerworms are the only tribes among whom I have not seen battles; and heaven itself, if we believe Hindoos, Jews, Christians and Mahometans, has not always been at peace. We need not trouble ourselves because of evildoers; but safely trust the "Ruler with his skies."

* * * * *

In wishing for your health and happiness, I am very selfish; for I hope for more letters; this is worth more than five hundred dollars to me, for it has already given me, and it will continue to give me, more pleasure than a thousand. Mr. Jay, who is about your age, I am told experiences more decay than you do.

I am your old friend.

John Adams

John Adams was born in the salt-box at right, built between 1675 and 1681; John Quincy was born in the house next door. Abigail Adams, below, was the only woman to be wife of one president, mother of another.

Thomas Jefferson

⭐ ⭐ ⭐ ⭐ ⭐

3rd President of the United States

Born: April 13, 1743, Shadwell, Virginia.
Occupation: Lawyer, farmer.
Wife: Martha Skelton. *Children:* One boy, five girls.
President: 1801-1809. Democratic-Republican party.
Vice-Presidents: Aaron Burr and George Clinton.
Died: July 4, 1826. *Buried:* Monticello, Virginia.

⭐ ⭐ ⭐ ⭐ ⭐

Thomas Jefferson was born in Virginia while it was still frontier country. His parents were well-to-do, and Jefferson was educated at William and Mary College.

He had a brilliant mind—he was an architect, an inventor and a musician.

> Like Leonardo da Vinci and Benjamin Franklin, he was amazingly many-sided, in a fashion which an age of specialization has outmoded. He was the greatest American architect of his time; a follower in the footsteps of the great Italian architectural stylist, Palladio. He was diplomat, statesman, writer, social revolutionist, scientist, musician, paleontologist, inventor, cartographer, educator, collector and farmer. It was impossible for him to look at a thing without wanting to improve it, to make it more convenient, to increase the variety of uses to which it could be put. If nothing had been invented up to that time to serve his purpose, he drew plans and supervised craftsmen while they made the contrivances he wanted.
> —*an ercerpt from an April 13, 1946,* Post *article written by Pete Martin.*

When John F. Kennedy was president and entertaining a group of 49 Nobel Prize winners, he told the guests, "I think this is the most extraordinary collection of talent and human knowledge that has ever been gathered at the White House, with the possible exception of when Thomas Jefferson dined alone."

Jefferson's political life lasted many years. He was only 26 when elected to the Virginia Legislature. Later he was governor of the state, Minister to France and Secretary of State under President Washington. He was not a good public speaker, and for this reason he wrote articles and letters instead of making speeches. This experience stood him in good stead for when he was named

Jefferson's concern with education led him to establish the University of Virginia in 1819, plan its curriculum and serve as its first president. His memorial at the University (above) displays his columned portico design.

The Howard Pyle Collection, Delaware Art Museum

to write the Declaration of Independence.

Historians rank Jefferson as a "great" or "near-great" president. He declared that all men are created equal, and he believed in religious liberty, that the people should govern themselves and in free schools. He was the first to advocate that all young people "whom nature hath endowed with genius and virtue" should be educated according to their talents "without regard to wealth, birth or other accidental condition."

During his administration, political parties were formed. Jefferson's party was called the Republican party, and the other party was known as the Federalist party. The Republican party of this period later became known as the Democratic party. Jefferson believed that a president had no powers except those put down in the Constitution. However, when he was offered the chance to buy the Louisiana Territory from France, he did so and asked Congress for permission afterwards. This treaty in 1803 more than doubled the size of the nation.

President Jefferson served two terms as president, turning down the chance to run again as he believed no president should serve more than two terms. He returned to his home, called Monticello, where he planned and helped build the University of Virginia. To John Adams he wrote: "I am mounted on a hobby, which indeed I could have better managed some thirty or forty years ago, but whose easy amble is sufficient to give exercise to an octogenarian rider. This is the establishment of a University." He drew the architectural plans for the buildings, selected the faculty and planned the curriculum.

On July 4, 1826, he died on the same day as John Adams, and exactly 50 years after he had written the Declaration of Independence. The death notices of the

The Declaration of Independence appeared in print for the first time in Franklin's Pennsylvania Gazette. The painting above, showing Jefferson deliberating over the Declaration, is by Howard Pyle, initiator of the Golden Age of American illustration which inspired Rockwell and others.

two friends appeared side-by-side in the July 8, 1826, issue of the *Post*. Jefferson's read:

> The venerable patriarch and sage, the immortal author of the Declaration of Independence, THOMAS JEFFERSON, Esq. expired at his seat, at Monticello, *on the fourth of July*, at ten minutes before one o'clock, just fifty years since the promulgation, in the Halls of Congress, of the Liberties of this country. His death had been looked for two or three days before it took place, as he was confined to his bed during that time by severe indisposition. He was sensible of his approaching dissolution, and prescribed the mode of his interment. Well might he have exclaimed in the language of the psalmist, "Lord, now lettest thou thy servant depart in peace, according to thy word, for my eyes have seen thy salvation." Mr. Jefferson had just reached the advanced age of eighty-three years, three months and two days, being born on the 2d of April, 1743. The flags of the shipping in the Delaware, were hoisted at half mast, and the bells of the different churches were muffled, in testimony of respect for the departed patriot.

Monticello, Jefferson's home for 56 years, is visited by thousands of people every year. It is a 35-room, red brick mansion with white pillars which sits on top of a mountain overlooking the university. As one visitor put it, "You wouldn't be surprised if he walked out of one of those doors." Certainly no man was ever so linked in his heart to the place where he dwelt. Only a man in love with a home could have uttered the touching phrase, "All my wishes end where I hope my days will end, at Monticello."

The Biggest Bargain in History

The Louisiana Purchase, one of the great take-off points for the American spirit, cleared the way for expansion to the Pacific and for the newly formed United States to attain the dimensions of a world power.

The Louisiana Purchase was also the biggest land bargain in history.

No commemoration can convey the drama and significance of the deal made in April, 1803, or the treaty which put this historic transaction into effect. But we can, at least, appreciate the significance of the event in terms of its consequences to us a century and a half later.

The ownership by a foreign power of the west bank of the Mississippi and its outlet port of New Orleans had long been a cause of concern. They constituted, as Jefferson said, the "one single spot on the globe, the possessor of which is our natural and habitual enemy." Two things happened almost simultaneously to bring this fact into focus. The Spanish Intendant of the province closed the Mississippi to navigation and trade by Americans. Shortly afterward Louisiana again passed into the hands of France.

War talk began to be heard along the western borders and in Congress. To avert it, Jefferson persuaded Congress to vote $2,000,000 to be used for the purchase of New Orleans and as much of the Floridas as could be obtained. The negotiations dragged on for months without result, but history was setting the stage for an entirely different outcome. New combinations were forming against Napoleon in Europe, and England was in control of the seas. Napoleon's continued possession of Louisiana was threatened.

Napoleon suddenly offered to sell it all. An awesome decision confronted the American minister, Robert R. Livingston. To buy the whole domain, he would have to obligate his Government for a much larger sum than had been appropriated. Livingston took the chance. It

was not without reason that Jefferson described this now all but forgotten figure as "the wisest American of his day."

Livingston and James Monroe, also on the scene as a special envoy, drove the hardest bargain they could, and on April 30, 1803, signed the papers. The consideration, in stock and absorbed claims of Americans against the French Government, was approximately $15,000,000, less than the value of a good day's run of cattle on the present Omaha market.

The news came as a troubling surprise to Jefferson. Strict constructionist that he was, he felt that signing the proposed treaty was "an act beyond the Constitution." But, with his vision of the incalculable future of America, he saw, too, what the extension of the westward frontier would mean. Jefferson sent the treaty to Congress on October 17, without amendment.

This provided a field day for the Federalists, smarting over the attacks on their own recent administrations. The treaty was clearly unconstitutional, they declared; it would destroy the sectional balance of the nation. One opponent asserted that the republican form of government would break down if attempted on so large a scale. But the purchase had fired the imagination of the people and two weeks after receiving the treaty Congress approved it and its conventions. The transfer of ownership was completed at New Orleans on December 20, 1803.

—excerpted from the April 25, 1953, issue of The Saturday Evening Post.

Political Buttons, Book III, by Theodore Hake

The original of the 1801 inauguration medal above goes for $1750 today. Below it, a cartoon by English artist James Gillray shows British Prime Minister Pitt and French emperor Napoleon carving up the globe.

The Conflict of Interest Case

In the early days of the Republic, Thomas Jefferson wrote in his own hand a strict rule of conduct for legislators. Published in 1801, it reads in part:

> Where the private interests of a member are concerned in a bill or question, he is to withdraw. And where such an interest has appeared, his voice has been disallowed, even after a division. In a case so contrary not only to the laws of decency, but to the fundamental principle of the social compact, which denies any man to be a judge in his own cause, it is for the honor of the House that this rule of immemorial observance should be strictly adhered to.

The "immemorial observance" continued for less than a generation. Jefferson was dead less than seven years when Senator Daniel Webster, otherwise one of the great legislators of all time, was writing the Biddle Bank in Philadelphia for money at the height of the Senate battle over the bank's controversial charter.

Wrote Senator Webster to Nicholas Biddle:

> I believe my retainer has not been renewed or refreshed as usual. If it be wished that my relation to the bank should be continued, it may be well to send me the usual retainers.

Senator Webster led the fight to renew the bank's charter.

As congressmen became more involved in the country's burgeoning economy, strict rules became more troublesome to apply. The crushing blow came April 11, 1874, when the Speaker of the House of Representatives ruled, in effect, that congressmen can vote their private interests if the measure is not for their exclusive benefit. The issue was whether three congressmen should vote on a national-bank taxation measure, since they were officers of national banks.

The House Speaker who promulgated the rule was James G. Blaine ("the Plumed Knight"), who even then was offering his services in Congress to the Little Rock and Fort Smith Railroad in return for their stock. Blaine's precedent remains in the rule books of the House today. There is no rule whatever in the Senate.

—reprinted from the November 17, 1961, issue of The Saturday Evening Post.

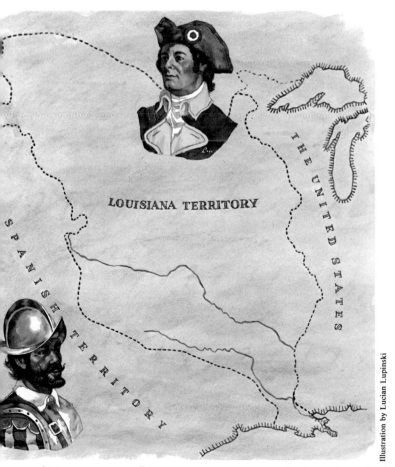

Livingston was sent to France to negotiate navigation and trading rights on the Mississippi. Monroe was sent to buy New Orleans and Florida. They returned with Louisiana: 828,000 square miles between the river and the Rockies. At the cost of four cents per acre, the purchase was a bargain by any standards.

Illustration by Lucian Lupinski

The Week That Was

Thomas Jefferson, who could never pass up a curious sight, paid a shilling to see a monkey. He didn't say what kind of monkey it was—probably some sailor's pet in a waterfront tavern. At any rate, he went to look at the monkey a few days before writing the Declaration of Independence. His account book showed the following notation: "pd for seeing a monkey 1/."

During the time he was actually writing the Declaration, Jefferson paid one shilling sixpence for a new pencil, seven shillings for a new map and six shillings for wine.

He was very proud of his version of the Declaration and his feelings were hurt when parts were changed or omitted on July 3rd and 4th. Old Doctor Franklin tried to soothe him. But for several days afterward, Jefferson was upset and a little angry. On the sixth, however, Jefferson must have felt better. His account book showed he had paid a shilling for beer.

—by Roger Butterfield, from the July 5, 1947, Post.

Jefferson's True Love

Jefferson—people still call him "Mr." Jefferson in Charlottesville, Virginia, not Thomas Jefferson or just Jefferson—was in love with a house. He loved the 580-foot-high mountain on which the house was built, but most of all he loved the mansion set on its scooped-off top. The mansion was the face of his love, the mountain was her curved body.

The place was never out of his mind. A day was a long time for him not to buy something for his mistress of wood and brick or to make an entry in his notebook about her. When he traveled in France and England and Italy, he shopped for her as a lover shops for a woman. Everything he saw—a garden, a carriage, a painting, even the silver and crockery from which he ate and the intricate French clocks which told him the time—he visioned as gifts for his home on its mountain.

He first settled at Monticello in November, 1770. His mother's house, Shadwell, burned in that year. He was twenty-seven years old, and building a house on the mountain which he had inherited from his father had been a dream for years. On vacation from William and Mary, he crossed the Rivanna River in a canoe and climbed to the summit of Monticello, a spot even then he was having leveled preparatory to building.

His best friend at college was Dabney Carr, who afterward married Jefferson's sister. As boys, it had been their habit to take their books to the slopes of Monticello and study there under the shade of a favorite oak. They made a promise, one to the other. The one who survived would see that the other was buried at its foot. When Carr died, Jefferson placed him beneath that tree. The location of the Monticello graveyard was decided in this way.

The first version of his home was completed in 1778. A French traveler who visited it described it by saying: "The house, of which Mr. Jefferson was the architect, and often one of the workmen, is elegant and in the Italian taste. Mr. Jefferson is the first American who has consulted the fine arts to know how he should shelter himself from the weather."

Jefferson's plan was novel in colonial home building. He placed a house on top of a mountain at a time when expediency and custom kept houses down in the lowlands close to the water. A part of the planning of any Virginia estate was the placing of the kitchens, stables, smokehouses, servants' quarters and carriage sheds. Jefferson placed these outbuildings so cleverly that, although they were attached to his house, they were invisible from the porches and lawns where he sat and walked and entertained.

Most of his years his public career kept him away from home. In Paris, as minister to France, he embarked upon the first great shopping orgy of his life. He roamed the city in search of furniture, damasks, *toile de Jouy*, table furnishings, paintings, books—enough of these to fill eighty-five packing cases. He bought fifty-seven chairs, two sofas, six mirrors, marble-topped tables, commodes, clocks, Venetian blinds, stoves, glassware, china, even wallpaper.

He had a passion for accessories and ingenious aids to living. He collected scientific implements and novelties with the acquisitive passion of a jackdaw. A lamp bought by Jefferson in Paris still hangs by slender brass chains in Monticello's entrance hall. Another Paris purchase was a pair of cylinder lamps, now standing on the mantel in the same room. In 1784 he wrote from Paris: "There has been a lamp called the cylinder lamp lately invented here. It gives a light equal, as is thought, to

An aerial view of Monticello, designed and built by Jefferson in 1770, shows the mansion nestled in the hills near Charlottesville, Virginia, facing the Blue Ridge Mountains.

Monticello was modeled in the style of Andrea Palladio's Villa Rotunda. At right, the front view of Jefferson's architectural creation; above, the clock in the entrance hall built and designed by Jefferson to tell the days of the week by a series of cannonballs suspended on pulleys.

that of six or eight candles. It requires olive oil, but its consumption is not great. The improvement is produced by putting the wick into a hollow cylinder, so that there is a passage for the air through the hollows."

He bought four French clocks. Not satisfied with these, upon his return home he imported a watchmaker from Europe to build for him a giant clock of his own design. It stands now above the entrance to the hall at Monticello. From it, on each side, by means of an arrangement of ropes and pulleys, heavy metal weights like small cannon balls climb up and down the walls past the names of the days of the week painted there. Watching the position of these weights, the owner of Monticello could tell what day it was. When Saturday arrived, the weights disappeared into holes cut into the floor on each side.

Among the legends about Monticello—one as hard to eradicate as wire grass from a lawn—is the story that Jefferson forgot to put in stairways until after his house was virtually completed, and that their steepness and lack of width are caused by the fact that they were made as an afterthought. Undeniably, they are inconveniently placed and dimensioned; those ascending to the upper floor are only twenty-two inches wide. But the legend of his forgetfulness is untenable, since stairways of some kind appeared in all his drawings for Monticello, even his earliest ones. The diminutive character of those he built indicates that Jefferson considered the second story of secondary importance. He planned to do most of his living on the first floor, and did.

Jefferson used a polygraph to make copies of his letters for his files, and its use has confused collectors of Jefferson-autographed letters. Every time he wrote one,

this device produced two identical letters. It was an ingenious double writing desk with duplicate pens and inkwells, built along the lines of the modern check signer used by treasurers of corporations. The pens were connected by jointed arms. In his old age, answering the flood of letters that came to Monticello became backbreaking drudgery. At his death his executors found 26,000 letters and 16,000 answers in his files.

Persuaded to remain in Washington's Cabinet for another year when he wished to retire, he wrote to one of his daughters, "The ensuing year will be the longest of my life. On the twenty-seventh of February I saw blackbirds and robin redbreasts, and on the seventh of the month I heard the frogs for the first time this year. Have you noted the appearance of these things at Monticello?" Such letters were the letters of a homesick man, exiled from the place he loved.

Despite the fact that multitudes of people seemed to regard Monticello as a free-loading resort hotel, the daily life there was simple. Jefferson once said that the sun had not caught him in bed for fifty years. He always made his own fire. He ate heartily, mostly vegetables. He never drank ardent spirits or brandy. His aversion to strong drink was such that when, in his last illness, his physician wanted him to use brandy, he could not induce him to take it strong enough. In summer he retired to his own apartments as the day grew warmer, and remained there until about one o'clock, reading and writing. At one o'clock he rode out, perhaps for two hours. Dinner was at half past three.

In 1923 the Thomas Jefferson Memorial Foundation was organized. Since then, Monticello has been maintained as a national shrine, open to the public.

—excerpted from an article by Pete Martin which appeared in the April 13, 1946, issue of The Saturday Evening Post.

James Madison

★ ★ ★ ★ ★

4th President of the United States

Born: March 16, 1751, Port Conway, Virginia.
Occupation: Planter, statesman, lawyer.
Wife: Dorothea Payne Todd. *Children*: One stepchild.
President: 1809-1817. Democratic-Republican party.
Vice-Presidents: George Clinton, Elbridge Gerry; Henry
  Clay, Speaker of the House of Representatives.
Died: June 28, 1836. *Buried*: Montpelier, Virginia.

★ ★ ★ ★ ★

James Madison had been a sickly, frail child and not able to take part in normal boyhood activities. He spent most of his time with books and became a known scholar of government. He completed a four-year course in two years at the College of New Jersey (Princeton University), which he chose because of its tradition against episcopacy [bishop hierarchy in the church]. He also found time to demonstrate against England while there.

He was a shy, serious man, only 5 feet, 4 inches tall and weighed 100 pounds. Washington Irving called him "a withered little apple-John." However, his wife, Dolley, made up for his lack, as she was the toast of Washington with her charm and gaiety.

Madison is known as "The Father of the Constitution." It was his Virginia Plan, put forward at the Constitutional Convention of 1787, which furnished the basic framework and guiding principles of the Constitution. Madison was the only participant to take day-by-day notes of the proceedings and the debates at the Convention, and therefore furnished the only comprehensive history of the event.

To promote ratification of the Constitution, Madison collaborated with Alexander Hamilton and John Jay in the publication of *The Federalist Papers*. He wrote 29 of the 85 that were published. In No. 44 he wrote:

> No axiom is more clearly established in law, or in reason, than that wherever the end is required, the means are authorized; whenever a general power to do a thing is given, every power necessary for doing it is included.

Madison was undoubtedly referring to his concept of the "implied powers" of Congress.

Elected to the new House of Representatives, Madison sponsored the first 10 amendments to the Constitution, known as the "Bill of Rights." In the debate which followed, he emphasized the freedoms of religion, speech and press. Indeed, his concept of liberty and republican theory proved to be his most lasting contribution. He fought against all government control over thought. Opinions were not legitimate objects of legislation to him. In 1793 he said, "If we avert to the nature of republican government we shall find that the censorial power is in the people over the government, and not in the government over the people."

In 1794 Madison took "vivacious and handsome" Dolley Todd, a young widow, as his wife. Sixteen years his junior, Dolley was raised a Quaker but she loved parties and was a charming and diplomatic hostess.

The election of 1809 found Madison the overwhelming winner over C. C. Pinckney, George Clinton (afterwards elected Vice-President) and James Monroe.

The War of 1812 took place during his administration. Madison's initial error at the beginning of the war was in giving the Army command to aging veterans of the Revolutionary War. By 1814, however, he lowered the average age of his generals from 60 to 36 years. But

The charred walls of the President's House (above) were saved only by a thunderstorm which broke the night of August 24, 1814. The mahogany, black leather Campeachy chair (right) was Madison's favorite.

it was the brilliant victories of the Navy, including those of "Old Ironsides" and Captain Stephen Decatur's *Wasp*, that turned the tide for the United States.

Despite repeated warnings of a British assault on Washington, D.C., Secretary of War John Armstrong ignored presidential orders for its defense. Dolley Madison, expecting her husband's return for their afternoon supper, was writing a letter to her sister as the British neared. She wrote, "Our kind friend, Mr. Carroll, has come to hasten my departure, and is in a very bad humor with me because I insist on waiting until the large picture of George Washington is secured, and it requires to be unscrewed from the wall."

Edward G. Lowry wrote in the May 9, 1931, issue of the *Post*:

> Dolly Madison is represented by what is said to be the oldest piece of porcelain in the White House. She is supposed to have saved it when she preserved Stuart's portrait of George Washington. When the British burned the White House and the Capitol in 1814, Dolly Madison saved this portrait of General Washington. It required courage, presence of mind and enterprise. Fortunately, there are fairly complete and authentic, verified accounts of her feat.
>
> . . .On the reconstruction of the building after the fire of 1814, Congress allowed President Madison $50,000 for refurnishing, and a portion of the sum was spent abroad. In 1841 Congress stipulated that "all articles purchased for the President's House shall be of American manufacture so far as may be practicable and expedient."

Madison served two terms as president and retired to his native Virginia. As he prepared to leave office in March of 1817, Madison was praised by his former political opponent, John Adams, who said, "Despite a thousand faults and blunders, his administration has acquired more glory and established more Union than all three of his predecessors."

Of his retirement to the beautiful Montpelier, Madison's 5000-acre farm, Beverly Smith, Jr., wrote:

> Over there is wispy little James Madison, five-feet-four, 100 pounds. Well on in his seventies, he enjoys his daily walk with his wife, the delightful Dolly Madison. When the weather is bad, she insists that he get his exercise. And so, quite indifferent to her dignity as former First Lady, she runs races with Madison on the sixty-foot-long piazza of their home. It must have agreed with him—he lived to be eighty-five.
>
> *May 6, 1961*, Post.

Besides entertaining, the Madisons worked the last 15 years of his life on his notes of the Constitutional Convention, which Congress purchased for $55,000.

Trend to Statism Wouldn't Astound "Elitist" Madison

A few months back, a sentence or two from James Madison was included in a *Post* editorial, the idea being to support a point with some solid authority. After the editorial appeared, we received a letter from a reader who is connected with a great American university, whether as student or teacher we don't know. The letter contained a sentence which seems to us a startling illustration of how far we have slipped away from "basic American doctrine."

The sentence in the letter was this: "Madison was an

27

Dolley, who had "a smile and a pleasant word for everybody," sent the first reply on Morse's telegraph: "Message from Mrs. Madison. She sends her love to Mrs. Wethered." The engraving is based on the Gilbert Stuart portrait.

ty are united by a common interest or passion, the rights of the minority are in danger." Madison followed Plato in feeling that some care should be taken to pick competent people to run the new country. As originally drafted, the Constitution reflected Madison's view that government should be carried on by officials selected in such a way as to make them as far as possible independent of the clamors and passions of the moment.

Furthermore he had the foresight to understand that "unbridled democracy" would inevitably produce such a situation as now confronts us, when 27 percent of the national income is expropriated to support government at all levels. He might not have imagined that an official publication of the Social Security Administration would one day describe social-security programs as "a basic essential for attainment of the socialized state envisaged in democratic ideology, a way of life which so far has been realized only in slight measure." (*Common Human Needs*, by Charlotte Towle, published by Social Security Board, 1945.) Nevertheless, the trend would not have astonished him, because he assumed that if the majority were left with the unimpeded right to shake down the minority, the shakedown would take place. He conceived it the business of government to prevent

elitist in the Platonic sense of the word—something you didn't choose to bring out."

Maybe there should be bigger dictionaries around here, but the best definition of the "elite" that we can find is "the choice or select part, the flower." The nature of an "elitist in the Platonic sense" is not entirely clear, even after a romp through the Dialogues, but we gather that it is regarded as unpleasant. In any event, the *Post* is charged with trying to slip in a quotation from the fourth President of the United States without telling the customers that Madison was some sort of Fascist Beast masquerading as a Founding Father.

All this may look like driving a small tack with a sledge hammer, but we have a hunch that this one correspondent's dismissal of Madison as some sort of remote and noxious reactionary is important in that it reflects the new set of assumptions which have grown up around the expression "democracy." It would be futile to deny that there is a great gulf fixed between the views of Madison and those at the Constitutional Convention of 1787, and those which prevail today.

Madison believed that "in all cases where the majori-

What's Going On Here?

The President of the United States has hurried from the capital on a wartime mission, accompanied by three ranking members of the Cabinet. Before his trip is done, he becomes the first United States Executive to serve actively in the field under gunfire as Commander-in-Chief of the United States armed forces.

What President, and what was the outcome of his mission?

Answer: *James Madison, fourth President, went personally to the battlefield at Bladensburg, Maryland, August 24, 1814, in a vain effort to turn back the British assault on Washington, D.C. Although not a military man, he is said to have directed the fire of Commodore Joshua Barney's naval battery, one of the few units that put up effective resistance. Two militia regiments broke and ran under fire from Congreve rockets, however, and the British captured Washington.*

—by Roger Q. Rodgers,
reprinted from the March 3,
1956, issue of the Post.

Mid-1800's engraving by Martin Johnson and Co.

The question now being decided is: Was Madison justified in his "elitist" forebodings? With government already taking a deep cut of the national income and with the Administration urging upon Congress new and dangerous grabs for power, it is easy to make a case for Madison's calculation that an unrestrained majority would soon pluck the minority of its rights and possessions. "Conscience," he opined, "is known to be adequate in individuals; in large numbers little is to be expected from it."

The pressure group of today was a future worry for Madison 160 years ago. It is our present and immediate danger. However you want to rate Madison in terms of current ideologies, it is urgently necessary to meet the challenge of his views.

—reprinted from the October 8, 1949, issue of The Saturday Evening Post.

Montpelier, named for the French city, was patented by John Maddison in 1653. When Dolley and "Jemmy" returned in 1817, the classic Jefferson portico with its 30-foot columns had been completed, and the interior refurbished.

such a development, not because he was an "elitist," but because he had read enough history to know what happens when majorities vote themselves "standards of living" with no practical suggestion for attaining them. Furthermore, as Felix Morley points out in his study of our political origins, *Power in the People* (Van Nostrand), Madison was no mere rural squire laying down the law for an agrarian colony. He believed that our population would reach 192,000,000 by 1930, and he anticipated changes "intellectual, moral and social, to which the institutions and laws of the country must be adapted."

Government, he thought, should provide a protective framework inside which individual men might better themselves spiritually as well as materially. Up to 1933 most people agreed that a man advanced, not by an act of Congress, but by application of his own industry, ability, character, luck and perseverance to his circumstances. Today, when it is possible for a Federal social-security employee to advise staff workers not to encourage children to take care of indigent parents on the ground that "the natural impulse toward emancipation may be unwholesomely checked," the "elitists" are under heavy fire.

29

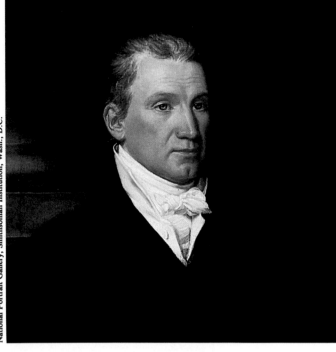

James Monroe

★ ★ ★ ★ ★

5th President of the United States

Born: April 28, 1758, Westmoreland County, Virginia.
Occupation: Lawyer.
Wife: Elizabeth Kortwright. *Children:* Two girls.
President: 1817-1825. Democratic-Republican party.
Vice-President: Daniel D. Tompkins.
Died: July 4, 1831. *Buried:* Richmond, Virginia.

★ ★ ★ ★ ★

James Monroe was studying at the College of William and Mary in Virginia when the call came to fight in the American Revolution. He was 17 years old. Wounded at the battle of Trenton, he carried a ball in his shoulder throughout his life. He spent the long winter at Valley Forge with General Washington. In the famous painting "Washington Crossing the Delaware" Monroe is depicted as the young man holding the flag.

Unlike his presidential predecessors, Monroe always wanted to be in politics. He studied law under Thomas

A Fragment of History

It may be a matter of interest to some of our readers, to recall the fact that Indiana voted for President and Vice-President of the United States before the act was passed which admitted her a member of the Union. Our younger friends have no personal knowledge of the circumstances, whilst it has doubtless escaped the recollection of most of our older ones. It was at the Presidential election of 1816, and a majority of the votes of the people of Indiana went for James Monroe, for President, and Daniel D. Tompkins, for Vice-President.

In the month of December following this election, Congress passed an act admitting Indiana as a State. Subsequently, in the month of February, the electoral votes thus prematurely cast, was allowed to be counted. The ground upon which this permission was asked and granted, was that a previous act had passed Congress allowing Indiana to form a State Government, provided that the Constitution adopted by her citizens should be Republican—that it should not be in violation of the ordinance of July 13, 1787—and, also, that such Constitution should be submitted to Congress. This was done—the Constitution was approved, and then followed the admission of Indiana as a State. Party excitement was not high at the time. Had it been, and could the electoral vote of Indiana have turned the scale, the case might have been different.

*—reprinted from the
July 13, 1850, issue of
The Saturday Evening Post.*

Jefferson and throughout his career held more political offices than any other president.

Monroe was serving in the Congress of the Confederation when he married Elizabeth Kortwright in 1786. As First Lady, Mrs. Monroe was the opposite of Dolley Madison, her predecessor, insisting on a return to formality at the newly painted "White" House.

In 1816 Monroe was elected to the presidency over Rufus King. The custom had been that the presidential oath be administered at a joint session of Congress on the floor of the House. Henry Clay, Speaker of the House at the time, flatly refused, he said, because the weight of the people expected to attend would collapse the floor. And so the custom of the oath taken on a raised portico in front of the Capitol was established.

Upon taking office President Monroe made a goodwill tour of the states. This was the first time many people had ever seen a president, and he was well received.

Monroe's first term as president became known as an "Era of Good Feelings" from a news caption in the *Federal Boston Centinel* dated July 12, 1817. There was peace at home and abroad. Agreements with England and Spain extended the United States' boundaries to the Pacific Ocean and between the 42nd and 49th parallels—the doors of "manifest destiny" had been opened.

James Monroe served as president for two terms. In the 1820 election only one vote was cast against him in the electoral college. The dissenter thought only George Washington deserved to be unanimously elected.

The President chose able men for his Cabinet, including John Quincy Adams as his Secretary of State. Aside from the purchase of Florida from Spain, Monroe's administration is known for the Monroe Doctrine and the Missouri Compromise.

Although southern citizens considered slavery an evil to be done away with at some future time, the controversy over the unbalance which the statehood of Missouri would cause, brought the southerners under northern attack. Southern reaction was bold, as Thomas Cobb of Georgia cried, "You have kindled a fire which all the waters of the ocean cannot put out, which seas of blood can only extinguish."

On February 17, 1820, the Missouri Compromise, forbidding slavery north of 36 degrees and 30 minutes north latitude in the future, was passed. Thomas Jefferson remarked that the compromise was "a fire-ball in the night. . . .We have the wolf by the ears, and we can neither safely hold him, nor safely let him go."

In the November 3, 1900, issue of the *Post*, the Hon. John W. Foster wrote of the importance of the Monroe Doctrine after 77 years:

...there is one principle or policy very vitally affecting our foreign relations which, announced more than three-quarters of a century ago, has been uniformly recognized by every succeeding Administration and firmly maintained whenever circumstances made it necessary. I refer to what is popularly known as the Monroe Doctrine, a declaration made in the annual message of President Monroe in 1823, which, broadly stated, is the non-intervention of European Governments in the political affairs of the American hemisphere.

At the time of its proclamation, Thomas Jefferson, our most astute politician, said, in prophetic language: "It sets our compass and points the course which we are to steer through the ocean of time opening on us."

In other words, with the lapse of time, the principle enunciated by President Monroe has proved so wise that it has become ingrained in the policy of the country and its application has been enlarged. A keen English observer of trans-Atlantic institutions has recently termed it a fixed and permanent state of American opinion.

Monroe retired to Virginia in 1825 with debts amounting to $75,000. In his final address to Congress Monroe said:

I have witnessed the great difficulties to which our Union has been exposed, and admired the virtue and courage with which they were surmounted. From the present prosperous and happy state, I derive a gratification which I cannot express. That these blessings may be preserved and perpetuated, will be the object of my fervent prayers to the Supreme Ruler of the Universe. JAMES MONROE.
Washington, Dec. 7, 1824.
—*December 11, 1824*, Post.

Monroe was the third president to die on the Fourth of July.

When James and Elizabeth (above) Monroe bought Ashfield (now called Ash Lawn) their neighbor, Thomas Jefferson, sent his gardener to plant trees for the orchard. The family lived in the small cottage which still stands adjacent to the larger house, from 1799 until 1819.

Photo by Dorothy Abner

John Quincy Adams

★ ★ ★ ★ ★

6th President of the United States

Born: July 11, 1767, Quincy, Massachusetts.
Occupation: Lawyer, statesman.
Wife: Louisa Johnson. *Children:* Three boys, one girl.
President: 1825-1829. Democratic-Republican party.
Vice-President: John C. Calhoun.
Died: February 23, 1848. *Buried:* Quincy,
  Massachusetts.

★ ★ ★ ★ ★

John Quincy Adams, eldest son of President John Adams, was trained from boyhood to be a statesman. He was a brilliant scholar, lawyer and diplomat. He proved his mettle and courage in the Senate and was offered an appointment to the Supreme Court. He helped

When Adams Left the White House

John Quincy Adams is the only President who left a published record of his emotions on quitting the White House . . . . the psychology disclosed by J. Q. Adams has a certain common application to all men who have reached the top in politics and receded. Sure that his public life was ended irremediably, that he had only a few months to live and that he would die gladly, he was elected to Congress a year and a half later, served there continuously for seventeen years and died in the Speaker's room, after being stricken on the floor of the House, in his eighty-first year.

On the August fifteenth previous to his election to the House he had been re-reading Cicero's reflections on death, and he wrote in his diary:

"I have read this dissertation at the most favorable moment of my life for giving it all its weight, when I have no plausible motive for wishing to live, when everything that I foresee makes death desirable, and when I have the clearest indications that it is near at hand."

On November seventh, on hearing of his overwhelming election, he wrote:

"No one knows, and few conceive, the agony of mind that I have suffered from the time I was made by circumstances, and not by my volition, a candidate for the presidency till I was dismissed from that station by failure of my reelection . . . . In the French opera, Richard Coeur de Lion, the minstrel, Blondel, sings under the walls of Richard's prison a song beginning:

> O Richard! O my King!
> · The world abandons you.

When I first heard this song, forty-five years ago, at one of the first representations of that delightful play, it made an indelible impression upon my memory, without imagining that I should ever feel its force so much closer home. But that call upon me by the people of my district, to represent them in Congress, has been spontaneous. I have received nearly three votes in four throughout the district. My election as President of the United States was not half so gratifying to my inmost soul."

—exerpted from an article by Irwin H. (Ike) Hoover, published in the September 1, 1934, issue of the Post.

negotiate the treaty which ended the War of 1812. As Secretary of State, under President Monroe, he played a leading part in formulating the Monroe Doctrine.

Yet this man, apparently so pre-eminently qualified for the presidency, had an unhappy four years in the White House. Factional fights beyond his control and virulent attacks on him by Jacksonian partisans clouded his administration. In those years he was variously described as irritable, petty, prejudiced, dogmatical, overbearing and discourteous. After his defeat by Gen. Andrew Jackson he was so embittered that he refused to attend his successor's inauguration in 1829.

In the following 18 months he was overwhelmed by new woes. His oldest son, George Washington Adams, who had fallen into dissipation and debt, committed suicide. Adams' own savings were swept away by the failure of his investments. He was tortured by nervous aches and pains. His wife suffered months of nervous prostration. In agony of mind, Adams read his Bible and compared his troubles to those of Job.

Then, in the fall of 1830, at the age of 63, John Quincy Adams took a fresh lease on life and began a new career. A friend urged him to run for Congress from his home district in Massachusetts. Other advisers said it would be "degrading" for an ex-President to take so modest a post. "No person," said ex-President Adams stoutly, "could be degraded by serving the people as a Representative in Congress." In the election he triumphed handsomely over two opponents.

"My election as President was not half so gratifying to my inmost soul," he wrote happily in his diary. He was in his element again, and on his way. His wife recovered; his own health and spirits improved. His subsequent 17 years in Congress were the brightest of his life. "Old Man Eloquent," as they called him,

The Old Mansion or Peacefield at Quincy (called the Old House by the family today) housed four consecutive generations of Adamses.

Photo by George Dow

Library of Congress

Though his father was President at the time, the marriage of John Q. Adams to Louisa Catherine Johnson on July 26, 1797, took place in London.

became a powerful and revered figure in the House, respected in the end even by his enemies.

No longer was he the fussy grouch of his White House days. As his biographer, Samuel Flagg Bemis says, "Mr. Adams mellowed like Madeira as the years advanced . . . . The diarist Philip Hone, congenial host to so many of the nation's elite at New York, tells of a dinner in 1841 where John Quincy Adams was the 'fiddle of the party' . . . gay, witty, instructive, entertaining, the privilege of a lifetime to listen to."

Like an ex-President of our time, Harry Truman, Adams was a devotee of early-morning walks. Doctor Bemis gives an appealing picture of him in July of 1846, as he entered his eightieth year. Adams, up at dawn, walked a mile to a secluded rock on the Potomac shore. "There he peeled off his apparel . . . . [He] swam about for half an hour before coming out and mounting his rock again, like the old pelican he was, to dry and dress in the morning sun."

Nineteen months later, vigorous to the last in his efforts to limit slavery and preserve the Union, he was stricken unconscious at his desk in the House. Two days later he died. In a brief return to consciousness he had murmured, "I am content."

—excerpted from an article in the May 6, 1961, issue of The Saturday Evening Post, *written by Beverly Smith, Jr.*

Andrew Jackson

★ ★ ★ ★ ★

7th President of the United States

Born: March 15, 1767, Waxhaw, South Carolina.
Occupation: Lawyer, soldier.
Wife: Rachel Robards. *Children:* Adopted son.
President: 1829-1837. Democratic party.
Vice-Presidents: John C. Calhoun and Martin Van Buren.
Died: June 8, 1845. *Buried:* The Hermitage, near Nashville, Tennessee.

★ ★ ★ ★ ★

Andrew Jackson grew up on the frontier. All the presidents who preceded him had come from the Eastern seaboard. The country was now expanding westward, and Jackson represented this movement.

He was born in a log cabin, joined the army at age 13, and was orphaned at 14. Young Jackson had an intense hatred for the English and a great loyalty to America. He fought in the American Revolution and was taken prisoner. He was still but a lad of 16 when he was finally liberated from the British pen at Charleston. He was without a friend, a relative or a dollar in the world.

After the American Revolution he moved west to Nashville, a frontier village, which suited Jackson and his rough disposition. Three years later he married Rachel Donelson Robards who was of a first family of the Cumberland Basin. By this act, Jackson acquired a network of relatives, many of whom became business partners and companions.

In an article in the May 6, 1961, issue of *The Saturday Evening Post*, Beverly Smith, Jr., Washington Editor for the *Post*, refers to the seventh President of the U.S. as "our duelist." He goes on to say:

> In earlier life he had fought three affairs of honor, in two of which he was wounded. In a duel . . . in 1806 he stoically received an almost mortal body wound, then coolly killed his opponent. He fought no duels while he was ex-President, but even after he had retired to The Hermitage, his known skill and readiness with his shooting irons were part of his towering prestige in a country still close to the frontier. The very day that he left the White House, in 1837, he had given notice that his fighting spirit was unimpaired. His sole regret, he growled, had been his failure to shoot Clay and hang Calhoun.

He became a hero during the War of 1812, when as a general, he won the Battle of New Orleans against the British.

By 1828, the people were ready for a president with whom they could identify and Andrew Jackson was known to be a man of the people. The Democratic-Republican party was breaking into groups. One part, led by Jackson, was called the Democratic party. John Quincy Adams was the leader of the conservative faction called the National Republican party, which later changed

Politics in the olden time, this drawing by Howard Pyle commemorates General Jackson's journey to Washington as President-elect in 1829.

its name and became known as the Whig party.

Jackson was elected president, and the "common" people from throughout the country came to his inauguration. They crowded the streets to see "Old Hickory," as he was called. The inside of the White House became a shambles, as the people reportedly stood on chairs with muddy boots and spilled punch on the rugs while cheering *their* president. Absent from the festivities was Jackson's wife, Rachel, who had died just months before Inauguration Day.

"To the victor belong the spoils" was the new cry. Jackson thought jobs should go to his followers, and he removed 2,000 old office holders. He was a strong president in that he assumed command and used the power of veto. He believed in a strong federal government as opposed to states' rights. He also refused to re-charter the Bank of the United States. This became the chief issue in the 1832 presidential campaign. Jackson said the bank did not have a "uniform and sound" currency.

The 1832 election was the first one in which national conventions nominated presidential candidates. State legislatures, general meetings or congressional caucuses had done this before. Jackson won the election easily and continued his fight as the champion of peoples' rights against corruption.

At The Hermitage, in his 70s, Smith tells us, the old warrior still exerted influence on his successors and on national policy. At 77, the year before his death, his support was decisive in nominating the first "dark horse," James K. Polk, thus setting the stage for the annexation of Texas and the start of the Mexican War.

Jackson and his pocket pistol (above) acquired a reputation for fighting Indians and duels.

devout hope which I cherish, that its labor to improve them may be crowned with success.

You are assembled at a period of profound interest to the American patriot. The unexampled growth and prosperity of our country, having given us a rank in the scale of nations which removes all apprehension of danger to our integrity and independence from external foes, the career of freedom is before us, with an earnest from the past, that, if true to ourselves, there can be no formidable obstacle in the future, to its peaceful and uninterrupted pursuit. Yet, in proportion to the disappearance of those apprehensions which attended our weakness, as once contrasted with the power of some of the states of the old world, should we now be solicitous as to those which belong to the conviction, that it is to our own conduct we must look for the preservation of those causes, on which depend the excellence and the duration of our happy system of Government.

Concerning the State of the Union, we have but to look at the state of our agriculture, manufactures, and commerce, and the unexampled increase of our population, to feel the magnitude of the trust committed to us. Never, in any former period of our history, have we had greater reason than we now have, to be thankful to Divine Providence for the blessings of health and general prosperity . . . we have every reason to feel proud of

The State of the Union

by Andrew Jackson

Entitled "The President's Levee, or all Creation going to the White House," this print depicts Jackson's infamous 1829 inauguration reception.

Editor's Note: Andrew Jackson's farewell address to Congress on December 7, 1835, covered every feasible aspect of the state of the union. There was much to be said about many important issues. He began as follows:

Fellow citizens of the Senate and House of Representatives: In the discharge of my official duty, the task again devolves upon me of communicating with a new Congress. The reflection that the representation of the Union has been recently renewed, and that the constitutional term of its service will expire with my own, heightens the solicitude with which I shall attempt to lay before it the state of our national concerns, and the

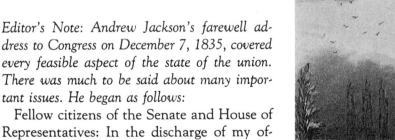

The White House Historical Assoc., photo by The National Geographic Society

The guitar-shaped drive leading up to The Hermitage was designed by R.E.W. Earl; the cedars lining it were planted by Jackson. The print above, circa 1840, shows The Hermitage as it looked in 1834 after it was rebuilt for the last time. The temple-shaped structure to the right is Rachel's tomb.

ourselves and of our country for its continuing prosperity.

The general state of our Foreign Relations has not materially changed since my last annual message. In the settlement of the question of the Northeastern boundary, little progress has been made. Great Britain has declined acceding to the proposition of the United States, presented in accordance with the resolution of the Senate . . . .

The internal contest continues still in Spain. Distinguished as this struggle has unhappily been . . . . No provision having been made at the last session of Congress for the ascertainment of the claims to be paid, and the apportionment of the funds, under the convention made with Spain, I invite your early attention to the subject . . . . The French Government having received all the explanation which honor and principle permitted, and which could in reason be asked, it was hoped it [the French Government] would no longer hesitate to pay the installments now due . . . . Not having received

The widower Jackson hung a portrait of his beloved Rachel in his bedroom that she "might be the first object to meet his eyes in the morning."

any official communication of the intentions of the French Government, and anxious to bring, as far as practicable this unpleasant affair to a close before the meeting of Congress, that you might have the whole subject before you, I caused our Charge d' Affairs at Paris to be instructed to ask for the final determination of the French Government; and in the event of their refusal to pay the installments now due, without further explanations, to return to the United States. . . . Whenever the advices, now daily expected from our Charge d' Affairs shall have been received, they will be made subject of a special communication.

The condition of the Public Finances was never more flattering than at the present period . . . . All . . . pecuniary engagements of the Government had been honorably and promptly fulfilled, and there will be a balance in the Treasury at the close of the Present year, of about nineteen millions of dollars.

As far as taxes are concerned, it is certainly our duty to diminish as far as we can, the burdens of taxation, and to regard all the restrictions which are imposed on the trade and navigation of our citizens as evils . . . .

In the area of our Nation's Security, I am gratified in being able to inform you that no occurrences had required any movement of the military force except such as is common to a state of peace . . . .

Your attention is also invited to the defects which exist in the Judicial system of the United States . . . . It is hoped that the present Congress will extend to all the States that equality in respect to the benefits of the laws of the Union which can only be secured by the uniformity

Jackson's administration stood in support of a strong party. The political cartoon at top is a spoof on the bronze statue above by Clark Mills. To make it clear where they stood on the issue of the spoils system, Jackson's opponents depict him and his administration as supported only by the back of a sow.

and efficiency of the Judicial system.

In conclusion, with these observations on the topics of general interest which are deemed worthy of your consideration, I leave them to your care, trusting that the legislative measures they call for, will be met as the wants and best interests of our beloved country demand.

—excerpted from the December 12, 1885, issue of The Saturday Evening Post.

A Gentleman

On the personal side history owes General Jackson reparation—his personality needs indeed complete reconstruction in the popular mind, which misconceives him a rough frontiersman having few or none of the social graces, whereas in point of fact he came into the world at heart a true gentleman, a born leader of men, a knight-errant who captivated women, deeply affectionate and tender.

I shared when a young man the common belief about him. But there is ample proof of the error of this. From middle age, though he ever liked a horse race, he was a regular if not a devout churchman. He did not swear at all, "by the Eternal" or any other oath. When he reached New Orleans in 1814 to command the army, Governor Claiborne gave him a dinner; and after he had gone Mrs. Claiborne, who knew European courts and society better than any other living American woman said to her husband: "Call that man a backwoodsman? He is the finest gentleman I ever met!"

There is another witness—Mr. Buchanan, afterward President—who tells how he took a distinguished English lady to the White House when Old Hickory was President; how he went up to the general's private apartment, where he found him in a ragged *robe-de-chambre*, smoking his pipe; how, when he intimated that the President might before coming down slick himself a bit, he received the half-laughing rebuke:

"Buchanan, I once knew a man in Virginia who made himself independently rich by minding his own business."

How, when he did come down, he was *en regle*; and finally how after a half hour of delightful talk, the English lady as they regained the street broke forth with enthusiasm, using almost the selfsame words of Mrs. Claiborne:

"He is the finest gentleman I ever met in the whole course of my life."

—an excerpt from an article that appeared in the March 1, 1919, issue of The Saturday Evening Post *written by Henry Watterson.*

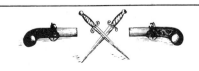

Martin Van Buren National Historic Site

Martin Van Buren

★ ★ ★ ★ ★

8th President of the United States

Born: December 5, 1782, Kinderhook, New York.
Occupation: Lawyer.
Wife: Hannah Hoes. *Children:* Four boys.
President: 1837-1841. Democratic party.
Vice-President: Richard M. Johnson.
Died: July 24, 1862. *Buried:* Kinderhook, New York.

★ ★ ★ ★ ★

Martin Van Buren's favorite pastime was politics. With Andrew Jackson's influence he was elected vice-president in 1832 and became the logical choice for president in 1836. After his nomination, Van Buren wrote a two and a half column letter stating his platform. It appeared in the paraphrased form in the September 2, 1848, issue of *The Saturday Evening Post* as follows:

> He enters into a long argument to prove the justice and constitutionality of opposing the extension of slavery into any of the territories of the United States; and expresses the opinion that while Congress has the right, it would be impolite to exercise the power of abolishing slavery in the District of Columbia; although he would not veto a bill for such an object, if passed by Congress.
>
> Mr. Van Buren advocates the improvement of rivers and harbors, though he inculcates a careful guarding against the great liability to abuse, in this respect. He approves of the doctrines of the late Silas Wright, upon this subject.
>
> He unites with the sentiments of the land reformers, relative to the public lands, with some slight differences.
>
> He prefers a system of direct taxation to the present one of collecting duties by imposts on goods imported, but for the present supports a tariff for revenue.
>
> On the whole, he adopts, with certain "explanations," that modify but do not essentially alter their character, the platform resolutions of the Buffalo Convention.

Van Buren had been in office only two months when the panic of 1837 caused a severe depression. This was not Van Buren's fault, but since he was the one in office, he was blamed for it. He did nothing to help correct the situation, because he believed that government was best which governed least.

An April 24, 1954, *Post* editorial tells that in 1839, Lincoln was serving his third term as a Whig member of the Illinois Legislature. At Springfield, he said this:

Angelica Singleton Van Buren, daughter-in-law of the widower President Martin Van Buren: Van Buren moved into the White House in 1837 with four bachelor sons. Dolley Madison, matriarch of Washington society, was visited by her young relative-by-marriage, Angelica Singleton, from South Carolina. Dolley took her to the White House to pay a call. Angelica's beauty, education and refined manner won the heart of the President's eldest son, Abraham. They were married in November 1838. Upon their return, Abraham served as the President's private secretary, and Angelica as First Lady. The only shadow over her reign as lady of the house was the loss of a baby girl— born at the White House—who only lived a few hours.

—The Van Buren National Historic Site, Kinderhook, New York

The White House Historical Assoc., photo by The National Geographic Society

Possibly no alterations on Lindenwald (left) were as great as those executed by Smith Thompson Van Buren, Martin Van Buren's son and heir. President Van Buren commented to Gorham A. Worth in 1849 on the many changes to the house: "What curious creature we are. Old Mr. Van Ness built as fine a House here as any reasonable man could . . . its taste of what was then . . . deemed the best. William P. came and disfigured everything his father had done. I succeeded him and pulled down without a single exception every erection he had made and with evident advantage. Now comes Smith and pulls down many things I had put up and makes alterations without a stint. The four operations will cost nearer fifty than forty thousand dollars for the buildings alone. What non-sense."
—Library of Congress
Reconstruction under Smith to change the 1797 house took over two years and, on several occasions, forced the Van Burens to live elsewhere. The main portion of the house today comprises a brick, two and a half-story structure on a stone foundation.

"I know that the great volcano at Washington, aroused and directed by the evil spirit that reigns there is belching forth the lava of political corruption in a current broad and deep, which is sweeping with frightful velocity over the whole length and breadth of the land, bidding fair to leave unscathed no green spot or living thing; while on its bosom are riding, like demons on the waves of hell, the imps of that evil spirit, fiendishly taunting all those who dare resist its destroying course with the hopelessness of their effort; and, knowing this, I cannot deny that all may be swept away. Broken by it I, too, may be; bow to it I never will."

What was the evil spirit that brooded over the Potomac with such dire results? None other than President Martin Van Buren. Many historians today, however, consider Van Buren's further development of Jacksonian Democracy to be one of his greatest achievements in office.

His political success was due largely to his managerial skills, as a publication by the Van Buren National Historic Site describes:

> His political genius lay in his ability to manipulate individuals and to organize groups skillfully. A true father of modern political science, he pitted faction against faction and molded consensus toward his own ends. Consequently, he earned the titles "Red Fox" and "Little Magician."

Van Buren was a small man, only five feet, six inches tall, and very fussy about his appearance. Renominated in 1840, he lost the election to William Henry Harrison. The campaign slogans were "Van! Van! Is a Used-up Man!" and "Tippecanoe and Tyler, Too!" The Whigs pushed a huge paper ball from city to city with campaign slogans on it, giving us the phrase: "Keep the ball rolling."

Rise 'n Shine

The Van Buren family are all dreadful sleepers; they sit up half the night, and lie in bed until noon. A droll scene occurred once at Washington when Mr. Van Buren was Vice-President. He lay in bed so late that he could not reach the Senate at 12 o'clock to call that honorable body to order. Lamenting his sleeping propensity to his son, John, he declared that there must be a reform, as they all slept too late.

"Let's make a bargain," said John. "The first who rises shall call the other up, with leave to pull the delinquent out of bed if not up in time."

"Agreed!" said the old gentleman.

One night John sat up playing brag with a parcel of roysterers until the morning's sun darted its rays through the green blinds. "Bless me," said he, "why, it's eight o'clock. I must go and call the old gentleman up." John went to his own chamber, made his toilet, and then went into his father's bed-room.

"Hallo! do you know how late it is, father? Past eight. Come, tumble up!"

"Oh, John! let me sleep a little longer!"

"Not a minute! You remember the bargain!" So he rolled the old gentleman into his blanket and sheet, deposited him very gently on the floor, and left him.

—an excerpt from the August 26, 1848, issue of The Saturday Evening Post.

William Henry Harrison

★ ★ ★ ★ ★

9th President of the United States

Born: February 9, 1773, Berkeley, Virginia.
Occupation: Farmer, soldier.
Wife: Anna Symmes. *Children:* Six boys, five girls.
President: 1841, one month. Whig party.
Vice-President: John Tyler.
Died: April 4, 1841. *Buried:* North Bend, Ohio.

★ ★ ★ ★ ★

The youngest of seven children born to Benjamin Harrison, one of the signers of the Declaration of Independence, William Henry was educated and reared at the illustrious Berkeley plantation in Virginia. At the age of 14 he entered Virginia's Hampden-Sidney College, but the following year transferred to the University of Pennsylvania Medical School to become a doctor as his father wished. He left the study of medicine in 1791 when his father died, and joined the Army.

Harrison fought in the Indian wars of the Northwest Territory (determined by the Ohio and Mississippi Rivers and the Great Lakes west of Ontario) for the next eight years. During this time he met and married Anna Symmes, with whom he fathered 11 children. His grandson, Benjamin, became America's 23rd president.

From 1798 until 1829 Harrison's political career was interrupted only by the War of 1812 when he distinguished himself by recapturing Detroit and invading Canada to end the hostilities there. He served as Secretary of the Northwest Territory, the Governor of the Indiana territory for 12 years, a U.S. Congressman, an Ohio Senator, a U.S. Senator and the Minister of Columbia under President John Q. Adams.

The presidential election of 1840 is well remembered for the carnival-like atmosphere and general excitement. Harrison had become a popular hero for defeating Tecumseh at the Battle of Tippecanoe on November 7, 1811; hence the slogan, "Tippecanoe and Tyler, Too!" Neither party developed a platform. The November 7, 1840, issue of the *Post* told of the election excitement in Philadelphia:

> The excitement among our citizens during the past week to learn the result of the Election in our state, we never saw equalled. The closeness of the vote—the contradictory nature of the returns—the rumors of victory for either side, alternating with every mail, kept the town in continual suspense, and daily made the interest intense. Crowds beseiged the offices of the

Uninvited Visitors

Harrison's life was threatened by a lunatic who got in through the south porch and the Red Room windows. Two doorkeepers had seized him when Harrison, attracted by the noise, came in and cut a window cord with which to tie him. Again, Harrison was sitting on the south porch one summer evening when a man leaped over the iron fence and came right up to the President and started to talk about getting a Government job. He was drunk and harmless. Harrison talked calmly with him, eventually ringing the bell to the ushers' room. When an usher came, the President asked him to show "the gentleman out."

> —*an excerpt from the Irwin H. (Ike) Hoover article that appeared in the October 8, 1934, Post.*

daily papers for slips, blocked up the avenues to the post-office, and filled the spacious hall of the Exchange to overflowing. The hour for the arrival of the Western mail was a signal for the excitement to begin, and with few exceptions, it continued the rest of the evening.

The newly elected president refused to wear an overcoat at a cold and rainy inaugural, and to show his good health, President Harrison rode on horseback in a parade for two hours. As a result, he came down with pneumonia and died just one month after taking office.

William Henry Harrison, at 68, was the oldest man to be elected president, the first to die in office and he served the shortest time as president.

If a House Could Speak

by Cathy L. Bergner

The most historic of the Great James River plantations, Berkeley (top) welcomed many important visitors in the great center hallway (above).

Tales of soldiers and statesmen, prosperity and plunder could fill volumes if Berkeley, the Harrison ancestral home, could speak.

Considered to be the oldest three-story brick house in Virginia (built in 1726) the Berkeley plantation lies along the historic James River between Williamsburg and Richmond. King James I granted the land in 1619 to the Berkeley Company and on December 4 of that year the 38 settlers aboard the ship *Margaret* stepped ashore.

It was their proprietor's wish that "the day of our ship's arrival . . . shall be yearly and perpetually kept as a day of Thanksgiving." And so it was that the first official Thanksgiving Day service was held by Captain John Woodlief at Berkeley more than a year before the *Mayflower* landed in New England.

The plantation was inherited by Colonel Benjamin Harrison, member of the Continental Congress, signer of the Declaration of Independence and three times Governor of Virginia. A close friend of the Colonel's, George Washington, often visited. In fact, all of the presidents from Washington to Buchanan, were entertained at Berkeley at one time or another.

Eighteen-gun battleships used in the American Revolution were built at the plantation "shipyard," but in 1781 Berkeley was attacked. On January 9th and 10th Benedict Arnold, along with 1,200 infantrymen on 27 vessels and 100 horses, ravaged the house, shot cattle and carried off 40 slaves.

During the Civil War General McClellan, Commander of the Army of the Potomac, used Berkeley as his headquarters and hospital after the Battle of Malvern Hill. The entire Union Army of 140,000 soldiers camped on the plantation during the summer of 1862. While quartered there General Daniel Butterfield composed "Taps."

It was that same summer that Count Von Zeppelin and his balloon, the *Intrepid*, made their maiden flight rising from the Berkeley lawn. Balloons made their debut into warfare during the Seven Days battles when Scotch Professor Low rented them to the Union Army.

The ancestral home of a signer of the Declaration of Independence and two U.S. presidents, a shipyard during the American Revolution and a camp housing the entire Union Army during the War Between the States, Berkeley stands as a monument to the courageous history of the United States.

Listen, there is a whispering within the walls, and off near the shoreline echoes the muted sounds of a bugle playing . . . . Indeed, Berkeley speaks!

John Tyler

★ ★ ★ ★ ★

10th President of the United States

Born: March 29, 1790, Charles City County, Virginia.
Occupation: Lawyer.
Wives: Letitia Christian, Julia Gardiner. *Children:* Eight boys, seven girls.
President: 1841-1845, Whig party.
Vice-President: Samuel L. Southard, President pro tempore of the Senate.
Died: January 17, 1862. *Buried:* Richmond, Virginia.

★ ★ ★ ★ ★

A graduate of William and Mary College by the age of 17, a member of the Virginia House of Delegates at 21, a member of Congress at the age of 26 and Governor of Virginia when 35, John Tyler became president at 51—the first man to become president due to the death of a president. He served nearly a full four-year term and set the

precedent that a Vice-President who becomes president in this manner is not a caretaker, but the president with full powers of the office. Soon after taking office Tyler wrote: "I am under Providence made the instrument of a new test which is for the first time to be applied to our institutions." And to Secretary of State Daniel Webster, he said:

April, 1841
"I never consent to being dictated to. I, as President, shall be responsible for *my* Administration. I hope to have your hearty cooperation in carrying out its measures. So long as you see fit to do this, I

shall be glad to have you with me. When you think otherwise, your resignation will be accepted.

Tyler was a southern Democrat who left his party to run with Harrison on the Whig ticket. As President, he vetoed almost every bill that the Whigs put forth. Tyler had no party organization to support him and his policies. His administration was one of infighting and disagreement, and his entire Cabinet resigned.

Because of Tyler's opposition with his inherited Cabinet, he relied chiefly on the advice of his famed "Kitchen Cabinet" of longtime Virginia friends such as 34-year-old Representative Henry A. Wise. It was Wise who, when Tyler's presidential status was questioned in the House, declared that Tyler was President "by the Constitution, by election and by the Act of God."

The Whigs became so angry with him that they tried to impeach him. This was the first time impeachment proceedings had ever been started against a president.

Among the high crimes charged to Tyler were (1) that he had agreed to two bank bills and then vetoed both; and (2) that he was using the veto power in a deliberate effort to ruin the Whig party.

It was Representative John M. Botts of Virginia, a former friend of Tyler's, who brought the resolution of impeachment to the floor of the House. But because "it might invest nothingness with consequence" by

swinging the public behind Tyler, the measure lost 83 to 127.

Historians now look upon Tyler as a courageous man who stood firm in his convictions, and did his best in a difficult situation. He once explained his firm stand:

> The Government was created by the states. It is amenable to the states, is preserved by the states and may be destroyed by the states. And any time they desire, the states may strike you [the Federal Government] out of existence by a word; demolish the Constitution and scatter its fragments to the wind.

The Two Jacks

John Dade had been a schoolmate of John Tyler—so intimate they were that at college they were called "the two Jacks"—and when the death of Harrison made Tyler President, the "off Jack," as he dubbed himself, went up to the White House and said: "Jack Tyler, you've had luck and I haven't. You must do something for me and do it quick. I'm hard up and I want an office."

"You old reprobate," said Tyler, "what office on earth do you think you are fit to fill?"

"Well," said Dade, "I have heard them talking round here of a place they call a sine-cu-ree—big pay and no work—and if there is one of them left and lying about loose I think I could fill it to a T."

"All right," said the President good-naturedly. "I'll see what can be done. Come up tomorrow."

The next day "Col. John W. Dade, of Virginia," was appointed keeper of the Federal prison of the District of Columbia. He assumed his post with *empressement*, called the prisoners before him and made them an address.

"Ladies and gentlemen," said he: "I have been chosen by my friend, the President of the United States, as superintendent of this eleemosynary institution. It is my intention to treat you all as a Virginia gentleman should treat a body of American ladies and gentlemen gathered here from all parts of our beloved Union, and I shall expect the same consideration in return. Otherwise I will turn you all out upon the cold mercies of a heartless world and you will have to work for your living."

—an excerpt from a March 1, 1919, Post article written by Henry Watterson.

John Tyler's home, Sherwood Forest Plantation in Charles City County, Virginia, has been a working plantation for more than 250 years.

James K. Polk

★ ★ ★ ★ ★

11th President of the United States

Born: November 2, 1795, Mecklenburg County,
  North Carolina.
Occupation: Lawyer.
Wife: Sarah Childress. *Children:* None.
President: 1845-1849. Democratic party.
Vice-President: George M. Dallas.
Died: June 15, 1849. *Buried:* Nashville, Tennessee.

★ ★ ★ ★ ★

James K. Polk, the eldest of 10 children, was born the
son of a prosperous farmer in Mecklenburg County,
North Carolina. The family moved to Middle Tennessee when James was 11. There he studied at Murfrees-
boro Academy and later at the University of North
Carolina, where he was named salutatorian of his class
of 1818, earning first honors in mathematics and class-
ics. He studied law in Nashville, was admitted to the

bar, and, at 28, was elected to the Tennessee legislature,
where he became friends with Andrew Jackson.

In 1824, Polk married Sarah Childress and continued
to devote himself to his political career. He was elected
to Congress in 1825, where he served for 14 years, the
last four as Speaker of the House. He was a strong supporter of the Jacksonian Democrats and used his
oratorical skills to serve as floor leader and leading
debator for his party.

James K. Polk was the first "dark horse" candidate to
reach the White House. The term *dark horse* refers to a
man who is little known before his candidacy. Polk was
chosen by Andrew Jackson to be the Democratic candidate in preference to Van Buren or Tyler.

According to Meade Minnigerode in the September 3, 1927, issue of *The Saturday Evening Post*, the
Democrats had a tough time deciding on a candidate in
1844. It was not until the eighth ballot at the convention that Polk's name was mentioned. But on the ninth
"in the midst of a furious uproar the first convention
stampede in American political history got under way,
and when it was all over Mr. Polk had all 266 votes."

In the election he defeated the famous Henry Clay,
the Whig candidate. "Who is James K. Polk?" the Whigs
had chanted throughout the 1844 campaign. They soon
discovered that as president, Polk could govern with
single-minded energy.

JAMES K. POLK.
THE PEOPLES CHOICE

*The campaign of 1844 matched the famed Henry Clay against little-
known James Polk. A close race, "little Hickory" won by 38,175 votes.*

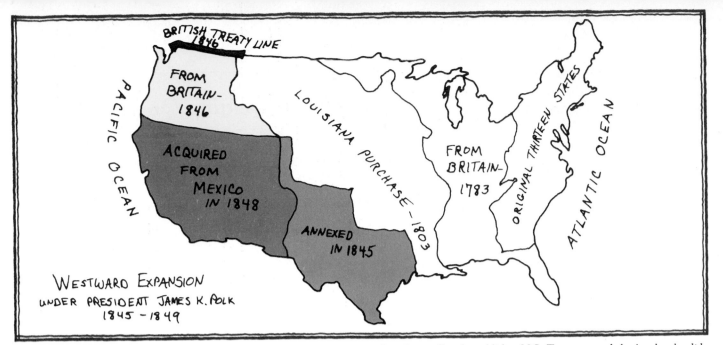

Polk promised the American people that he would settle Oregon and Texas, reduce the tariff and establish a U.S. Treasury—and that's what he did.

James Polk was more interested in issues than people; a hard worker, but suspicious. He did everything himself rather than trust anything to his aides. Nevertheless, historians rank Polk as a near-great president because he acquired the West for the United States. In all, Polk added 800,000 square miles to the country. This included California, New Mexico, Arizona and the extension of Texas to the Rio Grande which were acquired from Mexico after the Mexican War.

Although the United States eventually paid Mexico for her lands, the respect gained by winning the war was considered the paramount victory by the President, as he says in this July 15, 1848, *Post* excerpt:

> The extensive and valuable territories ceded by Mexico to the United States constitute indemnity for the past, and the brilliant achievements and signal successes of our arms will be a guarantee of security for the future, by convincing all nations that our rights must be respected. The results of the war with Mexico have given to the United States a national character abroad which our country never before enjoyed. Our power and our resources have become known, and are respected throughout the world; and we shall probably be saved from the necessity of engaging another foreign war for a long series of years.

In addition to this annexation, Polk also came to an agreement with England over the Oregon territory. The boundaries between Canada and the United States were set where they are today.

It was during this period in history, known as the Fabulous Forties, that Easterners migrated west and gold was discovered in California. News traveled slowly from the West to the East, but the gold rush made many exciting headlines:

> Large Lumps of Gold—Some astonishing large pieces of gold are reported to have been found at the Stockton mines, in California, within the last two weeks of January. A letter of January 31, to the *New York Tribune*, says:—One piece weighing *twenty-three pounds* was brought to Stockton; that another piece of incredible size and weight was also reported to have been brought to Stockton on Friday—it was said to weigh *ninety-eight pounds*. I saw a number of persons on board the Stockton boat who have seen the lump weighing twenty-three pounds. The gentleman who carries the express between Stockton and San Francisco, told me *he saw and had in his hands the piece weighing ninety-eight pounds*. If this be true, it is the largest piece of gold ever found, excepting one found, in the Ural Mountains, which weighed nearly one hundred pounds, troy.
>
> —*March 23, 1848*, Post.

Unrest and economic upheaval in Europe forced the Germans and Irish to come to this country in great numbers. Regular transatlantic steamship service was started, the first telegraph line was established and railroads were being built across the United States. The great literary figures of this period were Emerson, Longfellow, Poe, Whittier, Lowell and Whitman.

While president, James Polk rose at daybreak and worked until midnight. He then recorded in his diary the details of the day. He did not seek a second term and, worn out from his hard work, died three months after leaving office.

The *Post* ran his obituary on June 23, 1848:

> *Death Of Mr. Polk.* We have the melancholy news to lay before our readers this week, of the death of James K. Polk, Ex-President of the United States. Mr. Polk had been ill for some weeks of Diarrhea, of which disease he died. It is probable that the arduous duties of the Presidency had snapped the constitution of Mr. Polk, and rendered it unable to withstand the inroads of a disease particularly fatal in the West the present season. Mr. Polk died at his residence near Nashville, on Friday evening. Doubtless the fitting honors will be paid by the people at large to his memory.

Unfortunately, despite Polk's own explicit instructions to hand it over to the state of Tennessee, Polk Place was demolished after Mrs. Polk's death. It is for this reason that the Polk Shrine is today located in Columbia, Tennessee, on land purchased by President Polk's father, Samuel, on May 18, 1816.

The Polk Ancestral Home was built with handmade bricks by Samuel Polk in 1816 when he moved his family to Columbia, Tennessee.

"Strikingly handsome" Sarah Childress, the daughter of a Tennessee farmer, served as her husband's personal secretary for many years.

What's Going On Here?

A high-ranking United States general, who has waged a victorious war characterized by a successful amphibious campaign, is suddenly removed from command by a Democratic President and summoned before an inquiry. The action follows disagreement over the conduct of the war. One commentator terms the ousted general "a large man, (who) has done a large work and merited large treatment." But there was nothing large about the Administration. The general returns home to popular acclaim, an ovation in New York City, and ultimate retirement with full rank, pay and honors. The following year another general defeats the Democratic candidate and becomes President of the United States. Who was removed? Who became President?

Answer: *Not Gen. Douglas MacArthur, whose removal from command in Korea in 1951 by Truman was followed by Eisenhower's election in 1952, but Gen. Winfield Scott. Pres. James K. Polk relieved Scott of command of the victorious United States Army in the Mexican War in 1847. The MacArthur removal more than a century later was a case of history's repeating itself. Scott and Polk had had a reconciliation, MacArthur and Truman a "friendly conference" on a mid-Pacific island. Scott made a daring amphibious attack near Vera Cruz, MacArthur at Inchon. Scott's disciplining of unruly subordinates was reversed by Polk. MacArthur's objections to a "limited war" and insistence that "there is no substitute for victory" were not recognized by Truman. Scott, like MacArthur, returned home a popular hero, while the Democratic Party lost prestige. In 1848, another Mexican War hero, Gen. Zachary Taylor, was elected President over the Democratic candidate, Lewis Cass.*

—from the August 13, 1960, issue of the Post, *by Olney Rhode.*

Progress—A Difference of Opinion

As the nation took its shape and began to link itself together with the telegraph and the railroad, a change in lifestyle was soon to emerge. The following excerpts from the August 26, 1848, *Post* illustrate a question that is still unsettled in many an American mind: Is "all for the sake of progress" really the best theory?

The Telegraph.—Our city papers now have news headed "Two hours from New Orleans. Seven days in advance of the Mail." Who will say now that this is not a "progressive" age! Two thousand miles in two hours! Our forefathers would as soon have believed in the possibility of a turnpike to the moon. We wish old Doctor Franklin could just be allowed to make a visit to these parts for a few months—would not the old gentleman be astonished! He would own up outright, that this nineteenth century, with its railroads, magnetic telegraphs, Oregon and California settlements, European revolutions, &c., &c., was about the most wonderful that has ever rolled along.

Manifest Destiny realized, Americans flocked westward as fast as the railroad ties could be laid.

Evils of Railroads.—Some canal stockholder has recently made the following powerful argument against railways. We have been inclined always to think well of this mode of conveyance; but we confess, since reading the annexed, we are greatly staggered in our faith.

"He saw what would be the effect of it; that it would set the whole world a gadding. Twenty miles an hour, Sir! Why, you will not be able to keep an apprentice boy at work; every Saturday evening he must take a trip to Ohio, to spend the Sabbath with his sweetheart. Grave, plodding citizens will be flying like comets. All local attachments must be at an end. It will encourage flightiness of intellect. Veracious people will turn into immeasurable liars, all their conceptions will be exaggerated by their magnificent notions of distance. 'Only one hundred miles off!—Tut, nonsense. I'll step across, madam, and bring you your fan!' 'Pray, Sir, will you dine with me at my little box in Allegheny?' 'Why, indeed, I don't know, I shall be in town until twelve, well I shall be there, but you must let me off in time for the theatre.' And then, Sir, there be barrels of pork, and cargoes of flour, and chaldrons of coal, and even lead and whiskey, and such like sober things that have been used to sober travelling, whisking away like a set of sky rockets. It will upset all the gravity of the nation. If two gentlemen have an affair of honor they have only to steal off to the Rocky Mountains, and there no jurisdiction can touch them. And then, Sir, think of flying for debt. A set of bailiffs mounted on bomb shells could not overtake an absconding debtor, only give him a fair start. Upon the whole, Sir, it is a pestilential topsy-turvy, harum-scharum whirl-gig. Give me the old fashioned, solemn, straight forward, regular Dutch canal—three miles an hour for express, and two for a jog and trot journey—with a yoke of oxen for a load. I go for beasts of burden; it is more primitive and scriptural, and suits a moral and religious people better. None of your hop, skip and jump whimsies for me."

—*August 26, 1848*, Post.

Zachary Taylor

★ ★ ★ ★ ★

12th President of the United States

Born: September 24, 1784, Orange County, Virginia.
Occupation: Soldier.
Wife: Margaret Smith. *Children:* One boy, five girls.
President: 1849-1850, one year, four months.
  Whig party.
Vice-President: Millard Fillmore.
Died: July 9, 1850. *Buried:* Louisville, Kentucky.

★ ★ ★ ★ ★

The Whig party elected only two United States presidents, and both times these men died in office. As an added coincidence, both men were popular war heroes.

Zachary Taylor, second cousin of James Madison, grew up in Kentucky during the Indian wars and gained his military reputation fighting the various Indian tribes. When the Mexican War broke out, Taylor was one of two field commanders. His soldiers affectionately nicknamed him "Old Rough and Ready" because of his slovenly dress contrasting with "Old Fuss and Feathers," General Winfield Scott. He won a brilliant victory over Santa Anna, the Mexican leader, at the battle of Buena Vista, and became a prominent national hero.

Henry Watterson, U.S. journalist, recalls in a 1919 article in *The Saturday Evening Post:*

> The Presidential campaign of 1848—and the concurrent return of the Mexican soldiers—seems but yesterday. We were in Nashville . . . Tennessee, a debatable state. I was an enthusiastic politician on the Cass and Butler side, and was . . . disappointed when the election went against us for Taylor and Fillmore.
>
> Though the next winter we passed in Washington I never saw him in the White House. He died in July, 1850, and was succeeded by Millard Fillmore. It is common to speak of Old Rough and Ready as an ignoramus. I don't think this: He may not have been very courtly, but he was a gentleman.

A grateful country elected him to the presidency which he did not seek. He was a simple man, unpretentious, with a great love of his country. He vowed to lead not just the Whig party, but the entire Nation. The September 2, 1848, issue of the *Post* printed the speech Taylor gave in Baton Rouge, Louisiana, on August 6, 1848:

"I never had any aspirations for the Presidency, nor have I now . . . nor would I have it on any other terms than I stated when the subject was first agitated . . . that my acceptance must be without pledges . . . so that I could be the President of the whole *Nation* and not of a *Party.*"

His stand on the slavery dispute was to allow each state to decide for itself. In the following speech, ex-

Taylor's boyhood home in Springfield, Kentucky, built circa 1785-1790, was sold in 1829 when his father died. Taylor lamented the fact in a letter, as he "was very desirous that it should have remained in the family."

The S.S. President Taylor

Many ships are christened with president's names. Here is the story of how a ship bearing the names of two presidents went aground in the Pacific to become a landmark:

On February 14, 1942, the 522-foot, 10,000-ton President Taylor, loaded with 1200 soldiers and mountains of supplies, tried to stand close inshore at Canton Island to avoid a reported Japanese submarine. While her accompanying destroyer scurried off to drop a depth-charge pattern, the Taylor touched bottom. And a heavy swell forced her hard aground.

The Taylor's cargo was removed, excess weight was jettisoned, and tugs pulled while pumps burned themselves out. Nothing worked. By March eighteenth, the chief engineer sadly reported, "All pumps were secured and machinery and boiler spaces were allowed to fill to sea level."

The ship, built for the transatlantic trade in 1921 as the Granite State—also later named the President Polk—now was only a line in the United States Hydrographic Office's sailing directions, which declared: "The most conspicuous objects on the (Canton) island from seaward are the wreck of the President Taylor, located on the western side of the island near its main entrance; a lone palm tree on the northwest point, and a large kou bush on the southwest point."

—an excerpt from a February 26, 1955, Post article by Jeanne Booth Johnson.

Zachary Taylor gives a command at the battle of Buena Vista in 1847. His army defeated Santa Anna and a Mexican force three times its size—a victory which gained him popularity and election as President in 1848.

cerpted from the January 26, 1850, issue of *The Saturday Evening Post*, he addressed the question:

"It is to be expected any attempt to deny to the people of the State the right of self-government . . . will . . . be regarded by them as an invasion of their rights . . . . To assert that they are a conquered people and must submit to the will of their conquerors . . . will meet with no cordial response among American freemen."

Unfortunately, President Taylor did not live to fulfill his promises. One night after eating heartily of cherries and wild berries, he was seized by cramps which took the form of violent cholera morbus. He said to his medical attendant on July 8, 1850:

"I should not be surprised if this were to terminate in my death. I did not expect to encounter what has beset me since my elevation to the Presidency. God knows that I have endeavored to fulfil what I conceived to be an honest duty. But I have been mistaken. My motives have been misconstrued, and my feelings most grossly outraged."

He referred, no doubt, to the slavery question and the manner in which he was criticized for the stand he took. His illness did prove fatal and the *Post* carried this account of the "melancholy event" of President Taylor's death:

Washington, July 10, 1850.—The capital is shrouded in mourning. President Taylor is no more. He breathed his last at thirty-five minutes past 10 o'clock, yesterday evening, and lies in State this morning at the Executive mansion, surrounded by his griefstricken and afflicted family.

His last words were:

I am about to die—I expect the summons soon—I have endeavored to discharge all my official duties faithfully—I regret nothing, but am sorry that I am about to leave my friends.

Taylor was the first president to die in office while Congress was in session, which may account, in part, for the wide news coverage and elaborate funeral arrangements. And, according to custom, his favorite war-horse "Old Whitey" followed the funeral carriage in the procession.

Millard Fillmore

★ ★ ★ ★ ★

13th President of the United States

Born: January 7, 1800, Summer Hill, Cayuga County, New York.

Occupation: Lawyer.

Wives: Abigail Powers, Caroline McIntosh.

Children: One boy, one girl.

President: 1850-1853, two years, eight months. Whig party.

Vice-President: Howell Cobb*, Speaker of the House of Representatives; William R. D. King, David R. Atchison, Presidents pro tempore of the Senate.

Died: March 8, 1874. *Buried:* Buffalo, New York.

*According to the Succession Act of 1792, Cobb was next in succession for only two days (July 9-11) until Congress had time to elect a President pro tempore of the Senate.

★ ★ ★ ★ ★

Upon the death of Zachary Taylor, Millard Fillmore succeeded to the presidency. Born in a log cabin of poor parents his boyhood was not an easy one.

The *Post* described the new President's earlier days in an article in the July 20, 1850, issue:

> Mr. Fillmore was born at Summer Hill, Cayuga County, New York, on January 7th, 1800, and is, accordingly, now a little over fifty years old. His father was a farmer in very limited circumstances. The family removed to Aurora, Erie county, in 1819, where the father still carries on a farm of moderate dimensions; the writer hereof has often passed the modest house where reside the family of the President, in a style not more pretending than is common to thriving farmers of that prosperous district.—The narrow means of the father did not permit the bestowal on the son of any other than a most limited common school education. When 15 years old, he was sent to learn the trade of a clothier, at which he worked for four years, improving all his spare time in reading books from a little library in the village where he lived.

Ambitious and bright, he studied law under a local judge, as was the custom. The *Post* continued:

> At the age of 19, he made the acquaintance of Judge Wood, of Cayuga County, who detected the latent talents of the young man, and induced him to study law, for which he generously furnished the means. Mr. Fillmore remained in Judge Wood's office about two years, studying with that industry and perseverance which have distinguished him through life; during this time he also taught school in the winter months, in order himself to provide for his expenses as far as possible. In 1822, he entered a law office at Buffalo, and passed a year studying and teaching, when he was admitted to the bar, and removed to Aurora to commence the practice of his profession.

He was interested in politics and while in the New York legislature took a leading part in developing the public school system.

As president, he had an almost impossible job to satisfy all factions in the slavery controversy. Taylor's Cabinet resigned and President Fillmore had to form a new cabinet. The Compromise of 1850 was about to become law, and debates in Congress over whether the western territories would be slave or not were at their peak. The following letter from Fillmore in reply to an invitation to be present at a Sons of Temperance Celebration of the Fourth of July, 1850, at Buffalo, shows his concern:

> WASHINGTON, June 10, 1850.
> *Gentlemen:*—I have received your kind invitation to attend a "Union Celebration" in the city of Buffalo, of the approaching anniversary of our National Independence. Nothing could give me more pleasure than to be permitted to mingle with my fellow citizens on that joyous occasion. Judging from the favorable reports which I have recently heard of the progress of the cause of Temperance in Buffalo, I infer that this "Union Celebration" implies a union

Just after his successor had been sworn in, Fillmore lost his wife, Abigail (top right). After he died, his possessions were sold and his only son burned his letters and papers. He was commemorated in marble (above) by Robert Cushing.

Political Buttons, Book III, by Theodore Hake

of Patriotism and Temperance—of cool heads and warm hearts—and such a *union* is greatly desired at this time, to save the *Union* to which we are all so devotedly attached. I do not, however, anticipate that it will be in my power to accept your flattering invitation, as my official duties will, in all probability, require my presence here.

I trust, however, that notwithstanding the present painful aspect of our political affairs and the jarring discord of sectional feeling, that the wisdom and conciliation of the present generation are equal to the preservation of the glorious Constitution, unimpaired, which they have received as the greatest blessing from their ancestors, and that this birthday of our nation shall ever find us *"one and inseparable."*

Truly yours, MILLARD FILLMORE
—July 20, 1850, Post.

Harriet Beecher Stowe's book, *Uncle Tom's Cabin*, was published at this time and had a great impact on the thinking of the general public. Mrs. Stowe had never been in the South, and her book was not an accurate account of southern life, but the northerners accepted it as fact.

The major positive action of this administration was the sending of Commodore Perry to Japan to open trade negotiations.

In the presidential race of 1852, the Whigs ran General Winfield Scott instead of Fillmore. He did enter the 1856 campaign on the "Know-Nothing Party" ticket but lost, carrying only the state of Maryland. He then retired to relative obscurity, but still felt the need to influence people in a positive way. Beverly Smith, Jr., in the May 6, 1961, *Post*, described the unusual route he

Curious Facts

It is a singular fact, that within a space of a little over nine years, there have been six Presidents of the United States:

Van Buren, March 3rd, 1841.
Harrison, from March 4th to April 4th, 1841.
Tyler, from April 4th, 1841, to March 4th, 1845.
Polk, from March 4th, 1845, to March 4th, 1849.
Taylor, from March 4th, 1849, to July 9th, 1850,
            and on the 10th of July, 1850,
Millard Fillmore succeeded to the office.

Previous to that time, there had been but eight occupants of the office during a period of fifty-two years. The periods of service, age, &c., of the various Presidents, from Washington to Taylor, inclusive, are given below:

	Service.	Retired.	Died.	Age at Ret't.	Age at Death
Washington	8 years.	1797	1799	66	68
John Adams	4 years.	1801	1826	66	90
Jefferson	8 years.	1809	1826	66	84
Madison	8 years.	1817	1836	66	86
Monroe	8 years.	1825	1831	66	72
J.Q. Adams	4 years.	1829	1848	62	81
Jackson	8 years.	1837	1845	70	78
Van Buren	4 years.	1841	——	59	—
Harrison	1 month	——	1841	—	69
Tyler	3 years. 11 mos.	1845	——	55	—
Polk	4 years.	1849	1849	54	54
Taylor	1 year. 4 mos.	——	1850	—	66

James K. Polk was the youngest of the Presidents at the time of his inauguration, being but 49 years and 4 months old. Mr. Fillmore is the next youngest; being at the present time 50 years old. Jackson was the oldest of the Presidents at the time of his retirement, and John Adams was the oldest at the time of his death. The youngest of the Presidents at the time of his retirement and his death was James K. Polk.

—reprinted from the July 20, 1850,
issue of The Saturday Evening Post.

took to accomplish this end:

And there is solem, moral, kindly Millard Fillmore, who as ex-President did his best to spread culture by reading Shakespeare to the workers in a Buffalo shoe factory.

Franklin Pierce

★ ★ ★ ★ ★

14th President of the United States

Born: November 23, 1804, Hillsboro, New Hampshire.
Occupation: Lawyer.
Wife: Jane Appleton. *Children:* Three boys.
President: 1853-1857. Democratic party.
Vice-President: William R. King.
Died: October 8, 1869.
Buried: Concord, New Hampshire.

★ ★ ★ ★ ★

Franklin Pierce is one of the least-known of our American presidents. His compromising stand on the slavery issue, in an effort to prevent a civil war, accounts, in part, for this undeserved distinction.

As a student at Bowdoin College in Maine, he found Henry Wadsworth Longfellow and Nathaniel Hawthorne among his classmates. By rising at four in the morning and working unrelentingly until midnight, Pierce managed to rise from the bottom of his class and graduate third. He then studied law and, in 1827, was admitted to the bar.

He joined his father, who was also in politics, as a member of the New Hampshire legislature and became speaker in 1831. From there he went to Congress (1834) and then, at 32, was elected senator—at the time the youngest member of that legislative body. Then, because his wife disliked Washington, he interrupted his career to resume his law practice in Concord. For the next 10 years (1842-1852) his only official public act was service in the Mexican War, where he enlisted as a private, was appointed colonel and then brigadier general.

A stalemate in the 1852 Democratic Convention brought about his unexpected nomination for the presidency. By the 35th ballot, the necessary two-thirds vote had not yet been achieved. To break the deadlock, the Virginia delegation brought forth the name of General Pierce. Pierce accepted the nomination only because he thought he had no chance of winning over his opponent, General Winfield Scott, his old Mexican War commander. With an electoral vote of 254-42, Pierce won—much to his surprise and his wife's displeasure.

During Pierce's administration the United States bought 45,000 square miles of land in the Southwest from Mexico. This large tract of land, known as the Gadsden Purchase, was bought so that a railroad could be built to the Pacific by way of the southern routes.

The most serious event that happened during these years, however, was the passage of the Kansas-Nebraska Act of 1854 which violated the Missouri Compromise. It allowed both northerners and southerners to settle in the territory and to vote whether they would be free or slave. Internal fighting began as the pro-slavery and free-state settlers rushed into the territory and the area

Elected to the House in 1832, Pierce married Jane Means Appleton (below), the daughter of the President of Bowdoin College, in 1834. He was the only President to complete his term without making any changes in his Cabinet (right).

The New Hampshire home (above) was built the same year Pierce was born.

became known as "Bleeding Kansas." Peace was not restored until 1856, as reported in the December 13, 1856, issue of *The Saturday Evening Post*:

> Official correspondence, which we find published in the Washington Union, conveys ... that peace prevails. A letter from General Persifer F. Smith, dated Fort Leavenworth, Nov. 11th, says that "the laws have again been put in operation, and the administration of justice revived."

It was not until 1861 that Kansas was admitted to the Union as a free state and the Kansas-Nebraska Bill proved to be the fateful factor in the North-South split. Because of this the Republican party was formed, and the anti-slave platform became a reality.

Pierce's stay in Washington proved a bitter experience, and was made even more so by family tragedy. While president, his sole surviving son (of three children) was killed in a railroad accident. Not re-elected in 1856, he returned home a disappointed man. His attempts to avert Civil War had earned him the reputation at home of being a pro-slavery Yankee. Seven years later, his wife, Jane, died of consumption and melancholia.

Franklin Pierce died October 8, 1869, and was buried in Concord's old North Cemetery beside his wife and three children. The state of New Hampshire did not erect the bronze statue of Pierce on the southeast corner of its capitol grounds until 1914 and, in 1946, a granite memorial was finally placed by his grave.

Franklin Pierce of New Hampshire, and William King, of Alabama, comprised the 1852 Democratic ticket. Inscribed below their portraits on the lithograph by Currier (right) are the words "The Union Now and Forever."

Political Buttons, Book III, by Theodore Hake

"Who the H———"

At Nashville the night of the nomination a party of Whigs and Democrats had gathered in front of the principal hotel waiting for the arrival of the news, among the rest Sam Bugg and Chunky Towles, two notorious gamblers, both undoubting Democrats. At length Chunky Towles, worn out, went off to bed. The result was finally flashed over the wires. The crowd was nonplused. "Who the hell is Franklin Pierce?" passed from lip to lip.

Sam Bugg knew his political catechism well. He proceeded at length to tell all about Franklin Pierce, ending with the option that he was the man wanted and would be elected hands down, and he had a thousand dollars to bet on it.

Then he slipped away to tell his pal.

"Wake up, Chunky," he says. "We got a candidate—General Franklin Pierce, of New Hampshire."

"Who the h———"

"Chunky," says Sam, "I am ashamed of your ignorance. Gen. Franklin Pierce is the son of Gen. Benajmin Pierce, of Revolutionary fame. He has served in both houses of Congress. He declined a seat in Polk's Cabinet. He won distinction in the Mexican War. He is the very candidate we've been after."

"In that case," says Chunky, "I'll get up." When he reappeared, Petway, the Whig leader of the gathering, who had been deriding the convention, the candidate and all things else Democratic, exclaimed: "Here comes Chunky Towles. He's a good Democrat; and I'll bet ten to one he never heard of Franklin Pierce in his life before."

Chunky Towles was one of the handsomest men of his time. His strong suit was his unruffled composure and cool self-control. "Mr. Petway," says he, "you would lose your money, and I won't take advantage of any man's ignorance. Besides, I never gamble on a certainty. Gen. Franklin Pierce, sir, is a son of Gen. Benjamin Pierce, of Revolutionary memory. He served in both houses of Congress, sir—refused a seat in Polk's Cabinet, sir—won distinction in the Mexican War, sir. He has been from the first my choice, and I've money to bet on his election."

—an excerpt from an article by Henry Watterson which appeared in the March 1, 1919, issue of the Post.

James Buchanan

★ ★ ★ ★ ★

15th President of the United States

Born: April 23, 1791, Franklin County, Pennsylvania.
Occupation: Lawyer.
Wife: None.
President: 1857-1861. Democratic party.
Vice-President: John C. Breckenridge.
Died: June 1, 1868. *Buried:* Lancaster, Pennsylvania.

★ ★ ★ ★ ★

James Buchanan, born in a log cabin near Cove Gap, Pennsylvania, spent 42 of his 77 years in political service. The eldest of 10 children, his father was a successful farmer and later a wealthy iron manufacturer. His mother had little schooling but loved to read and so inspired her children. The family moved to Mercersburg, Pennsylvania, when James was seven. He was then allowed to attend school.

Buchanan entered Dickinson College at the age of 16 and began to smoke and drink with the other boys. Though his grades were exceptional, he was expelled for bad conduct after his first term. He pleaded, promising to "turn over a new leaf," and was allowed to return. James was graduated with honors and later admitted to the bar in Lancaster, Pennsylvania.

Within three years Buchanan was a candidate for the Pennsylvania legislature and could boast of a law practice earning him over $11,000 per year. But the War of 1812 delayed his entry into politics as Buchanan dutifully joined a volunteer cavalry company. He did return in time to win the seat and an additional term.

Young and successful, Buchanan fell in love with Anne Coleman, the beautiful daughter of a Lancaster millionaire. However, because of the suitor's somewhat "carefree" reputation, her parents disapproved. And, because of a carefully planted rumor, a heartsick Anne broke the engagement. She died in December of that same year, 1819, and Buchanan vowed never to marry.

Emersed in politics to ease his sorrow for Anne, Buchanan served in the House of Representatives for 10 years. A member of the Federalist party when first elected, he later joined the Jacksonian Democrats and became one of the leaders of that party. Jackson appointed him Minister to Russia in 1831, where he participated in the first trade agreement between the U.S. and Russia. On his return in 1833, Buchanan was elected to the Senate and served there for 10 years.

In 1844 President Polk appointed him Secretary of State. He helped to arrange the Treaty of Guadalupe Hidalgo ending the Mexican War in 1848 and expanding the United States' territories from west Texas to the Pacific Ocean. Two years earlier he had helped to avoid

"Hands off by Congress" and by the Executive branch did not prevent war.

Two pet eagles used to walk the stately grounds of Wheatland, whose "front-porch" was conveniently located between Philadelphia and Gettysburg.

a war with Great Britain via the Oregon Treaty which settled the Northwestern boundary dispute. When Polk left office Buchanan retired to his newly acquired home, Wheatland, near Lancaster, Pennsylvania.

Buchanan bought his beloved Wheatland, built in 1824, for $6,750 in 1848. Named for the sweeping view of surrounding wheatfields, the house was usually filled with his many nieces and nephews, some orphaned, who would come to stay with Uncle James.

Not able to resist, Buchanan sought the presidential nomination in 1852. Franklin Pierce defeated him but made him Minister to England the following year. Under Pierce's direction, Buchanan and the American ministers to France and Spain devised the Ostend Manifesto which declared that the U.S. wanted Cuba from Spain and would have it either by purchase or seizure. It was immediately repudiated but the effort won him the support of the southerners back home since it was understood that Cuba was to become slave territory.

The Democratic party was split in the nominating convention of 1856 due to the recent passage of the Kansas-Nebraska Act and the only candidate that would suit both the northerners and the southerners was James Buchanan. The Republican party was formed from the split and their nominee was John C. Frémont.

Buchanan conducted one of the first "front-porch" campaigns from Wheatland, which was also the campaign emblem for "Old Buck." He won easily but he was warned that he was sleeping on a volcano and that

unless he took prompt action he would be the last president of the United States.

No sooner had James Buchanan been inaugurated than the Dred Scott decision was handed down by the Supreme Court. It stated that the states, not Congress, had the right to legislate slavery and that Dred Scott, a slave, could not plead his case in court.

The slavery question came to a head during the Buchanan administration. Buchanan said that no state had a constitutional right to secede from the Union, but at the same time said that no state could be compelled to stay in the Union. He lacked the courage to take a stand some thought, but he had hoped that if he did not interfere, the problem would correct itself. During the 1860 Democratic Convention, Buchanan said:

> The people of the Southern States, can never abandon this great principle of State equality in the Union without self-degradation .... What then have the North to do? Merely to say that ... they will yield obedience to the decision of the Supreme Court and admit the right of a Southern man to take his property into the Territories, and hold it there just as a Northern man may do; and it is to me the most extraordinary thing in the world that this country should now be distracted and divided because certain persons at the North will not agree that their brethren at the South shall have the same rights in the Territories which they enjoy .... Let [the] principle of [Congressional] nonintervention [with slavery] be extended to the Territorial Legislatures ... and then the controversy is, in effect, ended .... Hands off by Congress and hands off by the Territorial Legislature.
>
> —*April 28, 1928*, Post.

55

In 1860 the U.S. received the Japanese delegation for the first time, the Pony Express was organized and Ft. Sumter was manned with Union troops.

High Rates of Interest?

Editor's Note: The effects of increases in the prime lending rates of the world's banks were debated 123 years ago.

The Bank of England has raised its rates to 8 percent, the Bank of France to 7½ percent, and the Bank of Hamburg to 9½ percent. In view of the recent doubling of the general rates of interest in Europe, it becomes a question whether the legal rate in this State, six percent, is not lower than what capital is fairly worth. Strange that the great increase of late years of the amount of coin and bullion, should thus have produced a corresponding increase, instead of decrease, of the rates of interest. We suppose it is in consequence of the immense impetus given by the abundance of capital to the business of the world.

—*an excerpt from the November 14, 1857, issue of* The Saturday Evening Post.

In an article by Henry Watterson in the March 8, 1919, *Post*, he summarized Buchanan's position:

> Mr. Buchanan was the victim of both personal and historic injustice. With secession in sight his one aim was to get out of the White House before the scrap began. It was not in Buchanan or Pierce, with their antecedents and associations, to be uncompromising Federalists. There was no clear law to go on. Moderate men were in a muck of doubt just what to do. With Horace Greeley Mr. Buchanan was ready to say "Let the erring sisters go."

Abraham Lincoln was elected president in 1861. The news of Lincoln's victory triggered the secession of South Carolina from the Union on December 20th. By February, 1861, six more states had withdrawn and the Confederate government was organized. Trying to keep the other eight states loyal, President Buchanan said he would not provoke war but must protect federal property. He asked Congress for men and money to do so but they refused.

Last-minute efforts to avoid war, by way of the Crittenden Compromise and the planned Peace Conference in Virginia, met with no success and Buchanan, sad yet relieved, left the White House in March.

"If you are as happy, my dear sir," Buchanan greeted Lincoln on Inauguration Day, 1861, "on entering this house as I am on leaving it and returning home, you are the happiest man in the country." "Mr. President," Lincoln replied slowly, "I cannot say that I shall enter it with much pleasure, but I can assure you that I shall do what I can to maintain the high standards set by my illustrious predecessors who have occupied it."

Buchanan returned to Pennsylvania to the sounds of roaring cannons of praise as that state's only president. He spent his last days at Wheatland reading his papers, playing cards, writing his presidential memoirs and dousing his gouty rheumatism in the mineral waters in nearby Bedford Springs. He died on June 1, 1868.

Divided Loyalty

John C. Breckenridge, Vice-President under Buchanan at the age of 35, "was the Beau Sabreur among statesmen," Henry Watterson wrote in the April 15, 1919, *Post*. But the Civil War was soon to claim him as another victim of rumor and circumstance, as Watterson recalled in the March 15 and April 5, 1919, issues:

"All through the winter of 1860-61 there had been a deal of wild talk. One story had it that Mr. Buchanan was to be kidnaped and made off with so that Vice-President Breckenridge might succeed and, acting as *de facto* President, throw the country into confusion and revolution, defeating the inauguration of Lincoln and the coming in of the Republicans. It was a figment of drink and fancy. There was never any such scheme. If there had been Breckenridge would not have consented to be party to it. He was a man of unusual mental as well as personal dignity and both temperamentally and intellectually a thorough conservative."

"There was never a man handsomer in person or more winning in manners. Sprung from a race of political aristocrats, he was born to shining success in public life. Of moderate opinion, brave and prudent, wherever he appeared he carried his audience with him. He had been elected on the ticket with Buchanan to the second office under the Government when he was but five and thirty years of age. There was nothing for him to gain from a division of the Union; the Presidency, perhaps, if the Union continued undivided. But he could not resist the onrush of disunionism, went with the South, which he served gallantly in the field and later as Confederate Secretary of War, and after a few years of self-imposed exile in Europe returned to Kentucky to die at four and fifty, a defeated and disappointed old man."

A Prince Visits the White House

When the Prince of Wales who later became Edward VII visited Washington as Baron Renfrew, he stayed with President Buchanan at the White House. After he left he wrote the President a polite bread-and-butter letter assuring his host that rarely "in a somewhat chequered career" had he so much enjoyed himself in any five days. That didn't tell the half of it. We only know the bare outlines of part of the story.

In those days the White House was not so large or so well furnished or so well ordered that it could entertain a guest of Baron Renfrew's rank and importance without considerable fixing up and rearrangement of its routine. The Prince was warmly invited, he was eagerly awaited, but undoubtedly he was a strain. Mr. Buchanan gave up his own bedroom to the royal guest and slept on a cot in the anteroom to his office.

Of course they did not let the Prince know this. Each night of his visit he stretched his short legs in a very long new rosewood bedstead that had been especially built for his visit. I don't think anybody knows what became of that cot. But the bed became known as the Lincoln bed, and the present legend is that it was made

for, as it was undoubtedly used by, the lengthy war President.

Miss Lane, Buchanan's niece, who was the Mrs. Edward Everett (Dolly) Gann of her day and the President's official hostess, was anxious to give a big dance for the Prince, but Mr. Buchanan wouldn't have it. He thought it might offend the sensibilities of some of his voting countrymen as being "profane gayety in the salons of the State." Presidents still have a quick regard for what the voters may think before they introduce novelties into White House entertainments.

Instead of a grand ball, the President and Miss Lane gave the Prince a formal dinner, followed by a reception and a musicale. This was a stiff party, but it turned out to be a notable one. The insufficient accounts seem to agree that nobody really enjoyed it except the author of a new song, dedicated to Miss Lane, called Listen to the Mockingbird, which was sung in public that night for the first time. It was what would now be called the world premiere of that enduring song. I am glad that ardent first-nighter, the Prince of Wales, was present. It somehow seems fitting.

To get up an appetite for the dinner, Miss Lane that afternoon took the Prince, heavily chaperoned, out to the gymnasium of a girls' school to play tenpins. That adventure in the bowling alley of the girls' school is a lost chapter.

—an excerpt from an article by
Edward G. Lowry which appeared
in the May 9, 1931, issue of
The Saturday Evening Post.

Bachelor James Buchanan's orphaned niece, the young and beautiful Harriet Lane, helped to make his personal and political career a social success.

Abraham Lincoln

⭐ ⭐ ⭐ ⭐ ⭐

16th President of the United States

Born: February 12, 1809, Hardin County, Kentucky.
Occupation: Lawyer.
Wife: Mary Todd. *Children:* Four boys.
President: 1861-1865. Republican party.
Vice-Presidents: Hannibal Hamlin, Andrew Johnson.
Died: April 15, 1865. *Buried:* Springfield, Illinois.

⭐ ⭐ ⭐ ⭐ ⭐

Abraham Lincoln is known as one of our "great" presidents. It is difficult to say just what makes a man great. It is not only what he does but also how he does it. Lincoln loved mankind, and he was more concerned for others than he was for himself. He believed in forgiveness and justice for all.

He was born in a log cabin near Hodgenville, Kentucky. When he was seven, his family moved to Indiana, and two years later his mother died. His father remarried and Abe and his stepmother became very close. She encouraged him to study, and took his part against his father, who did not like him spending so much time on "eddication" instead of doing the work that needed to be done.

The family moved to Illinois in 1830. Abe studied law, was elected to the state legislature for four terms and to Congress for one term. The question of slavery was being discussed all through the nation. Lincoln was very much against the Kansas-Nebraska Act which a young lawyer, Stephen A. Douglas, had authored. This act would let each new state decide for itself whether it would be free or slave. Lincoln and Douglas debated this question in a number of speeches which became known as the Lincoln-Douglas debates. In these debates Lincoln made his famous speech "that a house divided against itself cannot stand."

The Republican party nominated Abraham Lincoln for president in 1860, and he won the election. Lincoln described the purpose and function of government as: "The legitimate object of government is to do for a community of people whatever they need to have done, but cannot do at all, or cannot so well do for themselves, in their separate and individual capacities. In all that the people can individually do as well for themselves, government ought not to interfere."

By the time he took office in March, 1861, several southern states had left the Union. The new president took no action for a month because he wanted to hold on to the border states, and there were still many people in the North who would not support a war.

However, on April 12, 1861, an event occurred which forced President Lincoln to take a stand. Southern soldiers fired on Fort Sumter in Charleston, South Carolina. The American Civil War had started, and the next four years became the bloodiest in our history.

Lincoln called for troops, ordered a

Washington and Lincoln, together on this 1860 campaign kerchief, both studied surveying in their youth.

The engraving by J. C. Buttre of Stephen Douglas, recalls the famous debates.

blockade of southern ports, spent money without authority from Congress and suspended the writ of habeas corpus which meant that anyone could be thrown into prison without a hearing. The Union must be preserved at all costs! Lincoln had the ability to make the common people understand this. If this government were to be destroyed, it would mean that free people could not govern themselves.

On January 1, 1863, Lincoln issued his Emancipation Proclamation giving freedom to the slaves in the South.

The Battle of Gettysburg was one of the decisive battles of the war and it was here, at a dedication of a national cemetery, that Lincoln got up to "say a few words." These words are known as the Gettysburg Address, called the greatest speech in history. In this speech he spoke of "government of the people, by the people, for the people" and of "a new birth of freedom."

Lincoln was elected for a second term with the campaign cry, "Don't swap horses." In his inaugural address he set forth his plan for bringing the states back into the Union: "With malice toward none, with charity for all, with firmness in the right, as God gives us to see the right, let us strive on to finish the work we are in—to bind up the nation's wounds. . . ."

This was not to be. On the evening of April 14, 1865, Abraham Lincoln attended a performance of *Our American Cousin* at Ford's Theatre in Washington. A shot rang out and the President slumped in his chair. He had been shot by John Wilkes Booth, a well-known actor of that time. President Lincoln was carried to a house across the street from the theatre, where he died the next day.

Concerning the assassin(s), the following "Third Official Gazette" was issued by Washington to *The Saturday Evening Post* at 4:10 A.M., April 15, 1865:

> It is now ascertained, with reasonable certainty, that two assassins were engaged in the horrible crime, J. Wilkes Booth being the one that shot the President. The other is a companion of his, whose name is not known. The deception is so clean that he can hardly escape.
>
> It appears from a letter found in Booth's trunk, that the murder was planned before the 4th of March, but fell through then because the accomplice backed out until "Richmond could be heard from."
>
> Booth and his accomplice were at the livery stable at six o'clock last evening, and left there about ten o'clock, or shortly before that hour. It would seem that for several days they have been seeking their chance, but

The Gettysburg Address, perhaps the most inspiring "few words" on American democracy and freedom ever written, was delivered on November 19, 1863. This copy was given to Edward Everett, the chief speaker of the day.

for some unknown reason it was not carried into effect until last night.

The American people mourned this president as they had never mourned before. Millions lined the railroad tracks as his body was brought back by train to Springfield, Illinois. His grave there in Oak Ridge Cemetery is visited by many each year. In Washington, D.C., the Lincoln Memorial, stands as a tribute to this great president.

Library of Congress

"I do order and declare that all persons held as slaves . . . are, and henceforward shall be, free," Lincoln issued the Emancipation Proclamation on January 1, 1863, to boost Union morale and to gain support in Europe. Daniel Chester French (right) carved the likeness for the Lincoln Memorial.

Assassination of President Lincoln Probable Murder of Mr. Seward

WASHINGTON, April 15, 1:30 A.M.—Major-General Dix.—This evening, about 9:30 P.M., at Ford's Theatre, the President, while sitting in his private box with Mrs. Lincoln, Miss Harris, and Major Rathburn, was shot by an assassin who suddenly entered the box and approached behind the President.

The assassin then leaped upon the stage brandishing a large dagger or knife, and made his escape in the rear of the theatre.

The pistol ball entered the back of the President's head and penetrated nearly through the head. The wound is mortal. The President has been insensible ever since it was inflicted, and is now dying.

About the same hour, an asssassin, whether the same or another, entered Mr. Seward's house, and, under pretence of having a prescription, was shown to the Secretary's sick chamber. The Secretary of State was in bed, a nurse and Miss Seward with him. The assassin immediately rushed to the bed, inflicting one or two stabs on the throat and two on the face. It is hoped the wounds may not be mortal. My apprehension is that they will prove fatal.

The noise alarmed Mr. Frederick Seward, who was in an adjoining room, and hastened to the door of his father's room, where he met the assassin who inflicted upon him one or more dangerous wounds. The recovery of Frederick Seward is doubtful.

It is not probable that the President will live through the night.

All the members of the Cabinet, except Mr. Seward, are now in attendance upon the President. I have seen Mr. Seward, but he is unconscious.

EDWIN M. STANTON,
Secretary of War.

Editor's Note: Seward's wife, an invalid, received such a shock that she died within two months, and his only daughter, who witnessed the assault, never recovered from the effects of the scene and died within the year. His son, Frederick, recovered, and Seward himself gradually regained his health and remained in the cabinet of President Johnson until the expiration of his term in 1869.

WASHINGTON, April 15, 2:30 A.M.—The President is still alive, but is growing weaker. The ball is lodged in his brain, three inches from where it entered the skull. He remains insensible, and his condition is utterly hopeless. The Vice President has been to see him, but all company except the Cabinet, his family, and a few friends, are rigidly excluded.

Large crowds still continue in the street as near to the house as the line of guards will allow.

Lincoln was 28 years old when he rode into Springfield; exactly 28 years later he was shot by John Wilkes Booth (top) who afterwards waved a dagger at the audience and shouted "Sic Semper Tyrannis!"

WASHINGTON, April 15, 3 A.M.—Major-General Dix, New York.—The President still breathes, but is quite insensible, as he has been ever since he was shot.

The screams of Mrs. Lincoln first disclosed the fact to the audience that the President had been shot, then all present rose to their feet, rushing toward the stage, many exclaiming, "Hang him! Hang him!"

The excitement was one of the wildest possible description, and of course there was an abrupt termination of the theatrical performance.

There was a rush towards the Presidential box, when cries were heard, "Stand back!" "Give him air!" "Has any one stimulants?"

On a hasty examination, it was found that the President had been shot through the head above and back of the temporal bone.

He was removed to a private house opposite the theatre, and the Surgeon General of the Army and other surgeons were sent for to attend to his condition.

An immense crowd gathered in front of it, all deeply anxious to learn the condition of the President. It had been previously announced that the wound was mortal, but all hoped otherwise. The shock to the community was terrible.

MIDNIGHT.—The President was in a state of *syncope*, totally insensible and breathing hardly.

The surgeons were exhausting every possible effort of medical skill, but all hope was gone.

The parting of his family with the dying President is too sad for description.

—*reprinted from the April 22, 1865, Post.*

61

The Lincoln family in 1861: Mrs. Lincoln, William, Robert, Thomas ("Tad") and the President. Right, Rockwell's "Lincoln for the Defense" which he did for the February 10, 1962, issue of the Post.

A Wicked and Vile Work

Never did such a pang of horror convulse the heart of the American people, as when the news, spread rapidly through the length and breadth of the loyal states, reached them that President Lincoln had been vilely murdered.

The evening of Good Friday—that day consecrated in the hearts of Christians the world over—was chosen by the assassins for their wicked and bloody work.

For this man, whom with cruel hands they have slain, was the personification of all that was most humane and merciful and forgiving in the North. He it was who, in connection with Mr. Seward—their other victim—was standing between the prominent agents of the rebellion and the justice of the violated Laws. He it was who was meeting the wild cry for vengeance from those whose sons and brothers had rotted and starved in the loathsome prisons of the South, and been blown to pieces on Southern battle-fields, with invocations for forgiveness, for forgetfulness, for the restoration of fraternal love.

And this man, so free from passion, from vindictiveness—whose only fault was always to lean too much towards gentleness and mercy—who did not need to practice forgiveness towards his enemies, because he

Tad's Medicine

It was March 10, 1862. Willie Lincoln had died only nineteen days ago; now Tad, recovering, but still seriously ill, wouldn't take his medicine. Things got so bad upstairs at the Executive Mansion that Tad's nurse took the problem to John Hay, and Hay called Lincoln from an important White House conference with a group of border-state senators and representatives.

Silently, the President and the young nurse walked down the long corridor. "You stay here," Lincoln told her, entering the sickroom and softly closing the door behind him. He was gone only a few minutes and—though Hay had seen him in one of his awful fits of gloom only a short time earlier—now the President was smiling broadly.

"It's all right. Tad and I have fixed things up," he announced cheerily as he hurried back to the waiting statesmen.

The nurse found Tad, beaming, with a bank check reading "Pay to 'Tad' (when he is well enough to present)—Five dollars" clutched in his hand. Tad took his medicine.

—an excerpt from a December 14, 1953, Post *article written by Ronald T. Carr and Hugh Morrow.*

Editor's Note: The original five-dollar Lincoln check is today one of the prized possessions of an "amiable scholar" in Kentucky.

never seemed to feel towards any man as towards an enemy—whose constant thought was to restore the Union by kindness and conciliation—has been basely stricken down from behind by a representative of those whom he was striving with all his might and influence to shield and benefit.

Was it an error then? Was he wrong in brain, who was so nobly right in heart? Is mercy at this time an error, a cruel clemency, a false humanity, from which would spring in a short period even greater and more awful fruits than those we have been gathering during the last four years? Has this cruel deed been allowed in the orderings of an all-wise Providence, that we may fully understand the hearts of these men with whom we have been contending, and waste no foolish maganimity on those who seem incapable of responding to it? Such are the sorts of questions which at this moment every reflecting loyal man in the North is putting to himself.

For our own part, we have coincided heartily heretofore with the President in his generous and merciful projects and desires. We have been among those who have constantly pleaded for generosity, for amnesty, for universal forgiveness. But in the horror engendered by this cruel deed, we feel as if all other feelings were swept aside by the single demand for JUSTICE—as though the voice of Mercy in our heart had been stilled forever by the same ball which silenced the tongue and deadened the thoughtful brain of its most powerful advocate.

Ah, tender and generous soul of Abraham Lincoln, little did it matter to thee that in one swift moment thy day's work was over—that toilsome labor of heart and brain ended, and the sweet rest of a true and honest man thy everlasting reward.

But for us, thy countrymen, what new and untried paths seem to open before us. Almost it seems as if a comforting voice has come down from the pitying heavens, saying as of old, "Mourn not for me; mourn for yourselves and for your children!"

—an editorial from the April 22, 1865, issue of The Saturday Evening Post.

Mary Lincoln

Lincoln purchased the oak-framed house for $1500 in 1884. When he and his wife left for the White House he spoke to his neighbors gathered at the railroad station, "I now leave, not knowing when or whether ever I may return." The silhouette of her above is from a drawing by Raymond Warren.

63

Andrew Johnson

★ ★ ★ ★ ★

17th President of the United States

Born: December 29, 1808, Raleigh, North Carolina.
Occupation: Tailor.
Wife: Eliza McCardle. *Children:* Three boys, two girls.
President: 1865-1869. Democrat. National Union party.
Vice-President: Lafayette Sabine Foster, Benjamin
   Franklin Wade, Presidents pro tempore of the Senate.
Died: July 31, 1875. *Buried:* Greeneville, Tennessee.

★ ★ ★ ★ ★

There are only four kinds of office that may be attained by a citizen under the Constitution of the United States—legislative, judicial, military and executive. Andrew Johnson is the only man in American history who attained to all these and was both Vice-President and President of the United States, yet he had no formal schooling. He was a tailor by trade, and his wife taught him to read and write.

His political career began in Greeneville, Tennessee, a town previously run by the wealthy and the aristocrats. "Why can't we mechanics have a hand in it?" the tailor had asked, whereupon he was elected alderman, and then mayor. Things needed attention at the state capital, so they next sent him to the House and Senate.

Elected by his state in 1843 to the United States Congress, he worked for the passage of the Homestead Act, which opened up vast, unsettled areas of the West. This is perhaps the greatest accomplishment of his long career as a public servant.

By the beginning of the Civil War, he was a U.S. Senator and would have remained so, had not Lincoln chosen him to be Vice-President. In this capacity, he served for three years as military governor of Tennessee, a perilous and exhausting position, and his official residence was his home in Nashville.

When sworn in as Vice-President the second time in 1864, it was said that he was drunk. Johnson, it was true, drank—as did practically all public men of his day. In truth, Johnson, ill with pneumonia, left his sick bed to make the three to four-day journey to the nation's capital for the inauguration. The one preventative for pneumonia in that day was whiskey, and Johnson's physician had faithfully plied him with it throughout the entire length of the journey by carriage—explaining

Believe It or Not

Johnson, in the saying of the countryside, "outmarried himself." His wife was a plain woman, but she came of a good family. One day, so the legend ran, she saw passing through the Greeneville street in which her people lived, a woman, a boy and a cow, the boy carrying a pack over his shoulder. They were obviously weary and hungry. Extreme poverty could present no sadder picture. "Mother," cried the girl, "there goes the man I am going to marry." She was thought to be in jest. But a few years later she made her banter good and lived to see her husband President of the United States and go with him to occupy the White House.

*—excerpted from an article
in the April 5, 1919, Post
written by Henry Watterson.*

his reportedly "drunken state" at the time of the inauguration and discrediting the allegation that he was "nothing but a drunkard."

Though a southerner from Tennessee, Johnson had a great loyalty to the Union and the Constitution. He did not believe in secession. When Lincoln died, he became president and carried on with reconstruction as Lincoln would have done, allowing the southern states back into the Union. Congress, however, in the hands of the radical Republicans, wanted the South punished.

Johnson refused to let the emotions of the time threaten the liberties of the American people, a stand which led to his impeachment. He was acquitted, but to this day he holds the dubious distinction of being our only president to be impeached. On June 6, 1868, *The Saturday Evening Post* carried this brief summary on the results of the trial:

> THE IMPEACHMENT.—The Impeachment Trial has ended by the acquittal of the President on three articles and the final adjournment of the Court without voting on the remainder.

Defeated by Grant in the election of 1868, he returned to his homeland. Years later, he was again elected to the United States Senate and took his seat in the same room in which he had been impeached.

He suffered a stroke at his home in Greeneville in 1875 and died four months later. He was buried on a

The engraving above from an 1868 Leslie's Magazine shows Senator Edmund Ross of Kansas standing (far left) to vote "Not Guilty" to charges brought against Johnson in the impeachment trial.

hillside there with a copy of the Constitution, which he had so loyally defended, beneath his head. After his death, this statement in his handwriting was found among his papers, written when he was stricken with cholera in 1873. It now hangs in the library of his home:

> All seems gloom and despair. I have performed my duty to my God, my country and my family. I have nothing to fear. Approaching death to me is the mere shadow of God's protecting wing. Beneath it I feel almost sacred. Here I know no evil can come; there I will rest in quiet and peace, beyond the reach of calumny's poisoned shaft, the influence of envy and jealous enemies, where treason and traitors in state, backsliders and hypocrites in church, can have no place; where the great fact will be realized that God is truth, and gratitude is the highest attribute of man.

The Johnson Home (below), restored in 1957, looks today as it did in 1869-75.

Andrew Johnson National Historic Site, National Park Service

In the cartoon below, vice-presidential candidate Johnson uses his tailor's needle and Lincoln's help to sew the Union back together.

Tennessee State Library

Ulysses S. Grant

★ ★ ★ ★ ★

18th President of the United States

Born: April 27, 1822, Point Pleasant, Ohio.
Occupation: Soldier.
Wife: Julia B. Dent. *Children:* Two boys, two girls.
President: 1869-1877. Republican party.
Vice-Presidents: Schuyler Colfax, Henry Wilson.
Died: July 23, 1885. *Buried:* New York City.

★ ★ ★ ★ ★

Jesse Root Grant and Hannah Simpson Grant named their oldest son Hiram Ulysses, but the future president was called Ulysses until after the surrender of Confederate troops at Ft. Donelson in 1862, when he became known to the world as "Unconditional Surrender Grant."

As a boy on the Ohio farm, Grant was hard-working

(by the age of seven he could handle a team of horses) and thrifty but in business he was lacking—a condition he never outgrew.

Grant was a graduate of West Point, where he excelled in math and horsemanship, and served in the Mexican War. In August of 1848 he married Julia Dent. And in 1854 he resigned from the Army.

The next six years were not successful ones. Grant tried farming, real estate and then ran for the office of county engineer, which he lost. Finally, he turned to clerking in his father's leather goods store, earning $25 a month. His family called him "Lys" but the neighborhood called him "Useless."

When the Civil War broke out, the north needed officers, and he was given command of a regiment. His success as a military leader is nearly unparalleled in American history. In 1864, at the age of 39, Lt. General Grant was given command of the northern army.

The night before Lee's surrender at Appomattox, Grant and his officers slept on the floor of a farmhouse nearby. It was a restless night for the General:

> Grant was suffering from one of the cruel headaches that he was subject to occasionally, especially in times of anxiety, and he sat a good part of the night with his feet in hot mustard water, mustard plasters on the back of his neck and wrists. He had not taken off his clothes, just his boots, and had only lain down on a sofa at intervals; he went outside in the first gray light to walk up and down with his hands pressed tight to his temples. It had been much too considerate of him to let the young officers thump on the farmhouse piano all the first part of the evening; it had made his head worse, for music in any form was noise that caused the general actual physical pain.
>
> When Grant got Lee's note the morning of the ninth saying that he would meet him for discussion of terms for the laying down of arms, his headache vanished in one swift heartbeat.
>
> *—excerpted from an April 7, 1951,*
> Post *article by Dorothy Kunhardt.*

Grant was scheduled to attend the Ford Theater with President Abraham Lincoln in 1865. John Wilkes Booth carried a big knife to use on Grant after shooting Lincoln. But Grant begged off from attending the theater in order to catch a slow train to Philadelphia to see his children. It probably saved his life.

After the war, Grant was a national hero and Congress appointed him a full general, the first to hold such rank since Washington. When the Republicans notified him of his nomination for the presidency he replied:

> If chosen to fill the high office for which you have selected me, I will give to its duties the same energy, the same spirit and the same will that I have given to the performance of all duties which have devolved upon me heretofore. *—June 6, 1868,* Post.

A cheering nation elected him President for two terms.

One of the achievements of his administration was the agreement with Great Britain over the *Alabama* claims dispute. The *Alabama* was one of several Confederate warships provided by Great Britain which fought the Union merchant marine. Congress demanded and was awarded $15,500,000 in compensation.

For the most part, however, the administration was smirched with scandal and corruption because, being incredibly honest himself, President Grant found it hard to believe that people he trusted could betray him.

Post editor Beverly Smith, Jr., wrote of the retirement years of Grant in an article in the May 6, 1951, issue:

"Retired to private life as ex-President, General Grant ran into various financial reverses. Thus in 1884 he found himself impoverished and in debt. If he died, he could see no way of leaving his beloved Julia with even a pittance.

"He tried an article for *Century Magazine* on the battle of Shiloh [and] when the editors persuaded him to write as he talked, he turned out a narrative which was clear, direct and engrossing.

"From November, 1884, into July of 1885, he wrote the famous *Personal Memoirs of U.S. Grant*, two volumes, 1231 pages, 295,000 words. It was a task to daunt a young man in the prime of his vigor. Grant accomplished it while in almost constant pain. At times, when he fell unconscious from coughing fits and hemorrhages [symptoms of his throat cancer], the doctors despaired of his life. He recovered and went on. In the latter months he could not sleep in bed because of the danger of choking to death. He spent his restless nights propped on two chairs. When sleep would not come, he would ask that his lamp be brought, and would write on until dawn.

"Toward the end he wrote, in a note to his doctor, 'I am thankful for the providential extension of my time to enable me to continue my work.' He completed his task just a few days before his death on July 23, 1885. The *Memoirs* brought to his estate the huge sum of $450,000 [thanks to the intervention of his friend, Mark Twain]—more than enough to take care of his family and his other obligations.

"Thus U.S. Grant, ex-war leader, ex-President, in his last eight months fought and won the most heroic battle of his life."

The Grant family at Galena from an 1868 engraving by Samuel Sartain.

Grant adored his charming, spirited wife, Julia Dent, despite her "cast left eye."

Grant Nearly Captured!

He was often on picket line all alone endeavoring to ascertain from personal inspection, more of the enemy's position and plans than he could obtain from the reports of his officers. On one of these occasions he came near falling into the hands of the enemy. It was at Chattanooga, while he was preparing for the battle of Missionary Ridge.

Wishing to get a nearer view of the enemy, he again rode out on the picket line, and was on the eastern bank of Chattanooga Creek, when a party of rebel soldiers were drawing water on the other side. They wore blue coats; and thinking they were his own men, Grant asked them to whose command they belonged. They answered, "Longstreet's corps;" whereupon Grant called out: "What are you doing in those coats, then?" The rebels replied: "Oh! all our corps wear blue." This was a fact which Grant had forgotten. The rebels then scrambled up on their own side of the stream, little thinking that they had been talking with the Commander of the national army.

—reprinted from the June 6, 1868, issue of The Saturday Evening Post *from* The Life of Ulysses S. Grant, General-In-Chief U.S.A., *by Hon. J.T. Headly.*

Rutherford B. Hayes

★ ★ ★ ★ ★

19th President of the United States

Born: October 4, 1822, Delaware, Ohio.
Occupation: Lawyer.
Wife: Lucy Webb. *Children:* Seven boys, one girl.
President: 1877-1881. Republican party.
Vice-President: William A. Wheeler.
Died: January 17, 1893. *Buried:* Fremont, Ohio.

★ ★ ★ ★ ★

Hayes was a war hero and governor of Ohio. In 1876 two good candidates were running for presi-

dent—Hayes, a Republican, and Samuel J. Tilden, governor of New York and a Democrat.

The election that followed proved to be one of the most memorable and controversial in our history. When it came to an end the result showed 196 in the Electoral College, 11 more than the majority, and a majority of 264,300 over Hayes in the popular vote. Watterson described the incredible series of events which followed in an article in the May 3, 1919, *Post.*

> The newspapers, both Republican and Democratic, of November 8, 1876, the morning after the election, conceded an overwhelming victory for Tilden and Hendricks. There was, however, a single exception. *The New York Times* had gone to press with its first edition, leaving the result in doubt but inclining toward the success of the Democrats. In its later editions this tentative attitude was changed to the statement that Mr. Hayes lacked the vote only of Florida—"claimed by the Republicans"—to be sure of the required 185 votes in the Electoral College.

Senator Barnum, of Connecticut, financial head of the Democratic National Committee, sent a telegram to the *Times* asking for the latest news from Oregon, Loui-

This painting of Lucy Webb Hayes, a copy of an 1880 original by Daniel Huntington, is on display in the Rutherford B. Hayes Library.

siana, Florida and South Carolina. The *Times* people, intense Republican partisans, reasoned that if Barnum did not know, why might not a doubt be raised concerning the count of the ballots.

Telegrams were sent to Columbia, Tallahassee and New Orleans stating to each of the parties addressed that the result of the election depended upon his state. The signature of Zachariah Chandler, a very prominent Republican politician of that time, was affixed on each telegram. Senator Chandler then issued the statement from National Republican Headquarters that "Hayes has 185 electoral votes and is elected." The result of the above actions was confusion about the returns and a disputed count of the vote.

After weeks of speeches and debates, an electoral commission of members of Congress was appointed. They voted along party lines and two days before the inauguration, gave the election to Hayes by one vote. It was clearly dishonest, but a deal was made with the Democrats to withdraw the last of the Federal troops from the South.

As president, Hayes complied with this request, and, in spite of the shadow cast on it by the contested election, his administration was an honest one and one of progress. During his term, the transcontinental railroad was constructed; oil and steel industries were developed; and the telephone, phonograph and electric lights were invented.

Mrs. Hayes prohibited the serving of liquor in the White House—a move which subjected her and her family to considerable criticism and earned her the nickname "lemonade Lucy." Hayes' diary suggests, however, that several factors entered into the first family's decision:

> A desire to set an example of moderation after the exuberant social events of the Grant administration, Lucy's life-long abstinence from liquor, a desire to keep temperance advocates in the Republican Party, and *most of all* Hayes' firm conviction that government officials should conduct themselves at all times with discretion and dignity.

Rutherford B. Hayes declined to run for a second term and chose instead to return to his home, Spiegel Grove, where he devoted much of his remaining years to the social reform causes of education, prison reform and veterans' affairs.

Hayes and "Man's Inspiration"

Rutherford B. Hayes married Lucy Webb in 1852. His love for her was expressed on more than one occasion in

Campaign Memorabilia

The stately Victorian mansion at Spiegel Grove, Fremont, Ohio, was home for Hayes the last 20 years of his life. During his presidency, it served as a summer White House.

his diary, as well as in numerous letters. He referred to his marriage to Lucy as "the most interesting fact of his life" and wrote to her on his 48th birthday, "My life

I Decline

Arthur Krock, noted journalist, tells the following story about his Uncle Fred, as a boy, and President Hayes:

The first meeting that I am aware of between a President of the United States and any member of my family took place in 1877 and involved Frederick Morris, my maternal grandfather's second son. He had been appointed to the Naval Academy at Annapolis, and his father took him there from Glasgow, Kentucky.

With his son in tow, my grandfather proceeded to the White House to pay his respects to President Rutherford B. Hayes. They were received with the graciousness characteristic of this bearded chief of state, who, after shaking hands with the father, extended the friendly gesture to the boy. Whereupon my Uncle Fred firmly joined his hands behind his back, and then compounded the rude gesture. "I decline," he said, "to shake hands with the man who stole the election from Tilden."

—*an excerpt from an article in the September 9, 1968,* Post, *written by Arthur Krock.*

Ex-President and Mrs. Rutherford B. Hayes with children and friends at their Spiegel Grove residence, August 1887. Fanny Hayes is shown holding child; son, Webb, is in front with tennis racket; son, Scott, is the first man on Hayes' left. The dog is "Dot," the family pet.

with you has been so happy—so successful—so beyond reasonable anticipations, that I think of you with a loving gratitude that I do not know how to express."

Despite his feelings for his wife and the fact that she was the first President's wife to hold a college degree, Hayes was not an advocate of women's rights. He viewed women as "an elevating influence—man's inspiration," and said that the American male should "go forth to duty" while the woman stayed at home "to weave the spell which makes home a paradise . . . ."[1] A review of Hayes' writings suggests that he was indifferent to the nineteenth century women's movement in general, and opposed to women voting, in particular.

During his second term as governor of Ohio in 1870, Hayes was visited by his wife's aunt Margaret Cook Boggs, who was en route to a women's rights convention in Dayton. Hayes wrote afterward in his diary that, in his opinion, woman's role as wife and mother was incompatible with political participation.

Ironically, the same Republican political leaders (Hayes among them) who were opposed to rights for women, had endorsed the Fourteenth and Fifteenth Amendments following the Civil War. During this postwar period, the women suffrage advocates organized

Rutherford B. Hayes and Lucy Webb at the time of their wedding in Cincinnati, Ohio, on December 30, 1852, taken from a daguerreotype.

the National Woman Suffrage Association and the American Woman Suffrage Association in an effort to obtain voting rights for women.

By 1876, at which time Hayes was nominated Republican presidential candidate, women's suffrage had become a major issue. Back in the 1872 campaign, the Republican party had come out in general support of women's rights, but by 1876, little trace of any backing remained. And, since the Democratic party offered little support, pressure for women's rights remained outside the realm of the political parties.

After Hayes was elected, Susan B. Anthony made the following plea at the Fourth of July Centennial celebration: "We ask our rulers, at this hour no special favors, no special legislation. We ask justice, we ask equality, we ask that all the civil and political rights that belong to citizens of the United States, be guaranteed to us and our daughters forever." Although her plea was virtually ignored, the suffragists drew up a declaration of rights at their 1877 national convention in Washington, D.C., appealing to the nation to enter into its second century with voting rights granted to all its citizenry. They attended a reception given by Lucy Webb Hayes at the White House on a Saturday afternoon and met with President Hayes the following Monday morning. At this meeting, Sarah J. Spencer, a resident of Washington, D.C., who had taken the question of women's suffrage to the Supreme Court, read a resolution from the suffrage association admonishing President Hayes for not supporting their cause.

And, though petitions supporting the women's movement continued to pour into the White House after the suffrage convention, Hayes and his administration continued the policy of making no specific commitments.

Hayes did, however, sign an act permitting women to serve as lawyers before the Supreme Court. He signed the act, though, with no peripheral comments on the topic of women's rights. Later, when his Third Annual Message to Congress stressed civil service reform and votes for Negro men (with no mention of women), it appeared he was not yet persuaded that women should have any official say in politics.

When Hayes retired from political life in 1881, the controversy over women's rights was still very much alive—particularly the question of voting rights. In 1896 the women of Wyoming, Colorado, Idaho and Utah were the only enfranchised women in the Union. It was not until 1910, 14 years later, that other states extended voting privileges to women. And, it was not until the year 1920 that the Nineteenth Amendment was passed—drawn from the very proposal that had been endorsed by suffragists 43 years before at their national convention.

—from "The Hayes Administration and the Woman Question," by Dr. Beverly Beeton, Spring, 1978, Hayes Historical Journal.

Lucy Webb Hayes and children in the White House Conservatory, 1879; l/r: Carrie Davis, friend; Scott Hayes, Mrs. Hayes and Fanny Hayes.

Colonel Rutherford B. Hayes (far left) in the mess hall with officers of the 23rd Ohio Volunteer Infantry in Western Virginia, 1862.

Rutherford B. Hayes Library

Rutherford B. Hayes Library

1 Beeton, Dr. Beverly, *Woman Suffrage in the Nineteenth Century American West,* the University of Utah Press, soon to be published.

James A. Garfield

★ ★ ★ ★ ★

20th President of the United States

Born: November 19, 1831, Orange, Ohio.
Occupation: Lawyer.
Wife: Lucretia Rudolph. *Children:* Four boys, one girl.
President: 1881, six and one-half months. Republican party.
Vice-President: Chester A. Arthur.
Died: September 19, 1881. *Buried:* Cleveland, Ohio.

★ ★ ★ ★ ★

James Abram Garfield was the last president to have been born in a log cabin. He left his home in the pioneer town of Orange, Ohio, when he was 16 to become a sailor on the Great Lakes; he ended up leading the horses that pulled the canalboat between Cleveland and Pittsburgh. It took 14 spills into the canal before Garfield mastered the job. He returned home after contracting malaria.

Recovering, Garfield worked his way through Geauga Seminary and Western Reserve Eclectic Institute (now Hiram College) in Ohio and in 1856 was graduated with honors from Williams College in Massachusetts. He returned to Eclectic Institute to teach and one year later, at the age of 26, became the school's president.

In 1858 Garfield married his childhood friend, Lucretia Rudolph. The following year he was elected to the Ohio Senate. When the Civil War broke out in April of 1861, the young lawyer/teacher volunteered and was commissioned a lieutenant colonel. Colonel Garfield had no military experience, so he drilled his Ohio regiment with a textbook in one hand. In December he was sent to lead a brigade in Kentucky where he defeated the experienced General Humphrey Marshall at Middle Creek. He became the youngest brigadier general of the Civil War.

Major General Garfield resigned his commission in December of 1863 when he was elected to the House of Representatives. He was a Congressman for 17 years, rising to the position of minority leader.

The Republican Convention of 1880 was deadlocked between former President Grant of the Stalwart faction,

Whoa Horse!

President James Garfield kept horses for himself and his family. His little daughter Molly especially liked to ride. At least she did at the beginning. Her favorite was a brown mare named Kit. According to the custom in those days she rode sidesaddle. One day a stable hand failed to tighten the girth properly and, while Molly was aboard Kit, the saddle slipped and tilted. The horse shied and bolted. Molly was thrown to the ground, but one foot was caught in the stirrup. For a few moments the screaming child was dragged around until the horse was caught by the bridle and Molly was released. Had someone told the youngster to get right back in the saddle, everything would have been all right, for Molly was unharmed. But nobody did, and Molly never rode again.

—an excerpt from a Spring 1978
The Country Gentleman article by
Margaret Truman.

In the background of James Hope's painting of the President's birthplace is the schoolhouse the four Garfield children attended three months a year.

and Senator James G. Blaine of the Halfbreed faction. On the 36th vote Garfield was named as a compromise candidate. Chester A. Arthur was his running mate. He defeated the Democratic nominee by fewer than 10,000 popular votes.

James A. Garfield was a large man—6 feet tall and impressive in appearance. As head of a divided party, the President appointed mostly Halfbreeds to government positions which greatly aroused the Stalwarts. He was interested in civil service reform because he thought people should take a written examination to get a government job. However, before he could do anything about it, he was shot in a railroad station in Washington, D.C., by a government office-seeker who had been denied the position of his choice.

Professor James MacGregor Burns described the ordeal in the January 25, 1964, issue of the *Post*:

> A madman named Guiteau shot Garfield in July, 1881. For 80 days Garfield lingered, bearing his ordeal with incredible grace. Fevers came and went; cheerful bulletins alternated with cautious ones; infection spread; the sick man rallied, then fell; he underwent operations without anesthesia. The President could do no work, though he went through a few motions. The Government drifted.
>
> "Arthur is President now!" Guiteau had shouted as he shot Garfield. But Vice President Chester A. Arthur did not become President during the 80 days. His position was awkward. A New York machine politician, he had been on the outs with the President. The day after the assassination he met with Garfield's Cabinet, but they greeted him so coolly that he almost left. Arthur did not know what to do, so he did nothing.

Garfield was the fourth president to die in office, and the second president to be assassinated. Chester A. Arthur became president upon Garfield's death and urged Congress to take clarifying action on the problem of a disabled president. Congress talked about it and—did nothing.

Golden Music

My mother was a singing evangelist—Savilla Kring—who when I came to know her had a voice like a gentle flute—a voice that at eighty was still soft and true. She first sang the hymn, "I'm the Child of the King," at Chautauqua, New York, in the '70s, and then made it a favorite of the now-long-forgotten national camp meetings from Old Orchard, Maine, and Round Lake, New York, to Ocean Grove, New Jersey.

She sang it one Sunday morning at the dedication of Ocean Grove's first pavilion. On this particular Sunday, President James A. Garfield lay mortally wounded at Long Branch, just a few miles away. In the afternoon mother was driven to the then-little railhead seaside village, where she sang for the dying President, who lay propped against his pillows as he listened to the golden music of an eager girl:

My Father is rich in houses and lands;
He holdeth the wealth of the world in His hands . . .
A tent or a cottage, why should I care?
They are building a palace for me over there.
—an excerpt from a May 7, 1955, Post
article written by Daniel A. Poling.

The scene at the Baltimore and Potomac Railroad Depot on July 2, 1881. The assasin was described as having "the face and intonations of a demon."

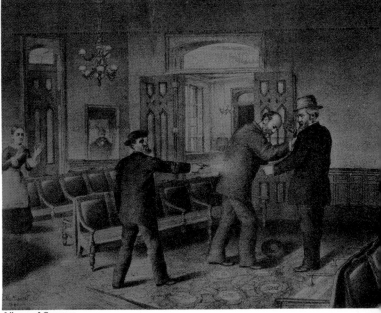

73

Chester A. Arthur

★ ★ ★ ★ ★

21st President of the United States

Born: October 5, 1830, Fairfield, Vermont.
Occupation: Lawyer.
Wife: Ellen Herndon. *Children:* Two boys, one girl.
President: 1881-1885. Republican party.
Vice-President: *Thomas F. Bayard, David Davis,
   George F. Edmunds, Presidents pro tempore of the
   Senate.
Died: November 18, 1886. *Buried:* Albany, New York.

★ ★ ★ ★ ★

Chester Alan Arthur was born in Fairfield, Vermont,
and, upon graduation from Union College in 1848, he
practiced law in New York City before joining the
political machine of Roscoe Conkling.

He had succeeded to the presidency as a Conkling
leader. A U.S. Representative (1859-63, following Garfield's assassination, 1865-67) and Senator (1867-81),
Conkling had come to be the undisputed Republican
leader in the state of Vermont. During the Grant administration (1869-77) he controlled Federal patronage.

The Great Auction of 1882

When Arthur succeeded Garfield, he wouldn't
move in until the house was drastically cleaned,
saying he would spend his own money if the
Government wouldn't pay for it. It was the first
time the attic had been cleaned out since
Buchanan's time. The subsequent housecleaning
resulted in the great auction of 1882.

Cast-off White House furnishings and the leav-
ings of many administrations included the rat trap
which was supposed to have caught the rat which
ate up Lincoln's suit of clothes, as well as a pair of
trousers, a battered silk hat and a carpet bag of
Lincoln's. The latter had held his inaugural
speech. Twenty-four wagon-loads in all were sold,
5000 attended the sale, the bidding was high and
$6000 was realized. All the East Room furniture
went at this auction. The relics dated as far back as
the Adamses, the first to occupy the original
house, a trunk belonging to Abigail Adams being
included in the sale.

—an excerpt from an article in the
October 6, 1934, issue of the Post,
written by Irwin H. (Ike) Hoover.

Arthur vigorously prosecuted the Star Route frauds, whereby misap-
propriations within the Post Office Department lost the government some
$4,000,000. No convictions were obtained in the 1882-83 trials.

*Due to some complex political moves, there was *no one* in line for succession from September 19 to
October 10, 1881, in accordance with the terms of the Succession Act of 1792!

A picnic in the woods along the St. Lawrence at Alexandria Bay—just what the doctor ordered, no doubt, to relieve the President from an exacting schedule.

A dispute with President Garfield over appointments that Conkling felt he should have controlled led him to resign his Senate seat and retire officially from politics, yet he continued to strongly influence the Republican party from behind the scenes.

Arthur was a tall, handsome man and the most stylish president since Martin Van Buren. He was also, like Jefferson, Jackson, and Van Buren before him, a widower. Henry Watterson described him in a July 12, 1919, *Post* article:

> Arthur was a man of surpassing sweetness and grace. As handsome as Pierce, as affable as McKinley, he was a more experienced and dexterous politician than either. He had been put on the ticket with Garfield to placate Conkling. All sorts of stories to his discredit were told during the ensuing campaign. The Democrats made him out a tricky and typical New York politician. He was, on the contrary, a manysided accomplished man, who had a taking way of adjusting all conditions and adapting himself to all companies.

He also loved good food and entertained a great deal. He thought the White House looked like "a badly kept barracks," and he asked that it be redecorated.

He is a good example of how the office of the presidency can change a man for the better. His earlier political activities had involved politics at the lowest level. He was put on the ticket with James Garfield with no thought of being president. The assassin's bullet changed that.

As president he realized his duty was to all the people. The job itself made him feel humble. He asked for civil service reform and signed the act creating the Civil Service Commission. He also updated the Navy and improved the postal service. He tried to give the country honest and efficient government. "It would be hard to better President Arthur's administration," said Mark Twain. Nevertheless, the leaders of his political party frowned upon his active social life and refused to renominate him in 1884.

But he went out in style. The final social event of the Arthur Administration turned into a free-for-all described by Edward G. Lowry in the May 9, 1931, *Post*:

> Beginning at three o'clock, the doors had not been open a half hour before the entrance hall, the corridor and anteroom were solidly packed. An hour after the opening the people began climbing in the windows to lessen the jam on the portico.
>
> Others sought entrance through the basement doors, and were met by those seeking egress in that way from the crowded parlors. The corridor, the conservatory and all the apartments on the main floor were solidly packed. The musicians were swept away from their places in the corridor, and 3000 women pushed, surged and struggled toward the Blue Parlor as their goal. An occasional man appeared here and there in the ocean of femininity.
>
> At 4:30 the President came part way down the private stairway and stood overlooking the surging crowd. Gathering courage, he made the start and conquered his way slowly to the Blue Parlor. As he entered, someone asked him, "How did you ever get in through that crowd, Mr. President?" and his answer was a question as to how in the world he was going to get out of it again.

Grover Cleveland

★ ★ ★ ★ ★

22nd President of the United States
and
24th President of the United States

Born: March 18, 1837, Caldwell, New Jersey.
Occupation: Lawyer.
Wife: Frances Folsom. *Children:* Two boys, three girls.
President: 1885-1889; 1893-1897. Democratic party.
Vice-Presidents: Thomas A. Hendricks, Adlai E. Stevenson.
Died: June 24, 1908. *Buried:* Princeton, New Jersey.

Grover Cleveland was the first Democrat sent to the White House after the Civil War. He was also the only president married in the White House, and the only president to be elected to non-consecutive terms.

He started his politics at the precinct level, became mayor of Buffalo and was then elected governor of New York. His rule of conduct was, "A public office is a public trust."

The Republican administrations after the Civil War had become weak and corrupt. In 1884, the Republican party nominated James G. Blaine for president. He had been connected with a financial scandal. Many Republicans were outraged and felt it was time to have reform. These Republicans, called *mugwumps*, said they would vote for a Democrat if he were an honest man. The Democrats responded by nominating Grover Cleveland who was known for his honesty and common sense, and had a reputation for good government. He won a close election.

As president he reformed the federal government and improved civil service. Believing in the reduction of high tariff, he fought a hostile Congress with many vetoes. He was a courageous, hard-working president. He did what he thought was right, and he performed his duty faithfully. One politician told him he might not be reelected and he said, "What's the use of being elected or reelected unless you stand for something?"

Benjamin Harrison won the election in 1888, but Mrs. Cleveland told the servants to take good care of the White House.

"I want everything just the way it is now when we

Grover Cleveland did not take a wife until he was 49. Her name was Frances Folsom and she was 21 when they wed. Therefore, what appears to be grandfather and grandchild above is actually father and son.

76

come back," she said. "That will be exactly four years from now." She was right.

During Cleveland's second term there was a depression, a railroad strike and hundreds of banks failed. Cleveland did not believe in trying to improve business or provide employment. He thought that natural laws would take care of that.

He did believe in honest and efficient government and left Washington a better place than he had found it. His words upon leaving were "I have tried so hard to do right."

David Graham Phillips describes him in the August 16, 1902, issue of *The Saturday Evening Post*, five years after Grover Cleveland had completed his second term:

> He stands and you note that he is about sixty years old—you would not be surprised if you heard that he was fifty-five; you are a little surprised when you read in the biographical dictionary that he was born sixty-five years ago. He has a large, substantial figure—broad shoulders, broad chest and a broad back, as you see when he leads the way into his library. You understand how he could sit at a desk more hours than any other President we ever had, how he could perform more labor with less assistance than any other. He is dressed in a baggy sack suit that comes up to a certain lowly ideal of "solid comfort." His is the dress of a settled father of a family.
>
> He speaks in a voice, you instantly feel, that has never listened to itself, has never modified itself to create an impression, has always been the untrained instrument of a mind determined to think for itself and to utter itself without fear or concealment. He is looking at you—squarely, keenly, with young eyes—the eyes of a young, alert mind. His is a serious, powerful face, even aggressive in some of its lines; yet the eyes twinkle. You have seen the same merry expression in the eyes of that wisest and best-natured of animals, the elephant; it is there even when, good-humoredly to end an annoyance, "my lord, the elephant," with a careless swing of his trunk, sends his annoyer tumbling. You feel that you would not, could not trifle with this man; could not ask an improper favor of him.
>
> He is sitting in a big chair at a desk covered with an array of books and papers—current economics and politics are the subjects of most of the print you see. He fills the chair, and his arms and strong hands rest upon the arms of it, and his feet are firmly and squarely planted upon the floor. And now you get two polysyllabic impressions—impenetrability and immovability.

The article ended with this tribute to Grover Cleveland:

"He was a man who spoke out courageously and sensibly; a man who did not fear to veto corruption, however ably disguised; and, above all, a man who attended to the public business with a fidelity that no amount of detail could weary or make careless. To him, great and small were alike important because both came within his conception of the obligations of his official oath."

A Defense of Fishermen

by Grover Cleveland

By way of introduction and explanation, it should be said that there is no intention at this time to deal with those who fish for a livelihood. Those sturdy and hard-working people need no vindication or defense. Our concern is with those who fish because they have an occult and mysterious instinct which leads them to love it, because they court the healthful, invigorating exertion it invites, and because its indulgence brings them in close contact and communion with nature's best and most elevating manifestations. This sort of fishing is pleasure and not work—sport and not money-grabbing. Therefore it is contemptuously regarded as no better than a waste of time. Generous fishermen cannot fail to look with pity upon the benighted persons who have no better conception than this of the uses and beneficent objects of rational diversion.

In these sad and ominous days of mad fortune-chasing, every patriotic, thoughtful citizen, whether he

fishes or not, should lament that we have not among our countrymen more fishermen. There can be no doubt that the promise of industrial peace, of contented labor and of healthful moderation in the pursuit of wealth, in this democratic nation of ours, would be infinitely improved if a large share of the time which has been devoted to the concotion of trust and business combinations had been spent in fishing.

The narrow and ill-conditioned people who snarlingly count all fishermen as belonging to the lazy and good-for-nothing class, and who take satisfaction in describing an angler's outfit as a contrivance with a hook at one end and a fool at the other, have been so thoroughly discredited that no one could wish for their more irredeemable submersion. But, although it may be true that these charges are unworthy of notice, it cannot be expected that fishermen, proud of the name, will be amiably willing to permit those making such accusations the satisfaction of remaining unchallenged.

At the outset, the fact should be recognized that the community of fishermen constitute a separate class or a sub-race among the inhabitants of the earth. Of course there are many who call themselves fishermen and who have not in their veins a drop of legitimate fisherman blood. In truth they are only interlopers who have learned a little fish language, who love to fish only when the fish are biting, who whine at bad luck, and who betray incredulity when they hear a rousing fish story.

In point of fact, full-blooded fishermen have ideas, habits of thought and mental tendencies so peculiarly and especially their own, and their beliefs and code of ethics are so exclusively fit-

Grover Cleveland authored 18 articles for the Post *between 1901 and 1906, more than any other president before or since. With topics ranging from politics to fish tales, the feature articles on the covers above reflect the diversity of the man evidenced both in his activities and in his character.*

ted to their needs and surroundings, that an attempt on the part of strangers to speak or write concerning the character or conduct of its approved membership savors of impudent presumption. None but fishermen can deal with these delicate matters.

What sense is there in the charge of laziness sometimes made against true fishermen?

Laziness has no place in the constitution of a man who starts at sunrise and tramps all day with only a sandwich to eat, floundering through bushes and briers and stumbling over rocks and wading streams in pursuit of elusive trout. Neither can a fisherman who, with rod in hand, sits in a boat or on a bank all day be called lazy—provided he attends to his fishing and is physically and mentally alert in his occupation.

It is sometimes said that there is such a close relationship between mendacity and fishing, that in matters connected with their craft all fishermen are untruthful. It must, of course, be admitted that large stories of fishing adventure are sometimes told by fishermen—and why should this not be so? Beyond all question there is no sphere of human activity so full of strange and wonderful incidents as theirs. Fish are constantly doing the most mysterious and startling things; and no one has yet been wise enough to explain their ways or account for their conduct. The best fishermen do not attempt it; they move and strive in the atmosphere of mystery and uncertainty. In these circumstances fishermen necessarily see and do wonderful things. If those not members of the brotherhood are unable to assimilate the recital of these wonders, it is because their believing apparatus has not been properly regulated

Assembled on the porch of Westland in Princeton, N.J. are, left to right, Esther, Francis Grover, Mrs. Cleveland, Ruth, Richard Folsom and the ex-president.

and stimulated. Such disability falls very far short of justifying doubt as to the truth of the narrative. The

Cleveland's Surgery

Cleveland's left upper jaw was vulcanized rubber for all but four months of his second term. A cancerous condition in his mouth was discovered in the early summer of 1893 and was operated on so secretly that when the news leaked out, two months later, no one would believe it. The panic was on, and Cleveland had called a special session, which meant a battle over silver. Conditions were so bad that no one dared let the country know its President would have to undergo a serious operation. Cleveland went to New York and boarded the *Benedict* yacht as if he were going fishing. While the yacht steamed up the Sound, the surgeons put him under ether and went to work. It took them half an hour. The yacht kept cruising until he could walk again, then it dropped him off at his summer home.

—*an excerpt from a March 31, 1934,* Post *article written by Irwin H. (Ike) Hoover.*

things narrated have been seen and experienced with a fisherman's eyes and perceptions. This is perfectly understood by listening fishermen; and they, to their enjoyment and edification, are permitted to believe what they hear.

Before leaving this branch of our subject, special reference should be made to one item more conspicuous, perhaps, than any other. It is constantly said that fishermen greatly exaggerate the size of the fish that are lost.

Actually, all the presumptions are with the fisherman's contention. It is perfectly plain that large fish are more apt to escape than small fish. Their weight and activity, combined with the increased trickiness and resourcefulness of age and experience, of course, greatly increase their ability to tear out the hook, and enhance the danger that their antics will expose a fatal weakness in hook, leader, line or rod. Another presumption which must be regretfully mentioned arises from the fact that in many cases it is the encounter with a large fish which causes such excitement, and such distraction or perversion of judgment, as leads the fisherman to do the wrong thing or fail to do the right thing at the critical instant—thus contributing to an escape which could not have occurred except in favor of a large fish. . . .

The defense of the fishing fraternity which has been here attempted is by no means as completely stated as it

79

should be. Nor should the world be allowed to overlook the admirable affirmative qualities which exist among genuine members of the brotherhood, and the useful traits which an indulgence in the gentle art cultivates and fosters. A recital of these, with a description of the personal peculiarities found in the ranks of fishermen and the influence of these peculiarities on success or failure, are necessary to a thorough vindication of those who worthily illustrated the virtues of our clan.

—*October 19, 1901*, Post.

Fish Tales and Other Folk-lure

Editor's Note: *Anecdotes in the* Post *concerning the colorful Grover Cleveland were numerous from the early to the mid-1900s. Particularly entertaining were the tales of his frequent fishing expeditions. Following are a few choice pieces which cover a wide range of subjects, yet best exemplify for the reader Cleveland's best-known traits—his sense of humor and forceful personality.*

Along the upper Potomac, between Great Falls and Harper's Ferry, Grover Cleveland, when he was President, found great delight in fishing. Among the canal men and fishermen of the vicinity many interesting incidents of the eminent visitor's outings are repeated.

At the place on the Potomac known as Point of Rocks the President was fishing one day and with democratic simplicity chatting with some canal boatmen. One of the latter remarked that people in that vicinity were very glad to see the President enjoying himself.

"Yes," said the President, "there are two ideal states of happiness in this world, and one of them is to fish and catch something," and he pointed to his string of bass.

"What's the other happy state?" ventured one of his auditors.

"The other great felicity," replied the President, pointing to one of the members of his party, who had been casting his line diligently and with great enjoyment but without other visible results, "is to fish and not catch anything."

—*November 29, 1902*, Post.

"When Grover Cleveland was President," said Mr. Joseph E. Ralph, of Washington, "he frequently enjoyed a day's fishing along the upper Potomac. On these outings he lodged at the house of a rough and hearty farmer.

She was the daughter of his law partner, open, winning and natural. He had been her guardian since she was 11. They were wed on June 2, 1886.

"The first morning he stopped there," continued Mr. Ralph, "the farmer, determined to show becoming attention to his distinguished guest, rapped at Mr. Cleveland's door at the unrighteous hour of four o'clock in the morning.

" 'What's the matter?' demanded the statesman.

" 'Mr. President,' said the farmer, 'we're goin' to hev fish in your honor for breakfast. Will you hev 'em skun or unskun?'

" 'I'll take 'em skun,' laughed the President, rolling over for another sleep."

—*August 9, 1902*, Post.

Mr. Cleveland was fond—not overfond—of cards. He liked to play the noble game at, say, a dollar limit—even once in a while for a little more—but not much more. And, as Dr. Norvin Green was wont to observe of Commodore Vanderbilt, "He held them exceeding close to his boo-som."

Mr. Whitney, Secretary of the Navy in his first administration, equally rich and hospitable, had often "the road gang," as a certain group, mainly senators, was called, to dine, with the inevitable after-dinner soirée or séance. I was, when in Washington, invited to these parties. At one of them I chanced to sit between the President and Senator Don Cameron. Mr. Carlisle, at the time Speaker of the House—who handled his cards like a child and, as we all knew, couldn't play a lit-

80

tle—was seated on the opposite side of the table.

After a while Mr. Cameron and I began bulling the game—I recall that the limit was five dollars—that is, raising and back-raising each other, and whoever else happened to be in, without much or any regard to the cards we held.

It chanced on a deal that I picked up a pat flush, Mr. Cleveland a pat full. The Pennsylvania senator, and I went to the extreme, the President of course willing enough for us to play his hand for him. But the Speaker of the House persistently stayed with us and kept on.

We could not drive him out.

When it came to a draw Senator Cameron drew one card. Mr. Cleveland and I stood pat. But Mr. Carlisle drew four cards. At length, after much banter and betting, it reached a show-down and, *mirabile dictu*, the Speaker held four kings!

"Take the money, Carlisle; take the money," exclaimed the President. "If ever I am President again you shall be Secretary of the Treasury. But don't you make that four-card draw too often."

He was President again, and Mr. Carlisle was Secretary of the Treasury.
—*August 23, 1919*, Post *article by Henry Watterson.*

Mr. Cleveland had a way of sudden fancies to new and sometimes queer people. Many of his appointments were eccentric and fell like bombshells upon the Senate, taking the appointee's home people completely by surprise.

The recommendation of influential politicians seemed to have little if any weight with him.

There came to Washington from Richmond a gentleman by the name of Keiley, backed by the Virginia delegation for a minor consulship. The President at once fell in love with him.

THE PROSPECTIVE HIGH PRIVATE.

" When my term of office is ended I wish for no more than to serve as a private in the ranks of my party."—*Cleveland's recent letter.*

As an outdoorsman, Cleveland ranked as fair game among political cartoonists. As president, he ranks among the great.

"Consul be damned," he said. "He is worth more than that," and he pronounced him Ambassador to Vienna.

It turned out that Mrs. Keiley was a Jewess and would not be received at court. Then he named him Ambassador to Italy, when it appeared that Keiley was an intense Roman Catholic, who had made at least one ultramontane speech, and would be *persona non grata* at the Quirinal. Then Cleveland dropped him. Meanwhile poor Keiley had closed out bag and baggage at Richmond and was at his wit's end. After much ado the President was brought to a realizing sense and a place was found for Keiley as consul general and diplomatic agent at Cairo, whither he repaired.
—*July 26, 1919*, Post *article written by Henry Watterson.*

When Grover Cleveland was President, Dr. Robert Maitland O'Reilly was the official physician at the White House.

Doctor O'Reilly is a Republican, but with Cleveland that was not to be weighed against his skill as a surgeon.

One day during the second Cleveland Administration a number of army officers at a social moment were talking informally to their Commander-in-Chief.

"Are you not afraid, Mr. President," ventured one jocosely, "to retain as your medical adviser a physician who is an uncompromising Republican?"

The President had just refused to sign the Wilson Tariff Bill, and the menace of defection from the ranks hung over the Democratic party.

"No," he laughed in reply; "Doctor O'Reilly is a physician of excellent judgment, and he knows that good Democrats are scarce."
—*August 30, 1902*, Post.

Benjamin Harrison

★ ★ ★ ★ ★

23rd President of the United States

Born: August 20, 1833, North Bend, Ohio.
Occupation: Lawyer.
Wives: Caroline Scott, Mary Scott Dimmick.
Children: One boy, two girls.
President: 1889-1893. Republican party.
Vice-President: Levi P. Morton.
Died: March 13, 1901. *Buried:* Indianapolis, Indiana.

★ ★ ★ ★ ★

Benjamin Harrison was a well-established corporate lawyer in Indianapolis and had served in the U.S. Senate from 1881-1887 before he was chosen by the Republican party in 1888 to run for president against Grover Cleveland.

He was a small man, five feet, six inches tall. During the campaign, the Democrats called him "little Ben," inferring that he wasn't big enough to be president. The Republicans, however, sang a campaign song, "Grandfather's Hat Fits Ben," making reference to his grandfather, William Henry Harrison, the ninth President of the United States. Cleveland received a popular plurality of 100,000, but Harrison won the Electoral vote—233 to 168.

Dignified, honest and conscientious, President Harrison lacked the ability to check the spoilsmen of his party, and Congress took over the reins of government.

During his administration, the high McKinley Tariff Act and the Sherman Silver Purchase Act were passed, Civil War pensions were augmented and Oklahoma was opened for settlement.

It was said of Harrison that if you pricked him, "he would bleed ice water," but in a March 3, 1934, *Post* article Ike Hoover suggests that, though "he was as aloof and reserved a man as ever filled the office," he was "not so cold as his exterior suggested."

Defeated for reelection in 1892 by Cleveland, Harrison returned to his law practice in Indianapolis. He died at his beloved Delaware Street home.

President Harrison and family took the train—the most expedient form of travel—to Washington, D.C. The above was taken en route in Bridgeport, Cumberland County, Pennsylvania, on February 25, 1889.

The large porch was not added to the Harrison Home (above) in Indianapolis, until 1895. The General's famous "front porch" campaign of 1888 was actually conducted from a small porch outside the parlor window.

The Obligations of Wealth

by Benjamin Harrison

Taxes are a debt of the highest obligation, and no casuist can draw a sound moral distinction between the man who hides his property or makes a false return in order to escape the payment of his debt to the State, and the man who conceals his property from his private creditors. Nor should it be more difficult to follow the defaulter in the one case than in the other. If our taxes were farmed out to an individual or to a corporation they would be collected. There would be a vigilant and unrelenting pursuit. The civil and criminal processes of the law would be invoked with effect, just as they were against fraudulent debtors under the bankrupt law. Is it not possible to secure public officers who will show the same activity?

If there is not enough public virtue left in our communities to make tax frauds discreditable; if there is not virility enough left in our laws and in the administration of justice in our courts to bring to punishment those who defraud the State and their neighbors, is there not danger that crimes of violence will make insecure the fortunes that have refused to contribute ratably to the cost of maintaining social order? If we are to admit that the obligations of public duty and of personal veracity and personal integrity are so little felt by our people, and that our administrative and judicial processes are so inadequate that tax frauds cannot, at least, be restrained, hope for the country is eclipsed.

I cannot believe, however, that it is impossible so to stir the consciences of our people, so to stimulate the in-dependence of our assessors and of our Courts and prosecutors, as to secure a fairly general enforcement of the personal property tax. I know that men hesitate to call a neighbor to judgment in this matter. We have too much treated the matter of a man's tax return as a personal matter. We have put his transactions with the State on much the same level with his transactions with his banker, but that is not the true basis.

Each citizen has a personal interest, a pecuniary interest, in the tax return of his neighbor. We are members of a great partnership, and it is the right of each to know what every other member is contributing to the partnership and what he is taking from it. It is not a private affair; it is a public concern of the first importance. Perhaps there should be a general proclamation of amnesty and a new start; for many men have been enticed into these offenses by the belief that all others were offending.

—September 24, 1898, Post.

Presidents Are People

The Harrisons renewed the agitation for a new White House to be built at the head of Sixteenth Street, or at least a drastic reconstruction, and it appeared for a while they would be successful. Plans were drawn, even a scale model was built of "Mrs. Harrison's place," as it was called. Sentiment defeated the effort. The press of the country quickly rallied around the old landmark, and the scheme died quickly.

Mrs. Harrison turned to making the house habitable and gave it such a going over as it had never had until then. Arthur's two bathrooms were converted from virtually public baths into private ones. The various bedrooms were divided into suites and the whole house was painted and refrescoed inside and generally refurnished. The kitchen was torn out and replaced, the various layers of basement floor torn up, concrete laid and the walls tiled shoulder high, making that floor sanitary for the first time. The engine room was rebuilt, a new area built around the entire house, the conservatory

Harrison entered the Union Army a lieutenant, left a brigadier general.

83

rebuilt and new greenhouses added. When the Clevelands came back after four years, they hardly recognized the old place . . . .

Life was much easier in the White House then . . . . Though Harrison was a great-grandson of a signer of the Declaration, grandson of a President and himself a former senator, they were simple folk who continued to live as they had in Indianapolis . . . .

An eight o'clock breakfast, one o'clock lunch, early dinner and early to bed was the rarely varied routine. Everyone of the large family appeared at the breakfast table and all attended family prayers, lasting half an hour or longer . . . . The President hired extra clerks to handle the Sunday mail so that the regular office staff might have their Sabbaths free. Despite their piety, the Harrisons are credited with having brought dancing back to the White House as a regular practice for the first time since it was discontinued in the Polk Administration, a bold move in the 90s.

After prayers, Harrison went directly to his office, the rest of the family about their duties, Mrs. Harrison to inspect the household and to confer with the steward

During the 1888 presidential campaign, a huge ball, 14 feet in diameter, covered with campaign slogans (below) was rolled from town to town to the following chant:

Old Allegany in 1840
Started the ball for Harrison:
In '88 as they did then,
We roll it on for Gallant Ben.

The saying, "Keep the ball rolling" originated from this form of campaigning.

Caroline Scott Harrison (above), Harrison's first wife, was also the first President of the DAR. Master Benjamin Harrison "Baby" McKee (left) was as famous as his grandfather, the President.

and the housekeeper. A son or a daughter, more often both, and their families lived with the Harrisons, while nieces and nephews, with their husbands and wives, stayed for weeks at a time. There were not enough bedrooms to go around and doubling up was necessary . . . .

Harrison was as systematic as he was thorough, and just as he always worked all morning, so he kept his afternoons for himself and family, barring a party crisis or state emergency. If the day were nice, a long stroll into the suburbs with Mrs. Dimmick, Mrs. Harrison's niece, or other younger members of the family, was the custom . . . .

The job of installing electricity was finished in about four months. On September fifteenth the current was turned on and away went the White House, blazing with electricity for all the world to see . . . . Electricity in practice was an unknown and fearsome quantity to the lay mind, and I found the family and servants afraid to touch the lights. I would turn them on in the halls

84

Baby McKee

One of Harrison's grandchildren, Baby McKee, was the best-advertised youngster ever in the White House, with the possible exception of the Cleveland babies. He was about two when the Harrisons came, and had been christened Baby McKee in Indianapolis by the reporters. His real name was Benjamin Harrison McKee, and because he was the grandson of a President who was in turn the grandson of a President, the newspapers seized upon him almost to the exclusion of his infant sister, Mary Dodge. The attachment between grandfather and grandchild was pumped up until readers had a right to suppose that the President spent his days in romping with his namesake. It was a pretty story, probably growing out of the party's wish to humanize so distant a man in the public's mind. The truth was that, though Harrison could unbend with his family, he was no doting grandpa.

The opposition, seizing the opportunity to capitalize on the publicity, contrived the following slogan:

> Wanamaker runs the Sunday School,
> Morton runs the bar,
> Baby McKee runs the White House,
> And, by God, here we are.
> —an excerpt from a March 3, 1934,
> article by Irwin H. (Ike) Hoover.

"The Raven" by Joseph Keppler in 1890 shows "little" Benjamin Harrison almost lost under the big hat of his grandfather William Henry Harrison. Perched on the bust of Benjamin's grandfather is Raven-Blaine. The cartoon was inspired by the disagreement between President Harrison and Secretary of State Blaine over the McKinley Tariff.

and parlors in the evening and they would burn until I returned in the morning to extinguish them. I discovered that the family still were using gas in their private quarters and had to persuade them as patiently as one does a child that no harm could come to them. They were timid even about pushing the buttons to call the servants. When such a crisis arose they would confer among themselves, and sometimes send one to the basement rather than risk electrocution. The more rash would touch a button gingerly and jump back.

In wiring the house I had worked in every room and had seen all and talked at length with the Harrison family. All were fascinated by this new thing, even if fearing it, and asked endless questions . . . .

Nothing could illustrate Mrs. Harrison's character better than her published explanation of why she had decided not to wear a low-cut, sleeveless gown at the inaugural ball: "If there is one thing above another I detest and have detested all my days, it is being made a circus of, and that is what has come to me in my old age, as it were," she told an interviewer. "I've been a show, the whole family has been a show since Mr. Harrison was nominated. If there is any privacy to be found in the White House, I propose to find and preserve it."

Beginning in the high spirits of children and young people, the Harrisons descended into tragedy . . . . Mrs. Harrison's health began to fail early and she died a month before her husband's defeat for reelection . . . .

I think Harrison had few regrets on quitting the White House. In the previous summer he had written Mrs. McKee, who was in Massachusetts: "Politics and business have been annoying me day and night, and this, with the anxiety about your mother, makes life just now a burden, and ambition a delusion."

> —excerpted from an article of the same
> title by Irwin H. (Ike) Hoover in the
> March 3, 1934, issue of the Post.

William McKinley

★ ★ ★ ★ ★

25th President of the United States

Born: January 29, 1843, Niles, Ohio.
Occupation: Lawyer.
Wife: Ida Saxton. *Children:* Two girls.
President: 1897-1901, four years, six and one-half
months. Republican party.
Vice-Presidents: Garret A. Hobart, Theodore Roosevelt.
Died: September 14, 1901. *Buried:* Canton, Ohio.

★ ★ ★ ★ ★

William McKinley, a native of Ohio, served as a major in the Union army during the Civil War. After the war, he returned to his state and practiced law in Canton. In 1876, he was elected as a Republican to Congress where, except for one term, he served until 1891.

The numerous writings in *The Saturday Evening Post* bring to surface two things about the man, William McKinley: his sparkling personality and his art of persuasion. Of his amiable temperament, Charles Emory Smith, former Postmaster-General says in the September 13, 1902, *Post:*

> ... McKinley had a keen sense of humor. His social traits were very marked, and he had great fondness for the freedom and the joys of social intercourse. He loved to be among his friends and to abandon himself to the relaxation and exhilaration of unrestrained communion with those he trusted. At such times he was the life of the company. His talk sparkled with fun and interest.

In the art of persuasion, Charles Smith said, McKinley was unequaled. "Much of it lay in his own deep sincerity and conviction. He convinced others because he was thoroughly convinced himself. But beyond this substantive foundation he had an extraordinary gift of putting things. His quick perception and his shrewd, saving sense enabled him to present a case in the strongest form and turn every point to his own account. His power in this direction was proverbial among all about him."

These two personal attributes account for his overwhelming popularity throughout his political life. As chairman of the Republican convention in 1892, he

In his lifetime McKinley, born above this store in Niles, would see the birth of the industrial revolution and the death of U.S. isolationism.

very nearly beat Benjamin Harrison, the Republican choice, and, in 1896 he was elected President of the United States with an electoral vote of 271 to 176.

The one shadow over his political success was the health of his wife, Ida, to whom he was devoted. An illness which followed the birth of her second child had left her subject to momentary seizures of unconsciousness which lasted only a second, but which might occur any time. For this reason, McKinley never let her out of his sight. Charles Howell, editor of the *Atlanta Constitution*, described a meeting with McKinley, then governor of Ohio, in which he (Howell) was asked to review an address McKinley was to give that afternoon at a banquet. He tells how every once in a while, McKinley would rise and walk to the side of his frail wife, who was sitting before the fire, pat her on the cheek and fasten the shawl around her shoulders. He then would return to the conversation with Mr. Howell. H.H. Kohlsaat, editor of the *Chicago Times-Herald*, quoted Howell's reaction to this incident in an article which appeared in the May 27, 1922, *Post*:

> . . . the one thing about that day that I will never forget and that has always endeared McKinley's memory to me was the beautiful, sweet solicitude of this strong, manly man to his sweet, frail wife as she sat by the fireside that day.

Because Mrs. McKinley was nearly an invalid, Mrs.

Fragile, petite Ida Saxton was a cashier in her father's bank when she met McKinley, thus making her the first career woman to become First Lady.

In 1898 McKinley, the last Civil War veteran to rise to the presidency, reconciled the North and South by declaring that the U.S. government would care for the graves of the Confederate dead.

Stark County Historical Center, Canton, Ohio

Garret A. Hobart, wife of the Vice-President, performed many of the duties in the White House as "Second Lady" during McKinley's administration. In the June 29, 1929, issue of the *Post*, Mrs. Hobart describes the relationship between her family and the family in the Executive Mansion: "It was an intimate friendliness that no Vice-President and his wife, before or since, have had the privilege of sharing with their chief administrator . . . though I constantly shared Mrs. McKinley's social duties, both she and the President understood I had no wish to usurp her place."

The true strength of character and high moral purpose which underlay McKinley's amiable manner and good humor were shown in the resolute and courageous firmness with which he restrained and held back the war impulse of Congress and the country in 1898. Spain's atrocities in Cuba, with the destruction of the *Maine*, had set the nation on fire. But for the unflinching determination of President McKinley, war would have been precipitated at once. When war finally was declared, Spain, only 100 days into the war, indicated a willingness to compromise. As a result, Cuba was granted independence and Puerto Rico, Guam and the Philippines were ceded to the United States.

As president, McKinley also strove to establish a cordial sentiment between the North and the South. His feeling on this subject was deep and he longed to see his country thoroughly united by a sense of nationalism. At the time the Spanish-American War broke out, he was quick to summon Southern as well as Northern leaders to the nation's defense.

Then, shortly after his second inauguration, McKinley was assassinated. He had gone to Buffalo, New York, to attend the Pan-American Exposition when a young man stepped up as if to greet him and shot him with a gun hidden beneath a handkerchief.

In an article in the August 30, 1902, *Post*, Charles Emory Smith gives the following tribute to William McKinley:

> President McKinley's life was so open, he was so much a man of the people, that no American was better known to his countrymen. He himself was unequaled in his popular sympathies. In turn the popular instinct quickly grasped and thoroughly understood his personality. He knew beyond any other leader of his time the mind and heart, the nature and impulse, of the American people. Through the same sympathetic chord the people came to know his character and qualities, his very being, better than that of any other man in public life. There was nothing inscrutable about him. He was frank, open, candid and sincere. There was reserve where reserve was needful for public purposes, but not reserve through lack of unison and fellowship. He was essentially the American people incarnate, and they instinctively knew their own.

Washington the Statesman

by William McKinley

Washington's public life is as familiar to the American student as the history of the United States. They are forever associated in holy and indissoluble bonds. Washington's character and achievements have been a part of schoolbooks of the nation for more than a century, and have moved American youth and American manhood to aspire to the highest ideals of citizenship.

But with all our pride in Washington, we not infrequently fail to give him credit for his marvelous genius as a constructive statesman. We are constantly in danger of losing sight of the sweep and clearness of his comprehension.

From the hour that Washington declared, in his Virginia home, that he would raise a thousand men and equip them at his own expense, to march to the defense of Boston, he became the masterful spirit of the Continental Army and the mightiest single factor in the Continent's struggle for liberty and independence.

A slaveholder himself, he yet hated slavery, and in his will provided for the emancipation of his slaves. Not a college graduate, he was always enthusiastically the friend of liberal education. He used every suitable occasion to impress upon Congress the importance of a high standard of general education.

And how reverent, always, was this great man. How prompt and how generous his recognition of the guiding hand of Divine Providence in establishing and controlling the destinies of the Colonies and of the Republic!

At the very height of his success and his reward, he emerged from the Revolution, receiving by unanimous acclaim the plaudits of the people, and commanding the respect and admiration of the civilized world, he did not forget that his first official act as President should be fervent supplication to the Almighty Being who rules the universe. It is He who presides in the councils of nations and whose providential aid can supply every human

The array of campaign paraphernalia (lower right) is a reminder that in the election of 1900 it was once again McKinley versus Bryan. However, the President's spotless record could not be beat. The following year he toured the states to address the Pan-American Exposition (below) where he was shot by Czolgosz and transported to the hospital by this ambulance (right).

defect. It is His benediction which we most want, and which can and will consecrate the liberties and happiness of the people of the United States.

Washington went further and spoke for the people, assuming that he but voiced the sentiment of the young nation in thus making faith in Almighty God, and reliance upon His favor and care one of the strong foundations of the Government.

Not alone upon days of thanksgiving and times of trial should we remember and follow the example set by the fathers. Never in our future should we forget the great moral and religious principles which they enunciated and defended as their most precious heritage. In an age of great activity, of industrial and commercial strife and of perplexing problems, we should never abandon the simple faith in Almighty God as recognized in the name of the American people by Washington and the first Congress.

In his inaugural address, Washington contends: (1) For the promotion of institutions of learning; (2) For cherishing the public credit; (3) For the observance of good faith and justice toward all the nations.

One hundred years ago, free schools were little known in the United States. There were excellent schools for the well-to-do, and charitable institutions for the instruction of children without means; but the free public school, open to children of the rich and poor and supported by the State, awaited creation and development. The seed planted by the fathers bore fruit. Free schools were the necessary supplement of free men.

How priceless is a liberal education! In itself what a rich endowment! It is not impaired with age, but its value increases with use. No one can employ it but its

Stark County Historical Center, Canton, Ohio

Best Wishes

A labor leader once asked McKinley for some favor he could not grant. The man was hurt and rather truculent. McKinley told him how pained he was to refuse his request, and as he shook hands with him asked him if he was married. Taking a carnation from his coat he gave it to him, saying, "Give this to your wife with my compliments and best wishes." The astonished man smiled and said, "I would rather have this flower from you for my wife than the thing I came to get."

McKinley made lifelong friends of that man and of his wife.

—an excerpt from an article by H.H. Kohlsaat which appeared in the May 13, 1922, issue of the Post.

rightful owner. He alone can illustrate its worth and enjoy its rewards. It cannot be inherited or purchased. It must be acquired by individual effort.

From the day our flag was unfurled to the present hour, no stain of a just obligation violated has yet tarnished the American name. This must and will be as true in the future as it has been in the past. There will be prophets of evil and false teachers. Some part of the column may waver away from the standard, but there will ever rally around it a mighty majority to preserve it stainless.

At no point in his administration does Washington appear in grander proportions than when he enunciates his ideas in regard to the foreign policy of the government: "Observe good faith and justice toward all nations; cultivate peace and harmony with all; religion and morality enjoin this conduct."

Today, nearly a full century since Washington's death, we reverentially study the leading principles of that comprehensive chart for the guidance of the people. It was his unflinching, immovable devotion to these perceptions of duty which, more than anything else, made him what he was and contributed so directly to make us what we are.

From four million, we have grown to seventy million people, while our progress in industry, learning and the arts has been the wonder of the world. What the future will be depends upon ourselves. That the future will bring still greater blessings to people I cannot doubt.

—June 4, 1898,
The Saturday Evening Post.

Theodore Roosevelt entered politics opposing injustice and corruption in government. He was first appointed assistant Secretary of the Navy, but, when the Spanish-American War broke out, he resigned his office to fight in the war. He came back a national hero, having led his regiment called "Roosevelt's Rough Riders" up San Juan Hill in Cuba.

He was then elected governor of New York and became known as a "trust buster," fighting the power of big business. The party bosses wanted him out of the way, so they backed his nomination for vice-president—considered a do-nothing job. But, when President William McKinley was assassinated in September, 1901, Vice-President Theodore Roosevelt became president.

The Saturday Evening Post, a non-political publication in 1901, printed the following brief commentary at the time of McKinley's death:

> Under the shadow of a heavy sorrow the Nation greets President Roosevelt. Younger than any man who before has held the Presidency of the United States, our new Chief Magistrate has on that account a fuller measure of the Nation's sympathy. Honest, personally brave, of a sincere Americanism, the Nation looks to him to lead it further in its career of honorable glory, of honorable success.

Theodore Roosevelt poses with his Rough Riders at the top of San Juan Hill in Cuba, after their decisive victory against the Spanish in 1898.

Theodore Roosevelt

★ ★ ★ ★ ★

26th President of the United States

Born: October 27, 1858, New York City.
Occupation: Public official, lawyer.
Wives: Alice Lee, Edith Carow.
Children: Four boys, two girls.
President: 1901-1909. Republican party.
Vice-President: John M. Hay*, Secretary of State; Charles W. Fairbanks.
Died: January 6, 1919. *Buried:* Oyster Bay, New York.

★ ★ ★ ★ ★

Theodore Roosevelt Collection, Harvard College Library

Barryman's now famous cartoon depicting the tenderhearted Teddy refusing to shoot a bear cub was published by The Washington Post *and inspired what is known to today's toymakers and toddlers as the "teddy bear."*

> Assuming his high office in a time of National grief, and under painful and delicate circumstances, all classes, all parties, all sections freely offer him their sympathy, their confidence, their encouragement.
>
> The assassination of its President has stirred the Nation to its depths. But while it is still sorrowing over the tragedy that has passed, it sees hope for continued prosperity, for continued National progress, in the accession of a man who has been tried in the balance of high office, who is conversant with important public affairs, and whose record thus far has been one of achievement and activity.

President "Teddy," as he was known, pushed through his "Square-Deal" program. He broke up trusts, started departments of Labor and Commerce, built dams to irrigate the West, and fought to preserve forests and wildlife. He is also given credit for the building of the Panama Canal. He believed in a strong centralized government, and he worked hard to make the United States a world leader. He backed this leadership with strong armed forces, strengthening the Navy in particular. "Speak softly and carry a big stick" was his motto. He became the first American to receive the Nobel Peace Prize because he was instrumental in bringing the Russo-Japanese War to an end.

Roosevelt loved being president and called the presidency a "bully pulpit." Cartoonists liked to draw him with his rimless glasses, bushy mustache, prominent teeth and jutting jaw. One cartoon showed him with a bear cub. Soon, toymakers across the country were producing adorable stuffed animals that are still known today as "teddy bears."

During the last year of Roosevelt's presidency the Republican party split into two factions—the progressive Republicans under Roosevelt, and the conservatives who opposed his program for social reform. Roosevelt had declared he would not run for president again, and he urged the delegates to support William Howard Taft. As a result, Taft won the nomination and the election of 1908.

Theodore Roosevelt was a big game hunter. After he left the White House, he went on an expedition to Africa which lasted a year. When he returned to the United States, he decided that he was dissatisfied with Taft's performance in the White House, so he formed a third party, called the "Bull Moose" party. It was called this because when a reporter had asked Mr. Roosevelt how he felt he had replied, "I feel as strong as a bull moose." The third party split the Republican vote and gave the election to Woodrow Wilson, the Democratic candidate.

Theodore Roosevelt died suddenly in 1919 of a blood clot in his heart. He was buried at Sagamore Hill, his home, in Oyster Bay, New York. It has since become a national shrine. Roosevelt is one of the four presidents whose faces are carved on the side of Mount Rushmore in South Dakota.

*A bill was passed in 1886 during Arthur's administration which established the Secretary of State as the first in the line of succession.

Named for Sagamore Mohannis, the Indian chieftain, Roosevelt's Sagamore Hill cost $16,975 to build in 1884. "I wonder if you will ever know how I love Sagamore Hill," Roosevelt murmured to his wife before he died.

National Park Service

Theodore Roosevelt, as he looked in 1880, his senior year at Harvard College, where he studied law, graduated with honors.

Theodore Roosevelt at Harvard

In Harvard College there was a joyful society to which the entrance lay through gates of tribulation. The society shall be nameless, but I may say that it belonged to the Sophomore year. For those lucky but alarmed youths who were serving their novitiate it had rites and processes extraordinary; but once the gates of tribulation were passed one entered instantly upon a land that was flowing with milk and honey. It was my fortune to be chosen into this society; and during the days of penance that were, so to speak, my preliminary examination, it was my still greater fortune to encounter Mr. Theodore Roosevelt. He would not be likely to retain the slightest memory of the occasion, for to him indeed it was not an occasion. He was an upper-classman. The days of his penance lay two years behind him, and he was only visiting the tortures of a younger generation, as all upper-class members of the society were expected and invited to do. This custom was supposed to lend dignity to the ceremonies.

You are to imagine an ordinary college room, with the usual books and pictures, filled with smoke, and seated on its floor four or five performing wretches. I was one of these; and for an hour I had been obeying the whims and inspirations of those members of the society who happened to be the torturers for that evening. But it is hard to make this sort of thing remain lively. An hour is a long time to keep imagination going; and you will readily see that the whole success of an exhibition in torture does not lie with the victims, but with their executioners. We were having a stupid time, and everybody was tired of it. Upon this dullness the door opened and Mr. Theodore Roosevelt entered with two or three of his friends. I had seen him before in the gymnasium, but never until now had been in a private room with him. I shall never forget the difference that his presence made in our spirits. He proceeded at once to torture us energetically. We were put through a number of perfectly new tricks; but, dear me, how I enjoyed it! Instead of the tiresome fooling that had so lately depressed me, I became filled with internal gayety that I dared not reveal. I longed to ask Mr. Roosevelt to do it some more, but this, of course, was impossible from a Sophomore and a stranger to an upper-classman. Therefore I had to be content with my silent enjoyment, and presently it was all over. Mr. Roosevelt soon had enough of us, and having performed his duty of visiting the games he went away.

During the whole of his stay, which I suppose was not

Roosevelt delighted in safaris, filled his home at Sagamore Hill with bronzes (left). The north room (below), added in 1908, was his favorite. TR designed the presidential flag in the background, bagged the antelopes himself; the Ethiopian emperor gave the tusks.

National Park Service

J.C. Leyendecker, in this October 26, 1912, cover for The Saturday Evening Post, *matches wits with the man of wit . . . and rimless glasses and prominent teeth . . . Theodore Roosevelt, of course.*

ten minutes long, there had been a breeze of robust good humor and geniality throughout the room. When he departed we all became again immediately as dull as ditch-water. I shall never forget it, this first impression of Theodore Roosevelt. . . .

> *—an excerpt from an October 12, 1901,* Post *article written by Owen Wister, a Harvard classmate of Theodore Roosevelt's.*

When Teddy Roosevelt Played Cowboy

On a certain Friday in September our country was struck dumb by the hand of calamity. We learned of the assassin's bullet. To no man in our nation could this news have been a greater shock than it must have been to Theodore Roosevelt. It was not yet a week since he had received a stunning shock followed by tension and suspense. Now these killing influences were over, and

what did he do? He took a long breath and he turned again to the serenity of Nature. He put away the newspapers, the railroad trains, the telegraph messages, the importunate visitors, the futile and endless conversations with which his world was vibrating, and we find him trying to regain composure in the healthy air of the mountains. No man ever did anything more like himself than this; and as long as he lives we may be sure that it is upon the mountain-tops he will find repose.

> *—taken from an article in the October 12, 1901, issue of the* Post *by Owen Wister.*

In the first year of Roosevelt's residence in the Bad Lands, the people of Medora were given a demonstration of his determination that will never be forgotten by any who witnessed it. Among the assets of the Chimney Butte outfit was a big bay bronco appropriately named The Devil.

From the first time Roosevelt came to the ranch and began to mix up with the horses, he held out the theory that a spoiled or bucking bronco could be "gentled" by kindness. As The Devil was the ugliest brute in all that section, Roosevelt picked him as the best subject by which to prove his theory. While the rest of us admitted that probably he could "gentle" The Devil by kindness in the course of time, we believed that at least 75 years would be required to accomplish that purpose. But Roosevelt insisted that we were wrong and began to put The Devil through a systematic course of kindness. I confess that when he one day called me out to the horses and showed me that he could walk straight up to The Devil and put his hand on him, I began to think that perhaps he might be able to prove his theory after all.

But the real show-down came one day when the horses were being tried out for the approaching roundup, and Bill Merrifield suggested that it would be a good chance for Roosevelt to show us how lamblike The Devil would act under the saddle. Roosevelt never could resist a challenge.

After his first wife died, Roosevelt headed for North Dakota and the life of a rancher and frontiersman.

"Good to the last drop," remarked President Theodore Roosevelt in 1907, upon completing his first cup of Maxwell House Coffee. Joel Cheek, creator of the famous blend named after the South's most celebrated hotel, caught the remark still heard in households today.

before. Four times that beast threw him, but the fifth time Roosevelt maneuvered him into a stretch of quicksand in the Little Missouri River. This piece of strategy saved the day, made Roosevelt a winner, and broke the record of The Devil, for if there is any basis of operations fatal to fancy bucking it is quicksand.

After that experience Mr. Roosevelt repeatedly rode The Devil, and his reputation for grit and determination was so well established in that country that it was often said that he "owned the Bad Lands after his turn with The Devil . . . ."

In the biographies of President Roosevelt, mention is seldom made of the fact that he once held office in Montana. At the time of which I speak he was the only regularly constituted representative of the law in that entire region. His office was that of Deputy United States Marshal. About the same time the better class of citizens in that locality determined to rid the community of a gang of toughs and desperadoes and to supplant old-fashioned "gun law" with rule by citizens' committee. It fell to my lot to serve as chief of police, and the one agreeable thing in connection with it was the coop-

"All right," answered Roosevelt, "I'll do it." At that he picked up a saddle, went up to the brute, and finally managed to get it on him. Then he mounted at a jump, but had no more than touched the leather when The Devil humped himself, drew his hoofs together, and came down like an antelope fighting a rattlesnake. Then he limbered up into a few fancy curves·and landed his rider on the ground a rod or two in front of him.

Roosevelt did not stay there, however, but sprang to his feet, whirled around, and made a rush for his mount. That was more grit than the best of us would have shown, and when The Devil once more began to cavort and put himself through all the fiendish calisthenics that he had acquired in a long and wicked lifetime, we simply stood up and shouted "Stick to the leather! Stay with the brute!"

About every other jump we could see 12 acres of bottom land between Roosevelt and the saddle, but now the rider stayed with the animal a little longer than

Noted for his sense of humor, Theodore Roosevelt would include drawings like the above in his frequent letters to his children. In 1907, his 13-year-old son, Archie, was the delighted recipient of this one.

94

Above, Roosevelt, the family man, in 1903 at Sagamore Hill. From left to right are: Quentin, age 5; Theodore, 44; Theodore, Jr., 15; Archie, 9; Alice, 19; Kermit, 13; Edith, 41; and Ethel, 11. Below, Roosevelt the hunter and his other great love—the outdoors.

eration and support of ranchman and Deputy United States Marshal Roosevelt. Theodore Roosevelt "owns the cow country," and will continue to do so until the range is only a recollection!

—reprinted from the March 4, 1905, issue of The Saturday Evening Post.

Teddy, Junior

President Theodore Roosevelt takes the keenest delight in eluding the Secret Service guardians, and apparently he has no fear whatever of personal danger. He cannot, however, escape the vigilance of his family. One of the most tireless guardians of the head of the nation is young Teddy, the President's oldest son.

Not long ago the President gave a dinner to some personal and political friends, and after coffee had been served the conversation turned to deeds of valor with firearms. The President, so the story goes, casually remarked that he had never owned a self-cocking revolver and did not even know how to operate one. The conversation drifted away to other things and the President forgot all about the neglected portion of his education, so far as self-cocking revolvers were concerned, until the next morning.

It was just a few moments before the President was to leave for a trip out of the city where he was to be the guest of a municipality which had made great preparations for his reception. There was to be an immense crowd and it was thought that the danger to the President would be greater than usual. He was talking to a friend in the Cabinet room when Teddy, Junior, came into the apartment. Drawing a self-cocking revolver from his pocket he presented it to his father with the remark that he did not propose to have his father go around unprotected. The President protested that he did not know how it worked. Teddy, Junior, thereupon withdrew the cartridges and in a matter-of-fact way said: "Well, father, I will show you."

He demonstrated that the mechanism of the firearm was all right. The President was an obedient pupil and after he had been thoroughly schooled by the youngster he tried the revolver himself. He found that it worked perfectly, and replaced the cartridges, putting the revolver in his pocket. Then throwing his arm about the boy's neck he said, in a voice filled with gratitude and pride: "It was very thoughtful of you, Teddy, my boy."

Teddy had gone out and bought the revolver himself out of his own pocket money.

—an excerpt from the August 9, 1902, issue of The Saturday Evening Post.

William H. Taft

★ ★ ★ ★ ★

27th President of the United States

Born: September 15, 1857, Cincinnati, Ohio.
Occupation: Lawyer.
Wife: Helen Herron. *Children:* Two boys, one girl.
President: 1909-1913. Republican party.
Vice-President: James S. Sherman.
Died: March 8, 1930. *Buried:* Arlington National Cemetery.

★ ★ ★ ★ ★

William Howard Taft was a large, jovial, easy-going man who was six feet, two inches tall and weighed 332 pounds—by far the largest man ever to be president. President McKinley had appointed Taft to be the first governor of the Philippines. While he was in the Philippines, a friend, concerned about his health, cabled him from the States. Taft replied, "I am well. I rode twenty-five miles this morning on horseback." The friend cabled, "How is the horse?"

William entered Yale in 1874. Twenty-five years later he turned down the presidency of that university in favor of his post as Federal Circuit Court Judge. This was in keeping with a family tradition, as his father and grandfather had both been judges.

As governor of the Philippines, Taft twice refused appointments to the Supreme Court, saying that his job was not yet finished. He did, however, accept a Cabinet position, Secretary of War, under Teddy Roosevelt, but continued the Islands' supervision as well. He also took charge of the building of the Panama Canal.

Taft was selected by Roosevelt to run for president. "The Roosevelt blessing was equivalent in 1908 to election, and he gave it to Taft over the opposition of most of the party leaders—a personal gift," Ike Hoover wrote in the March 17, 1934, *Post.*" Yet before Taft took office a wall had risen between them, and four years later their enmity split the Republican Party and made Woodrow Wilson President."

Taft did not seek to become president, but when Roosevelt asked, he agreed. Mrs. Taft had influence as well, as Ike Hoover recalled:

> The ambition of Taft's life, finally gratified by Harding, was a place on the Supreme bench. Roosevelt was waiting for the first vacancy to appoint him. By temperament, Taft hated competitive politics and all that it involved; he loved the law and could conceive of no higher destiny than Chief Justice. Everyone in the house knew the exact hour of the famous call made by Mrs. Taft on Roosevelt when she dramatically pleaded with him not to appoint her husband to the Supreme Court and thereby destroy his political future. She didn't leave until she had T.R.'s promise. As Nellie Herron, of Cincinnati . . . . Mrs. Taft had visited often in the White House—one of many young Ohio girls with whom Aunt Lucy Hayes surrounded herself. The story went that she had told Mrs. Hayes that she intended to return some day as mistress of the house.

As president, Taft tried to carry out Roosevelt's policies. There were as many noteworthy events in Taft's term as there had been in Roosevelt's administration. However, Roosevelt did everything with a fanfare, whereas Taft was quiet. He did not believe that the president should take over powers that really belonged to Congress.

Taft's administration saw the admission of Arizona and New Mexico as states, the establishment of the Tariff Board limiting tariffs on foreign imports, strengthened control of the Interstate Commerce Commission over the railroads and a continuation of "trust-busting." The President wrote in the October 19, 1912, issue of *The Saturday Evening Post:*

When Taft married Helen Herron in 1886, she wanted to be First Lady and he wanted to be a judge. When this picture was taken in Canada, she was an ex-First Lady and he was Chief Justice of the Supreme Court.

"During the seven and a half years preceding this Administration forty-four cases against trusts were instituted. During the less than four years of this Administration twenty-two civil suits and forty-five criminal indictments have been brought under the Anti-Trust Law."

Unlike Teddy Roosevelt, Taft did not enjoy being president. On September 6, 1911, he confessed to his brother Charles: "I am not very happy in this renomination and reelection business. I have to set my teeth and go through with it . . . . But I shall be willing to retire and let another take the burden." He got his wish. The Taft-Roosevelt split in the Republican party caused the election of 1912 to fall into the hands of the Democrats for the first time in 15 years. In his article in the *Post* on February 28, 1914, Taft wrote:

> When I laid down the office on the fourth of March, I ended an official career of continuous public service of twenty-six years, in which the responsibilities of my successive offices became more and more heavy. During that time I was inclined to think that a nervous system was lacking in me; but upon leaving office, for two or three weeks I was made aware of the existence of nerves in a positive and acute way. It was not until this reaction had ceased that I came to realize what a tremendous official responsibility had been lifted from me. I felt like a boy out of school. I have not gotten over that feeling yet.

Upon his retirement from the presidency, Taft accepted the position as Kent Professor of Constitutional Law at Yale and during World War I he was joint-chairman of the National War Labor Board.

On June 30, 1921, President Harding named Taft Chief Justice of the Supreme Court, and the next nine years were probably his happiest. "The Court," Taft once wrote, "next to my wife and children, is the nearest thing to my heart in life." Under his direct supervision, the building which houses the Supreme Court was constructed in the late 1920s. According to Stewart Alsop, in an article in the October 21, 1967, *Post*, "Taft knew what he wanted—a building that would impress the humble citizenry with the power and majesty of his beloved Court. And that is what he got."

Taft's sons followed him into politics, Robert as a Senator from Ohio and Charles as mayor of Cincinnati.

The Bigness of Big Bill

Editor's Note—We know of no one better qualified to write sympathetically of the bigness of Big Bill and of fat men in general than Mr. Blythe. Like the illustrious candidate from Ohio, he too, for years, found it necessary to weigh himself on hay scales.

There are two kinds of fat men—fat men, and men who are fat; or, to make a closer analysis: (a) fat men in whom the fat predominates, and (b) fat men in whom the man predominates. Fat men of type a are of no con-

sequence. You could set up a row of them a block long and blow them over by waving a straw hat at them. They are the chaps who have no shoulders, no chests , no legs—nothing but paunch. Fat men of the other type are big fellows, with broad shoulders, fine chests, sturdy legs and some stomach, men who do not look as if they had swallowed a bass drum, but have their weight evenly distributed over them, albeit there may be a trifle too much about the equator. All the fat men in history have been of this type, and history, it may be remarked in passing, has been made by fat men, and unmade, too, if that side of it should

97

Special arrangements were often made to accommodate "Big Bill"—big bathtubs, large chairs, extra-wide car doors—but his wit matched his weight. He once telegraphed a train conductor, "Stop at Hicksville. Large party waiting to catch train."

porting that huge body and supporting it firmly and forever. To be sure, there were a few chins more than were absolutely necessary, but that was a detail. The ensemble was magnificent.

[Eventually] they came around to Taft and said: "Bill, you are getting too fat. Better do something for it."

No man has attained the majesty of three hundred and thirty pounds without going through reduction torments in various forms. Taft has had his share. He had been fighting fat, off and on, for years, and he had seen the fat win every bout. This time he did not jump wildly at a diet or hire himself out for a punching-bag to a physical torture artist. He had been a judge and was then a statesman, so he looked at the matter in a calm, sage manner and canvassed the world for a process that would do what was necessary . . . . He scoured the world for a man who had a record for eliminating extra flesh, and secured him in England.

bother any. The whole world is divided into two classes, generally speaking: Thin people who are constantly trying to get fat and fat people who are always trying to get thin.

Occasionally there is a philosopher who doesn't give a hoot. That philosopher is always a man. No woman ever was content to be fat, or thin, either, although most of them are one or the other. The lack or abundance of a waist-line is the cause of more secret sorrow than anything in the world, unless it is money; but thin people and fat people can get money—sometimes—and it is mighty hard to upholster a bony frame; harder, indeed, than any other human project except decushioning a padded one.

Now, Taft is a real, honest fat man, too. He is fat. That is all there is to it. And he admits it, which shows he is a philosopher. When he first arrived from the Philippines to be Secretary of War, somebody asked him how heavy he was. "No gentleman," Taft replied solemnly, "weighs more than three hundred pounds."

When Taft first burst on our view, he certainly could cast a shadow. He was big everywhere. His head was big enough for his shoulders and his shoulders wide enough for his chest. His chest merged grandly into his stomach without one of those outward abdominal flares observed in the fat men who are only fat in the center, and his legs were veritable pillars of solid flesh, capable of sup-

Mr. Taft was never a great eater, but it took a reasonable supply of food to keep that three hundred and thirty pounds energized. One morning he rose, sniffed at the breakfast that was in preparation, gazed out at the green trees and greener grass, sighed and said: "Good-by, hot biscuits and wheatcakes. Farewell,

It was Mrs. Taft, here seated at a White House garden party, who conceived the idea of the thousands of flowering Japanese cherry trees in Potomac Park.

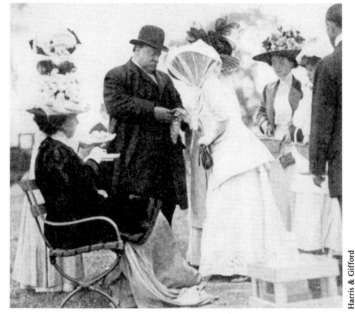

Political Buttons, Book III, by Theodore Hake

A postcard from the 1908 campaign pictures Taft's warm, quick smile.

sausages and lamb chops. Au revoir, eggs and everything else that make for the joy of living. Here, at this moment, I enter on a dun-gray existence. Here I begin to play it low down on my faithful palate. Avaunt food and quit my sight. I am now on a diet."

And he was on a diet, for fair. "You will understand," said the English expert, "that sugar is entirely debarred, and that fats, milk, cheese, cream, eggs and all bread and farinaceous foods are cut off." That was a running start, but it was merely the preliminary.

The fight went on for months. A few ounces of lean meat or a few ounces of chicken or white fish! Day after day he sat down to that unvarying round. He always had some of his biscuits with him and nibbled at one now and then. But when he went to bed he knew he would get up to lean meat, lean fish and lean chicken. Everything in the world seemed lean but himself. He loathed breakfast, hated luncheon and despised dinner. Still, he had set the mark, and he didn't quit. Daily visits to the scales showed him he was falling off. The weight went rapidly at first and then slower and slower, but it disappeared. After months of it he stepped on the scales one day and found he had lost eighty pounds. He had suspected as much, for he had kept a force of tailors busy altering his clothes, an incident in dieting, by the way, which is not so inexpensive as may be thought! Walking over to the window he threw his biscuits out as far as he could throw them, and for dinner that night he had everything he could think of that had been interdicted by his reduction expert.

It wasn't necessary for him to continue the diet, although he did not drop it entirely.

Every morning he does his little series of exercises, which shows, in another way, how thoroughly his mind is in control of his body. Next to stopping eating the hardest thing in the world to do is to perform those involuted convolutions the physical culture professors charge fifty dollars to teach you. It is easy enough to exercise if a professor is standing by, to make you, but to go into the bathroom, with nobody on earth to know whether you shirk or not, and perform that sickening series of bending over and touching the floor with your finger-tips without bending your knees a few score of times, and lying down on your back and bringing up your legs until you think they are going to break off at the hips, requires moral courage of the kind few people have. Taft has it, and he doggedly does his stunts, whereupon his waist-line continues at about the right figure, say fifty inches or thereabouts.

There are still about two hundred and sixty pounds of Taft, two hundred and sixty pounds well disposed on a big frame. Maybe he runs to two hundred and seventy, for there have been no bulletins lately. At any rate, he is a fat man of type *b*—a fat man in whom the man predominates, not the fat—Big Bill—Fit, Fat and Fifty.

—excerpted from a June 13, 1908, Post
article written by Samuel G. Blythe.

Votes for Women
by William Howard Taft

Two generations ago woman suffrage was not much discussed. Noble women, like Lucretia Mott, Lucy Stone, Elizabeth Cady Stanton, Mrs. Livermore and Julia Ward Howe, went about the country lecturing in its favor. But the issue seemed rather an academic one, and was not then believed to be pressing or within the range of practical politics. I had the privilege of hearing some of these presentations of the question. My father and mother were both in favor of women's voting, and I wrote a commencement address, when I graduated from Woodward High School, in Cincinnati, in which I advocated it. I had read John Stuart Mill's essay on the subjection of women, and it seemed to me that the case was a clear one for this reform.

That was more than forty years ago. In the interval I have had occasion to study more intimately the nature of our popular government, and have noted the argu-

William H. Taft devoted over 40 years to public service and was the first man to head both the Executive and Judicial branches of the government.

Library of Congress

99

Taft felt women deserved a voice in the government. He was not sure, however, that the majority of women had had sufficient education and experience to warrant the privilege, not the right, to vote.

ments *pro* and *con* on the Woman Suffrage issue. When I hear the arguments of ardent suffragists as to the good things that are to flow from the voting of women, many of them seem to me so fanciful and unattainable that they incline me against their cause. On the other hand, when I hear from antisuffrage champions the dire results that are permanently to follow such a political change, I find myself out of sympathy with their views also. In considering the arguments of the suffragists for the immediate extension of the ballot to women it will help the clearness of thought to define the nature of the electoral suffrage and to point out certain distinctions between it and citizenship that are often confused.

Under the Federal Constitution the qualification for suffrage had been left to the states without limitation until the Fifteenth Amendment, when they and the United States were forbidden to deny the suffrage to anyone otherwise entitled to vote, merely because of his race, color or previous condition of servitude. The franchise has never been regarded as an inalienable right of an American citizen . . . . [and] has been granted or withheld by the states as seemed best to them to secure the best government for the majority of the people.

The question, then, whether women shall be given the suffrage is to be argued and determined on the issue whether it would be better for the Government, for society and for the women that they should vote . . . . With all classes represented in the government it is likely to be stronger . . . . Popular government, then, is the best means of securing happiness for all people, because by representation of all classes it tends to secure justice

for all classes, and by being the result of the action of all classes it commands the greatest strength to do the thing that government must do.

Why, then, will it be asked, upon these two premises, should women not at once be granted the suffrage? They constitute a class in number equal to half the adult population. Will their welfare not be better secured if they are given a voice in the government charged with protecting it, than if it be left to men alone?

In the end I think these questions must be answered in the affirmative. If the suffrage is sufficiently delayed to give better preparation to women as a class for the exercise of the franchise, its advantages will outweigh its probable injurious consequences.

. . . It was long ago settled that the word "citizen" in the Federal Constitution included not only men and women, but children, and that the protection of the Government, the guaranties of life, liberty and property and the pursuit of happiness were secured to all. Since our Government was founded, however, women have been taxed and have had no voice in the government through the franchise.

Why did not Thomas Jefferson and those who strongly upheld the widest democracy in government and the extension of the franchise suggest that women should be allowed by the states to vote? If it was true that to withhold suffrage from them was really taxing them without representation, would it not have occurred to our ancestors that they were guilty of a glaring inconsistency? Now what was the reason for not giving the franchise to women? The family formed a unit in which the members had a common interest and, when the father and the sons were given votes, it was thought that the interests of the other members of the family, the mother and sisters and the daughters and the minor children, had proper political representation.

The women, on the other hand, accepting the duty of bearing children and nurturing them, and engaged in domestic matters, never in any considerable number until recently conceived the idea that they were in any way deprived of privilege because they did not vote. Women were not educated in the early days of the Republic with any view to enabling them to take an interest in public affairs. It is only within seventy-five years that the higher education of women has had any encouragement. Marriage and the institution of the family made a conflict of political, social or economic interest between members of

The "Lighter Side" of the Presidency

When Taft came to the White House, a larger tub had to be installed in his bathroom. He would stick in the other tub and have to be helped out.

* * * * *

Young Charlie Taft took a copy of *Treasure Island* to the Senate on Inauguration Day to read in case the speech bored him, he said.

* * * * *

The President was a tremendous goer; he loved to travel, to dine out, to mingle. His ability to sleep at any time enabled him to survive such a regime. He would go to sleep while talking with the Speaker, the Chief Justice, a delegation or a pretty woman, at the theater, a funeral or while playing cards. He and Justice White both went sound asleep at a funeral while sitting alongside each other, and snored too.

* * * * *

Once Taft, Butt [a military aide] and a newspaperman went for a walk soon after Mrs. Taft was taken ill. Coming to the Botanical Gardens, the President decided to pick a bunch of flowers for Mrs. Taft. A watchman saw them, and came on the run. He didn't recognize the President at first and dressed him down properly.

> —*excerpts from a March 31, 1934,* Post *article by Irwin H. (Ike) Hoover.*

if given a voice in the government . . . . The error is in the assumption that legislation can cure all inequalities which they conceive to be wrongs. The inequality in this case is not found in the law. The inequality and injustice, if it be one, is in the attitude of society toward the subject, and statute law is helpless to control the view of society . . . .

The ballot would be a defense for the woman, some thought, but would it mean "domination" for the man, as others feared?

But though I am opposed to woman suffrage now I recognize that it is likely to come some time. If it can be delayed until a great majority of the women desire it, and have become better prepared to exercise it, I think it will be a correct and useful extension of the democratic principle . . . . I believe that the campaigns will increase the number of women favoring suffrage until a majority will join in the demand.

Women are more independent than they used to be. It is not physical disability, but convention, that has excluded them from many avenues of livelihood . . . changes have not come because of the movement for woman suffrage. That movement has been only one of the results of the necessary enlargement of woman's sphere in life. The theory that each woman ought to be a wife and a mother and dependent on a man, and that those who are not are useless burdens on society, has been seen to be unjust to women and unwise socially and economically.

. . . Let us, for the sake of argument, concede that . . . the average man's mental strength and capacity is greater than that of the average woman . . . . The important difference in the capacities of men and women to vote is in the lack of experience and education that the women have had . . . .

On the whole, however, if . . . I were called upon to vote I would vote against giving the suffrage . . . the longer the extension of the franchise to women waits, the better they will be prepared for it and the more good and less harm it will do. Let us, therefore, not force the ballot into their hands on theory, but let it come as a growth in their own conception of the part they ought to play in the political life of the country.

> —*September 11, 1915, issue of* The Saturday Evening Post.

the same family of different sexes seem impossible.

Of course this view failed to take into consideration the women who were not married and who never were to be married, and those who had no men so related to them as really to constitute them their representatives. Such women, however, were in the small minority. In

the popular mind the young women who were not married were expected to be married, and the women who did not marry were looked upon as failures . . . .

The movement for woman suffrage has had its great source and impetus in the belief that great reform in the condition of women can be effected by law which men are reluctant to enact, but which woman will secure

Woodrow Wilson

★ ★ ★ ★ ★

28th President of the United States

Born: December 28, 1856, Staunton, Virginia.
Occupation: Educator, lawyer.
Wives: Ellen Axson, Edith Galt: *Children:* Three girls.
President: 1913-1921. Democratic party.
Vice-President: Thomas R. Marshall.
Died: February 3, 1924. *Buried:* Washington, D.C.

★ ★ ★ ★ ★

Thomas Woodrow Wilson was a southerner (extremely fond of chicken and charlotte russe), a son of a Presbyterian minister and a scholar. He graduated from Princeton University, taught there and was later its president. Sir Harry Lauder described Wilson in the February 25, 1928, issue of the *Post:*

> Woodrow Wilson looked to me exactly what he was—a schoolmaster. That long, clean-shaved face, the cold logic in his eyes, the lines about his mouth, in fact every outward aspect of the man savored of the university classroom. If you had put on his head a mortarboard, underneath his arm a couple of books and in his right hand a cane, you would have got the perfect dominie.

Wilson was the governor of New Jersey when he became a candidate for president. Because of the split in the Republican party, he won a decided victory.

Mr. Wilson was the last president to ride to the inauguration in a horse-drawn carriage. He and his wife did not like large parties so there was no inaugural ball. Mrs. Wilson became ill and died six months after her husband took office. It is said that the President himself arranged her body on a sofa and sat up two nights alone with her in death. A year later, Wilson married Edith Bolling Galt.

As president he was concerned with the rights of all the people and against special privileges for a few. Breaking custom, Wilson personally appeared before Congress demanding that the Democratic campaign promise—reform of the tariff, the tax on imports—be fulfilled. He was a very active president, and was instrumental in the passage of the Underwood-Simmons Tariff Act of 1913, the Federal Reserve Act of 1913, the Federal Trade Commission Act and the Clayton Antitrust Act of 1914, and in 1916, the Child Labor Act, the Federal Farm Loan Act and the Adamson Act.

During his administration, World War I broke out in Europe, and Wilson tried to keep the United States out of this war. When he was nominated for his second term, his campaign slogan was, "He kept us out of war."

The election was so close that his opponent, Charles Evans Hughes, went to bed thinking he had won. Later that night, a reporter called his house and his son said, "The President is asleep." "When he wakes up, tell him he isn't the President," the reporter replied.

Wilson tried to live up to his campaign promise, but Germany had submarines in the Atlantic, and they were sinking American ships. Five months after his second inauguration (April 2, 1917), with a sad heart, Wilson asked Congress to declare war on Germany "to make the world safe for democracy."

As a wartime gesture, a flock of sheep grazed on the White House lawn and the Wilsons traveled to church in horse-drawn carriages.

Even as the war was going on, Wilson was determined to make this "a war to end war." He worked on a treaty with a 14-point program. His great dream was to form a League of Nations that would put an end to war forever.

He went to the peace conference in Versailles, France, and convinced the European countries to create such a league. In an article in the August 16, 1919, issue of the *Post* William Allen White wrote of Wilson's fight for the League:

> The League of Nations before President Wilson came to Europe was a pacifist's dream—iridescent but also evanescent. He made it real. For it he gave everything—even his good name. He sacrificed profoundly for the idea, and saved it to the world. He could not have done this by delegating his power. His influence from Washington would have been negligible. But in Paris—grotesque figure though he was in European eyes—he was powerful. His words had weight. They prevailed. They have made a world league for peace and not for war one of the inevitable things which humanity will bring into being by the very act of longing for it.
>
> It matters little what happens right now to the idea of the League of Nations. Time is long, and the deep aspirations of men will wait. But our American democracy may be honestly proud that it has raised up one who put into the hearts of all the world, because we sat him high where he could speak to all the world, the aspiration of our hearts for the coming of a peace of good will among men of good will.

When he returned to the United States, Congress refused to ratify the treaty. Wilson started out on a speaking tour of the West to win support from the people. The trip was to have lasted 27 days and cover 10,000 miles, but on the 26th of September, while speaking in Wichita, Kansas, Wilson collapsed. He had suffered a cerebral thrombosis that paralyzed his left side. For days he was in a coma and for months he lived in seclusion, attending to business only when Mrs. Wilson thought advisable. During the last 18 months of his presidency, his near-disability cost him the Senate battle for the League of Nations.

Wilson's remaining years were spent as an invalid. He is buried in Washington Cathedral, Washington, D.C.

Courtship and Marriage of a President

Dr. Cary T. Grayson had been the naval surgeon assigned to the *Mayflower* in the Roosevelt and Taft administrations, and now was the President's physician and companion. Grayson was a suitor for the hand of a

Although Wilson gives his birthday as the 28th of December, the family Bible records it as 12:45 a.m. on the 29th. Below, the rear view of Shadow Lawn in Virginia and bottom right, a front view.

Above, Franklin D. Roosevelt visits with Wilson on the porch at Shadow Lawn during the 1916 campaign against Hughes.

Washington belle, Miss Alice Gordon, who was a much-courted young woman. Through Miss Gordon, he met her friend, Mrs. Edith Bolling Galt, widow of a Washington jeweler. In turn, he introduced Mrs. Galt to the ladies of the White House, with whom she soon became a favorite. They returned her calls, had her to tea a number of times and occasionally took her riding.

The President regarded these afternoon teas as strictly women's affairs and stayed away, but he must have heard talk and praise of their new friend. An attractive lady she was; good to look at and handsomely turned out. The President's cousin, Miss Bones, was especially attracted to her. Finally, the President looked in on one of these teas and met Mrs. Galt. He shared the favorable impression of his womenfolk, but no suspicion of a special interest was roused until he began to make rather a point of happening in to tea.

Casual meetings with Mrs. Galt now became appointments, and she came for the first time to dine in the evening. The President was all expectancy and had arrayed himself with care. A White House car was sent for his guest. She, too, evidently had taken unusual pains with her appearance. She made a pretty picture, set off with a single purple orchid, pinned high on the left shoulder. Her voice was soft with a Southern accent, her manner charming. We all shared the President's admiration. At the end of the meal, he and the ladies went for a long ride before dropping Mrs. Galt at her home. From now on it was a courtship.

He now had no plans which did not include Mrs. Galt. Where he was to go, provision must be made for her. When he went to New York to a naval review, she was a member of his party. When she drove to Baltimore with the ladies of the White House, the President met them halfway in another car and returned with her. A President in love is no different from any other man in love. Woodrow Wilson was a gallant lover, an ardent wooer. His anxiety that he make a good impression was delightful to onlookers. He seemed no more certain of success than another man might be, and he exhausted all the tricks of this old trade. The employees had a very human interest in a love affair as such, particularly one that involved a president. Every covert squeeze of the hand, every little special attention was seen and reported.

The President had instructed Secretary Tumulty to announce the engagement at eight P.M. of October sixth, for release to the morning papers of the seventh. That night the President dispensed with a chaperon and took his fiancée home, not returning until after midnight.

The announcement cards were a model of simplicity. Designating himself as plain "Mr. Woodrow Wilson," he, with Mrs. Norman Galt, née Edith Bolling, announced their marriage on December 18, 1915, at 8:30 o'clock at the bride's home.

The wedding supper menu included:

Oyster Patties

Boned Capon   Virginia Ham   Rolls

Chicken Salad   Cheese Straws

Biscuits With Minced Ham

Pineapple Ice   Caramel Ice Cream

Cake   Fruit Punch   Coffee

Bon Bons   Salted Almonds   Chocolates

Brown Brothers

Courtesy of the Woodrow Wilson House, a property of the National Trust for Historic Preservation

The last detail to be rehearsed was the plan for a secret get-away after the wedding. The honeymoon was to be spent at Hot Springs, Virginia, and the train was to be boarded by prearrangement at Alexandria, Virginia. The President had great fun in making these plans, took into his confidence only the few who must know, and did not tell anyone all.

The wedding day dawned clear and pleasant both inside and out. Arriving at the Galt home, the President went directly to the front room on the second floor, which had been converted from a bedroom into a living room. The Marine Band orchestra struck up the Lohengrin Wedding March above stairs and the President and his bride descended the steps unaccompanied. As the music died, the voice of the minister took up. Every other sound ceased, every neck was craned. None present ever will forget it. Both the bride's and the groom's faces were set and serious. He assisted her when it came time to kneel on the *priedieu*, and little gasps of approval ran among the women.

Only when the final words were uttered and the orchestra struck up again was the spell broken. The family of the bride rushed forward to kiss her, Mrs. Galt's mother likewise kissing the President.

The orchestra continued to play; the bride and groom made their way to the table where stood the great wedding cake. With a silver knife with which her mother had cut her wedding cake, the new Mrs. Wilson expertly cut her own, serving several slices herself to those near by, the President included. The newly married couple mixed freely among the guests and it became a homey sort of affair, with everybody talking at the same time.

A great cheer went up from the throngs in the street as the President and Mrs. Wilson emerged from the house . . . . Now the wild ride to the railroad station.

Time demonstrated the wisdom of his choice. The President and his wife moved together in perfect accord, each much the better for having met and joined the other.

—excerpted from a June 23, 1934, Post *article written by Irwin H. (Ike) Hoover.*

As president of Princeton, where he and his family were photographed (top left), Wilson introduced the preceptorial system of education where students and teachers get together in small discussion groups. One year after Ellen Wilson's death, the President wooed and won the hand of Edith Galt. The couple was photographed at the White House reflecting pool (bottom) and at the 1919 World Series (top right). On November 11, 1921, they rode in a horse-drawn carriage in the procession which carried the Unknown Soldier's body to Arlington (above).

Cut Out Privilege

by Woodrow Wilson

I am glad to have an opportunity to state briefly and directly what I understand the Democratic platform and policies to mean for the people of the United States. The most striking thing, to my mind, about the present situation is that the Democratic party should at last have attracted the attention of the country to a program which it has proposed, at any rate in all its larger features, for half a generation. The Democratic party did not wait until the year 1912 to become progressive. It did not wait until the year 1912 to discover that the Government was being enslaved by the special privileges it had been granting to the beneficiaries of the tariff. It did not wait until this moment of final critical choice to foresee what the choice was ultimately going to be. The choice which the voters have now to make is simply this: Shall they have a Government free to serve them, free to serve all of them, or shall they continue to have a Government that dispenses special favors, and that is always controlled by those to whom the special favors are dispensed? The choice is simple.

There are many things proposed in the Democratic platform upon which I suppose practically all thoughtful citizens will agree. The programs of parties are nowadays in many particulars singularly alike. We all know what ought to be done for the equalization of conditions in the United States, for the conservation of our natural resources, for the protection of the lives and health and energy of our people, for the development of transportation facilities, and for the protection of the people against extortionate charges in the service of corporations which they must all employ. All thoughtful men must concur also in the judgment that not all of the social betterment of our time must be left to voluntary effort, but that the Government itself should lend a hand to improve conditions of life. But only the Democratic platform perceives what are the necessary first steps—namely, to cut out privilege absolutely, and absolutely prevent monopoly. Neither the Republican party nor the party that has now assumed the name "Progressive" goes straight at these matters or seems to understand that it is necessary to go straight at them. They both admit that some of the tariff duties are too high and ought to be lowered, but they fail to see the principle upon which they must be lowered. That principle is that every part of the tariff that has afforded a covert to those who have organized monopoly in this country and have thereby created high prices, shall be cut out as quickly as it can be cut out without risk of business disaster. That is the heart of that matter. And with regard to the trusts, nothing more is proposed by those two parties than this—that we shall accept the consequences of the evil developments that

---

"You'll Catch Your Death!"

It is to be remembered that Woodrow Wilson had given his whole adult life to the study of government, being one of the few presidents to take office with a fully formed political philosophy. Where a tenet of this philosophy was concerned his mind stood locked. State's rights, for instance, was one of these deep convictions, and although a firm believer in equal suffrage, he could not bring himself to indorse the constitutional amendment demanded by the women.

Courage always appealed to him, and instead of frowning upon independent thought, he delighted in it.

We argued the matter many times during the wild days of 1917, for I was a violent supporter of the measure, and though agreeing with me that victory was inevitable, he refused steadily to capture the popularity that would come from his assumption of leadership.

"They are doing the right thing in the wrong way," he insisted. "It is a matter for the decision of the states."

Even so, he had only admiration for the women who picketed the White House gates day after day, careless of heat and cold, rain and storm. Many of the banners that they carried were downright abusive, attacking him as a czar, but never once did he manifest irritation or resentment. On the contrary, he worried no little about the comfort and health of the pickets. I sat with him one afternoon when the very heavens opened, and after fidgeting around, with repeated trips to the window, he finally summoned a messenger.

"Please go out there and ask those women to come inside," he said. "They'll catch their death of cold."

—*excerpted from a March 28, 1931,*
Post *article written by George Creel.*

When the Wilsons left the White House in 1921 they retired to "S" Street in Washington, D.C. (center top, bottom). Scott, his valet (above), accompanied Mr. and Mrs. Wilson (right). Now the ex-president could find time to read and write his books. His most noted work was a five-volume History of the American People. *He also wrote* Division and Reunion, *a history of the U.S. between the Jackson era and Reconstruction.*

have characterized the last decades in this country, shall assume that it is impossible to prevent monopoly, and shall merely set the Government to preside over it, see that its processes are assuaged and rendered less cruel, see that monopoly becomes a providence for the people as well as a master over them.

On such a program what the country has hoped and waited for is impossible. Apparently only the Democratic leaders know that it is impossible. They are not blind to the new developments of business. They know that modern business cannot be conducted as business was conducted a generation ago; but though they are quite aware that business must be upon a great scale, they know that the only sound way of conducting business is to let it grow big by natural growth, based upon efficiency, economy, intelligence, enterprise, and that when business is big because allowed a brutal control, based merely upon combination and monopolistic agreement, it is unwholesome and dangerous and arbitrary in all its processes.

The claim of the Democratic party to the confidence of the country is based upon its perception of these things, upon its determination to attack them frankly and directly, and upon its unhesitating courage in the enterprise. It is not embarrassed by alliances. Its leaders are absolutely free. Its purpose is clear and has been forming through half a generation. It has the impulse of conviction, and is sutained in its enterprises by demonstrable facts.

The present situation of business in this country is wholly abnormal. To carry out with soberness and discretion the program proposed by the leaders of the Democratic party will be to release American business from artificial conditions and to give it a new era of freedom and expansion and a new variety in enterprise. No government, however beneficent, can do for a people what they can do for themselves. No government, however beneficent, can safely be intrusted with the determination of the courses business should take and the enterprise of its citizens. I am a Democrat because I feel the deepest conviction that only the principles and purposes avowed by the Democratic party afford any hope or prospect of a genuine restoration of liberty, equality and justice in the United States. Who that knows the forces now in contest can question this conclusion?

—reprinted from the October 26, 1912, issue of The Saturday Evening Post.

All photos courtesy of the Woodrow Wilson House, a property of the National Trust for Histoic Preservation

Warren G. Harding

★ ★ ★ ★ ★

29th President of the United States

Born: November 2, 1865, Corsica, Ohio.
Occupation: Editor.
Wife: Florence DeWolfe. *Children*: None.
President: 1921-1923. Republican party.
Vice-President: Calvin Coolidge.
Died: August 2, 1923. *Buried*: Marion, Ohio.

★ ★ ★ ★ ★

As a boy, Warren Gamaliel Harding was a farm boy and the eldest of eight children. At the age of 14 he entered Ohio Central College. Upon graduation he took employment as a schoolteacher, but quit after one term saying it was the hardest job he ever had.

The following year the family moved to Marion, Ohio, where Warren studied law. After a few months he decided he didn't like it; likewise with real estate.

In 1884, Harding and two friends bought the Marion *Star*, a newspaper without reputation or circulation. About this time he married Mrs. Florence Kling DeWolfe, a widow five years his senior. More ambitious and industrious than her husband, she played a large role in the prosperity of the *Star*.

As one of Marion's leading citizens, Harding won a Republican seat in the Ohio Senate, was later elected Lt. Governor of Ohio and in 1914 to the U.S. Senate.

Harding became a presidential candidate in 1920 because everybody liked him. He was tall, good-looking and looked like some thought a president should look. Since he was chosen in the infamous "smoke-filled room," the Republican bosses thought they could control him. But, according to Samuel G. Blythe in an article in the July 2, 1921, *Post*, this was not to be the case: "The one thing about the President that most people have not yet learned is that though he is genial and smiling and affable and glad-handed, there are times when he puts down those 10½-D feet and keeps them down."

"No President up to his time was as popular with newspapermen as Harding," wrote Wesley Stout in the January 26, 1935, *Post*. "He revived the press conferences which Wilson had dropped. Each year he played in the newspapermen's golf tournament and religiously attended all other press functions.

"Harding's appointment list at the office was longer than that of any previous President . . . . On May 2, 1921, the President saw twenty-one visitors between 10:00 and 12:45."

World War I had been over for two years and Harding promised a "return to normalcy." The Republican Congress was in session almost continuously during his administration. Wartime restrictions were lifted, taxes were cut, a federal budget system was created, the high protective tariff on imports was re-established and, for the first time, immigration was restricted. A senator at the time, George Wharton Pepper commented on the advances of the administration:

> The financial legislation was even more significant. To reduce the interest-bearing public debt by nearly seven billions of dollars and to refund, at a reduced interest rate, more than four billions of the remainder was in itself a stupendous achievement.
>
> —*August 23, 1930, Post.*

Instead of cooperating with Europe through the League of Nations, Harding called the Washington Arms Conference of November 11, 1921. The Five

Power Naval Treaty resulted. This prevented a Japan/Great Britain alliance and avoided the controversial covenant by which a majority vote of the League could obligate all members to take action against an aggressor.

Harding's administration has the reputation of being one of the most corrupt in history. He brought in his old Ohio "cronies," known as the "Ohio gang." Congress, however, approved the appointments, as Mr. Blythe commented:

> It is quite true that Congress, in many of its powerful individual units, raged over some of the appointments Mr. Harding made. They did not meet either the plans or the expectations of those powerful individual units; but was there lack of confirmation and support? Not that was noticeable. Not in important particulars. An incoming President must be obeyed; an out-going President may be flouted. The one is a prospect for patronage, the other a worked-out vein. And the gentlemen up on the Hill in Washington are expert miners, each and every one.

In an article in the May 8, 1954, *Post*, Alben W. Barkley, Vice-President under Truman, summarized the results of the appointments:

> President Harding was a personally likable man who was cursed by an unfortunate inability to say no to his cronies. What the members of the "Ohio gang" [namely Sec. of Treasury Andrew Mellon and Attorney General Harry Daugherty] did to their chief and to their country with their wholesale spree of bribery and general corruption, culminating in the infamous Teapot Dome and Veterans' Bureau scandals, is one of the more sordid stories of American political history.

The ordeal greatly upset Harding, who put stock in honesty. Showing signs of fatigue in San Francisco while on a cross-country trip with his wife, Harding remarked privately: "I have no trouble with my enemies . . . But my . . . friends . . . keep me walking the floor nights!" He developed pneumonia and died suddenly on August 2, 1923.

The women's vote in 1920 helped Harding win by the greatest majority ever obtained in a presidential election. Harding the golfer (upper right) and the sportsman (far right with Babe Ruth) brought the "just folks" attitude back to the White House by reopening the grounds to the public and shaking hands with many.

WOMEN'S
FIRST VOTE

VOTE
THE
STRAIGHT
REPUBLICAN
TICKET

A Calm Review of a Calm Man

AP San Francisco, August 3, 1923.—"That's good! Go on—read some more."

These were the last words uttered by President

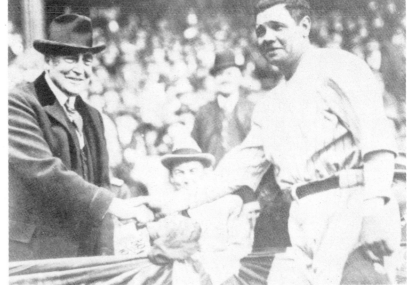

Harding to his wife.

Mrs. Harding was reading aloud to the Chief Executive Samuel G. Blythe's article, "A Calm Review of a Calm Man," in which he was the man reviewed, when the stroke of apoplexy brought an end to his life.

Mrs. Harding paused and looked at the President. His hand was raised as he asked her to continue reading. Instantly his expression changed. He was dead.

No President is a hero to his politicians. He is a producer to them. Nor is any President a hero to the other party's politicians. He is a usurper to them. Consequently, as the public view of a President—any President—is largely influenced by what is printed about him, and as what is printed about him is largely influenced by the politicians, the popular esteem, or disesteem, of the man who occupies the White House has three fundamental sources: Applause contrived to make him produce; censure because he has not produced; and general opprobrium because he is in a position to keep the opposition out of the fruits of production.

This public view gives rise to a situation that works two ways against the President: If he is a politician he offends all who belong to the opposition party; if he is a nonpolitical he offends all who belong to his own party. The office of President of the United States is the most powerful, dignified and important political position in the world. Also, it is the position that brings to the incumbent of it the keenest realization of the plight of those who hold high place—the plight of being damned if they do and damned if they don't.

Mr. Harding is now in the third year of his term. He has been President for two years and three months as this is written. The beginning of the latter half of a President's term is the lowest ebb of his political and official fortunes. There can be no complaint over that. It has been the lot of all official mankind since the dawn of time, because criticism lingers and censure persists long after acclaim has died down the winds. It goes with the job.

After hearing all this criticism of the Harding Administration, reading yards of it in the press and then sitting down and trying to analyze it, the conclusion is reached by any unbiased investigator that the real defect of the Harding Administration, as it reacts on the people, is that it doesn't make noise enough. It is too calm. Conversely, the criticism is loud and vociferant.

We are a volatile and an impressionable people, and noise gets us. Hearing these demonstrations we say to one another: "Prob'ly there's something into it. I guess this man Harding ain't what he's cracked up to be."

Probably he isn't, but, so far as that goes, he isn't what he's cracked down to be either. And the present seems to be an opportune moment for stating the judicial fact that there is a Harding mean which the President as President of the United States, and not as a Republican or as a partisan or in any political

Unlike his predecessor, Harding enjoyed having his likeness sculptured and painted. He was sitting for his first portrait within three months of taking office. On Memorial Day, 1922, Harding accepted the artistic and inspiring Lincoln Memorial on behalf of the people.

A pianist all her life, Florence Harding jeopardized the essential tools when she stood at a New Year's reception and shook 6567 hands in five hours.

sense whatsoever, is entitled to have spread on the minutes. This man Harding is neither noisy nor brilliant, in the showy acceptance of that term. He is not loud and declamatory. He is a modest man—too modest no doubt—and a calm man, and a man with a philosophy that has not worked out so badly, as will be shown. He undoubtedly has made mistakes, and undoubtedly will make more mistakes, but his Administration hasn't been all mistakes.

The great grievance seems to be a general assumption that he doesn't work as hard as he should, when the facts are that he works harder, longer hours, over greater problems and under more strain than any critic, bar none; and the further fact is that inasmuch as he finds time for recreation he must work rather efficiently, which is what he does. It makes no difference how many of us, in the crowd, loaf on our jobs. The President is different. He isn't human. He is merely a machine who is expected to grind at a desk for the benefit of those who deride him.

This country, under Harding, has come to be the only legitimately prosperous country in the world. It doesn't take much of a memory to go back to 1921, nor much of a business training to realize that business was bad in this country at that time. Nor does it take much experience of economics or commerce, general trade, manufacturing or labor conditions to make it plain that this country, at this time, is really, legitimately, solidly and nationally prosperous. This prosperity is not sectional. It is not geographical. It extends from coast to coast, from the Canadian border to Mexico. Labor is universally employed at high wages. Money is plentiful. All lines of business are flourishing. And there is no other country in the world of which this can be said.

What, to repeat a question asked some time back, do the people want? They have prosperity. They have economy in government. They have a fine type of American for President, a human, understandable, modest, kindly man, with all the reserve force needed to govern capably.

Why let a lot of self-seeking politicians, with no other motive than their own advancement, and with their own interests paramount to those of the country and the people, obscure the real facts with fog of denunciation and theory and demagogism? Why not give the President an even break?

—*excerpted from the July 28, 1923,* Post.

Ante Up!

Man displays his temperament and details his disposition of mind more directly in his diversions than elsewhere. He is off watch when he is playing, and more nearly himself. In his senatorial days in Washington Mr. Harding occasionally played poker with some of his colleagues. It was a friendly game and a relaxation from the hard work of the Senate. In this poker game there were one or two players of the sort known as hardboiled—technicians, fellows who look after the ante and always know when the pot is right and whose bet it is, and so on, pests in a friendly game and no exception because they are senators.

Frequently in these games the hardboiled would tangle up the play with disputes as to what had happened, what might happen or what couldn't happen. Invariably Harding would say, "Well, let's settle it by dealing a hand of stud," and he'd deal it, and by the time the hand of stud was played the dispute was forgotten. You watch the great political, governmental and national poker game that is played at Washington during these four years. The President of the United States will compose many a situation by dealing a tranquilizing hand of stud.

—*an excerpt from a July 2, 1921,*
Post *article written by*
Samuel G. Blythe.

Calvin Coolidge

★ ★ ★ ★ ★

30th President of the United States

Born: July 4, 1872, Plymouth, Vermont.
Occupation: Lawyer.
Wife: Grace Goodhue. *Children:* Two boys.
President: 1923-1929. Republican party.
Vice-President: Charles G. Dawes.
Died: January 5, 1933. *Buried:* Plymouth, Vermont.

★ ★ ★ ★ ★

John Calvin Coolidge, born on Independence Day in 1872, was raised in the Green Mountains of Vermont. His ancestors immigrated to America in 1630 and moved to Plymouth Notch in the 1780s. His father, John, fought in the Revolutionary War.

Though the nation was growing into a country of cities and factories in the 1870s and '80s, the little village nestled in the Green Mountains was little affected. Calvin was raised on policies of honesty, thrift and hard work. The family was generally self-sufficient, and Calvin helped with the chores on the farm until he went away to Black River Academy in Ludlow, Vermont, at the age of 13.

In 1891 Coolidge was admitted to Amherst College in Massachusetts. Excelling in debate and public speaking, he was graduated in 1895 with honors. By the age of 25 he opened his own law office in Northampton, Mass., and it is noted that he made $500 his first year. That same year Coolidge was elected to his first office—city councilman. During his career he would be elected to 19 offices, more than any president since Monroe.

Coolidge met Grace Goodhue, a teacher of the deaf in Northampton, and married her in 1905. She was the opposite of her husband, gay and full of fun. They had two sons, John and Calvin, Jr. Young Calvin died from what began as a mere blister on his foot, acquired while playing tennis at the White House, on July 7, 1924.

As Governor of Massachusetts, Coolidge worked to reduce excess government spending and to quell the Boston policemen's strike by calling out the National Guard, declaring that "There is no right to strike against the public safety by anybody, anywhere, any time."

Elected Vice-President of the United States in 1920, Coolidge succeeded to the presidency upon the death of President Harding, on August 3, 1923. The 30th President of the United States was administered the oath of office by his father, a notary public. This historic event took place in the Vermont farmhouse home at 2:00 a.m., by the light of kerosene lamps.

"Silent Cal," as he was known, was a popular president because he did nothing to disturb the general feeling of well-being in the country. The President said, "When things are going all right, it is a good plan to let them alone." Coolidge did not believe that the government should interfere too much in the private affairs of its citizens. "The people cannot look to legislation

Derby and cane lend a distinquished air to young Calvin, a student at Amherst in 1895.

generally for success. Industry, thrift, character are not conferred by act or resolve. Government cannot relieve from toil. It can provide no substitute for the rewards of service. It can, of course, care for the defective, and recognize distinguished merit. The normal must care for themselves. Self-government means self-support."

As president, Coolidge was conservative in his economic policies. He attempted to reduce the national debt, government spending and taxes. He supported the high protective tariff, which aided American business, but vetoed a bill to raise the declining prices of farm products. He favored the World Court but due to his own lack of enthusiasm and Congress' insistence on certain specifics before ratification, this was not accomplished.

The Kellogg-Briand Pact, an agreement between 15 nations to substitute arbitration for war, was ratified by the United States during the Coolidge administration. A great deal of the business of the country was taken care of in that "cool Coolidge" manner:

> After his succession to the presidency he asked President Harding's secretary, George Christian, to carry on for a while until the new Administration should have established itself. Nobody could be more impressed than Christian by the difference between his two chiefs.
>
> "If I stayed much longer with the new President I should come to love him for the way he handles problems," he said, after a few weeks of contact.
>
> "One day," he added, "I responded to the President's bell and found Mr. Coolidge looking out of a window opening on the White House grounds while he smoked a big cigar. 'Mr. Christian,' said he, 'it is about time for many people to begin to come to the White House to discuss different phases of the coal strike. When anybody comes whose special problem concerns the state, refer him to the governor of Pennsylvania. If his problem has a national phase, refer him to the United States Coal Commission. In no event bring him to me.'" Mr. Coolidge resumed his cigar. As far as he was concerned, the strike was over.
>
> —excerpted from an August 23, 1930, Post article written by George Wharton Pepper.

Coolidge presided over a period in history known as the "Roaring Twenties," when business was booming and everyone was happy to "keep cool with Coolidge." Also known as the Jazz Age, it was the era of Prohibition. The unpopular Volstead Act, prohibiting the sale of alcoholic beverages, gave rise to "bootleggers" and "speakeasies" and gangsters like Al Capone. It was during the '20s that women were granted the right to vote via the 19th Amendment; Charles A. Lindbergh became the first man to fly nonstop and alone across the Atlantic (after which he

Coolidge was sworn in at his Vermont farmhouse at 2:00 a.m. The lamplight in the interpretation above casts appropriate shadows upon the somber event, after which, Coolidge walked alone in the misty dawn.

and his mother were entertained as guests of the Coolidges); the first talking movie, *The Jazz Singer*, was produced; Babe Ruth was hitting home runs and Gene Tunney defeated Jack Dempsey for the heavyweight boxing championship.

Coolidge himself was very thrifty and never spent a cent that was not necessary. The American people, however, were buying stocks and expanding the economy. Some people said that if something wasn't done to slow down the boom, a depression would surely follow.

Coolidge did nothing. Alben W. Barkley commented on the Coolidge administration in an article in the May 8, 1954, *Post*.

> My principal censure of the Coolidge Administration is that it did nothing positive and even went so far as to accentuate the negative. As the hot air began to leak out of the Coolidge balloon of false prosperity, the President failed to take effective steps to stop the

drift toward economic disaster. He merely camouflaged the situation—I doubt that he ever really knew what was coming—by starting a practice, continued by his successor, Herbert Hoover, of issuing reassuring statements, telling the public that all was well.

Every time there was a drop in the stock market or some other ominous economic portent in that Coolidge—Hoover period, we could count on a reassuring statement from either Secretary of the Treasury Mellon or one of the two Presidents. But no real remedies were offered and the situation worsened.

Mr. Coolidge was elected easily in 1924, but with his usual brevity said, "I do not choose to run for president in 1928." He is quoted as saying that it was best to get out while he was ahead.

After Coolidge left the White House, he returned to quiet Northampton, where he spent the remaining years of his life in the first home he ever owned. He wrote articles giving his opinion on current events and politics, and he published his autobiography. On January 5, 1933, he died suddenly of a heart attack.

Debts and Taxes

by Calvin Coolidge

Almost all units of government from the national treasury down are faced with a deficit. This comes at a time when many of them feel the necessity of enlarging relief expenditures. The result is a scramble for new means of raising revenue.

Some years ago it became apparent that tangible personal property and real estate were paying about all the taxes they could bear. To meet the cost of war, resort was had to very high income taxes, which were levied on the theory that those who had income could and must afford to make large contributions to public expenses. That seemed fair. With the increase in prosperity that the country enjoyed, large incomes increased rapidly, so that there was a great temptation to load more and more of the burden upon that source and release or disregard other and more stable sources of revenue. Now that large incomes have greatly diminished, something must be done in a hurry to pay the expenses of government.

This situation raises questions of extraordinary difficulty. It is evident there are but three things to be done—increase taxes, increase debt, or reduce expenses. Not much thought has been given to curbing the cost of government. Increasing the debt means borrowing money to meet current expenses, which leaves the

Coolidge enjoyed throwing out the first ball of the baseball season, a popular presidential duty, much more than he did shaking hands.

treasury in the precarious position of having an unbalanced budget.

That is always demoralizing. It can be done to meet a temporary emergency or for a specific purpose, but to borrow to pay ordinary running expenses of a government breaks down public confidence and very soon destroys credit. Some of our municipalities are already dangerously near this position. While no one questions the credit of the United States, a violent decline in government bonds recently gave warning that there is a limit to the borrowing power even of the strongest treasury in the world. When people saw that the national receipts last year were but $3,317,000,000, and that $236,000,000 of that came from foreign-debt payments, which are now suspended, while the expenses were $4,220,000,000, a cold shiver went down the financial spine of the public. Last year a deficit of more than 21 per cent and this year a threatened deficit of about

The One That Didn't Get Away!

When the President accepted our invitation to summer in the Hills, it was up to us to provide some amusement for him.

We did not want him to go hunting and shoot our buffalo, deer or elk that roamed around the Game Lodge in our state park. Since the Black Hills streams furnished the finest trout fishing in the world, we decided that was the sport. Upon inquiry, we learned that the President had never done any trout fishing, and, that being the case, we knew that he never would be able to catch one of our Black Hills trout. Oscar Johnson was our state game-and-fish warden—the best game warden that any state ever had. He knew trout. He said we had far too many old trout in the Spearfish hatchery.

So it was arranged that he should pick a couple of deputy game wardens to help him—deputy wardens who could keep their mouths shut and who could see well on dark nights. They were to round up and sort the trout in the Spearfish hatchery, and all the fish that were fifteen years old or older were to be penned up in one pond away from the rest.

Then they were to get a couple of big tank trucks and seine these aged trout out of the pond into the tanks and, when nobody was looking, they were to haul these trout down to the state park and turn them loose in the creek by the Game Lodge. They were also to stretch a wire netting across the creek under the bridge east of the Game Lodge—so that these trout could not come right up into the lodge—and another netting under the bridge two miles down the stream.

These two miles were set aside as the special private fishing ground of the President, in which no one else was allowed to fish unless by special invitation from Mr. Coolidge. The two miles of creek became the best trout fishing in all the world. Those trout would fight and battle one another to see which could grab the President's hook first. He became the nation's foremost trout fisherman.

—an excerpt from a January 4, 1947, Post *article written by William J. Bulow.*

40 per cent were not pleasant to contemplate.

While it may not be possible to demonstrate by any known statistics of trade, it would seem perfectly apparent that high taxes stimulate overproduction and underconsumption. If the farmer finds his taxes are high, very naturally he seeks to pay them by increasing the amount he has to sell. In the long run, if he is to sell more farm produce to industry, he must himself directly or indirectly purchase more manufactured goods, for in the end trade is an exchange of commodities. But high taxes take so much of his production that he is unable to buy much from industry. At the same time, industry has been increasing its production in order to meet its own high taxes. But when the farmer and the manufacturer attempt to sell their goods they find the tax collector has taken so much of the money of their customers that there is little left with which to make purchases.

If we resort to borrowing, it must be on the theory that, as we have no reserves, we anticipate future prosperity and spend now what we think we may be able to save in the coming years. That may turn out well, but it is extremely hazardous. No one can be sure that public confidence will be restored and business thrive at the prospect of a large debt and future enlarged taxes.

Scarcely anyone questions the necessity of some increase of tax rates and the imposition of new taxes by the National Government to pay the present deficit. But it seems apparent that such remedy ought only to be for the existing emergency that must be met to protect the public credit. The nation has the resources to

Bettmann Archives

The state dinner given for Queen Marie of Rumania (right) in 1926 was one of the smallest in modern times, with only 46 guests.

provide for such action, and they must be used. But the only permanent remedy, the only relief for high taxes, is a reduction of public expenditures. Such a reduction must be made. Almost all our governmental units have been taxing, borrowing and spending beyond the means of the people to pay. Taxes are remaining unpaid. That causes forced sales of property and destroys values. The credit of many units is exhausted, so that no more money can be borrowed by them. The local governments, on the whole, have been the worst offenders and find themselves in the most serious difficulties. Nothing but drastic retrenchment will restore them to financial health. It will be a painful operation requiring a good deal of executive energy, but it can be done. Unless it is done, the suffering and want that will result are beyond estimation.

The time has come for a combination, on a nonpartisan basis, of wage earners and business men for their mutual protection. They need to be organized, alert and vocal. Then the Congress and other bodies will listen because they will feel they have some support in resisting further expenditures and some encouragement in pursuing a policy of retrenchment.

—excerpted from the March 26, 1932, issue of The Saturday Evening Post.

Bettmann Archives

A Man of Few Words

In some parts of the country natives who had never known New England had some little difficulty in their efforts to understand Calvin Coolidge, the man. They had no difficulty as to his utterances. His words are clear, crisp, specific—and few.

It was the fewness of his words which made him a mystery. That a man in public life could be so saving of words and still have a full working equipment of human feelings was not readily understandable to men and women who were at no more pains to conceal their emotions than their clothes.

One of these puzzled men once remarked to Forrest Crissey, a New Englander, "I wish I knew the truth about that man. I don't want to think of him as a Vermont brook trout breathing cold mountain spring water instead of air—but that's the picture that comes to me."

Crissey's reply was, "That's because you don't understand Vermont nature. A throughbred Vermonter, of real top-shelf quality, is like a prize New England pie—a lot of sweet and juicy insides entirely surrounded by crust. Crust, not shell!" Witness the following:

As a child, Cal didn't like to bring in wood any better'n Dell Ward or Ed Blanchard or any other boys. He wasn't lazy and he didn't mind fillin' the box most of the time. But he'd strike times when he hated to be held to that task, and he'd do his

Mrs. Coolidge was the opposite of her husband, gay and full of life. Shown above in the Inaugural Parade of 1925 with Senator Charles Curtis, the President once told a White House visitor that "I have always noticed that the remarks I don't make cause me the least trouble." Right, the First Lady meets the famous Helen Keller on January 12, 1926.

116

best to shirk it. That was just the boy of it. What's more, he had an odd way, even as a little tad, of getting back at anybody who forced him to do work that he had tried to get out of. Time and again, when chided for failing to fill the wood box, I've seen him leave all the doors open behind him, way out into the woodshed. Of course that made everybody uncomfortable—which was just what he intended.

Once when he did this I didn't call out to him to shut the doors behind him. Instead I never said a word but went and closed the door myself. It was stinging cold that night and the room was cooling off fast. When he came back and saw what I'd done he said nothing, but braced the door open and gave me a lesson by bringing in all the wood the boxes and the stoves would hold. It was his way of answering me. I most froze.

—October 25, 1924, *Post.*

President Coolidge spent one summer up at Paul Smith's, in the Adirondacks, and Governor Al Smith, of New York, went to pay him a visit.

In order to have a quiet and undisturbed talk, the President and the Governor took a ride in a rowboat, with a guide at the oars. The conversation turned on the reputation President Coolidge had then for saying very little. Smith asked him how it worked.

"First rate," said Coolidge. "It really isn't necessary to say anything. I've discovered that the average man can tell all he knows in 10 minutes, so why interrupt him?"

—*August 22, 1931,* Post.

In the early days of their married life a smooth book agent sold Mrs. Coolidge a volume entitled *The Family Physician*, which was recommended as a compendium of remedies to deal effectively with every ailment. When Mrs. Coolidge had, so to speak, come out from under the ether she found herself in the possession of the book and a sense of guilt at having parted with six dollars of family funds at a time of small and uncertain income. Then there was the further disturbing thought that she had done this without consulting her husband, thereby breaking a family precedent.

How to justify herself in her husband's eyes was a difficult problem. Finally she decided to adopt a Coolidge method and say nothing. She simply deposited the bulky volume on the center table and awaited results. When the young lawyer came home his eye was quick to catch the addition to the family store of knowledge, and he promptly settled himself in the Boston rocker and gave himself up to a painstaking study of the book.

Later they went out together and he made no men-

Grace Coolidge's love of animals is well recalled. She had a raccoon named Rebecca and with her in Christy's portrait is Rob Roy, her collie.

tion of his conclusions on the new medical accession. Several days passed and he did not speak of it—much to the relief of the young wife, who concluded that she had not made so great a mistake as she had feared.

But the day came when she opened the volume, and on its flyleaf found this line penciled: "I find here no cure for suckers."

It is said that no book agent has ever induced Mrs. Coolidge to sign on the dotted line since.

—October 25, 1924, *Post.*

Herbert Hoover

★★★★★

31st President of the United States

Born: August 10, 1874, West Branch, Iowa.
Occupation: Engineer.
Wife: Lou Henry. *Children:* Two boys.
President: 1929-1933. Republican party.
Vice-President: Charles Curtis.
Died: October 20, 1964. *Buried:* West Branch, Iowa.

★★★★★

Herbert Hoover, the first president born west of the Mississippi River, was a mining engineer by profession and a multimillionaire. After World War I, he took on the task of feeding and clothing millions of Belgians who were victims of the German invasion in 1914.

In 1928, after serving creditably as Secretary of Commerce under the Harding-Coolidge Administrations, he was elected president by the largest majority since George Washington, during a period of economic optimism. Arthur Krock describes the prevailing attitude of that time in a 1968 *Post* article:

> Herbert Hoover was swept into office in 1928 in an atmosphere of euphoria and a belief that an ever-soaring condition of national prosperity was an established fact. Two automobiles in every garage. Two chickens in every pot.

"We in America today are nearer to the final triumph over poverty than ever before in the history of the land," Hoover had declared in his inaugural speech.

But in 1929 the economic crash came, followed by the big depression of the 1930s. Hoover did not believe in federal welfare programs—banks closed, 30,000 businesses failed in one year and the gross national income dropped from 80 billion to 40 billion. "Prosperity is just around the corner," Hoover promised, but it wasn't.

In 1919, Franklin D. Roosevelt wrote in a letter:

> I had some nice talks with Herbert Hoover before he went west for Christmas. He is certainly a wonder, and I wish we could make him a President of the United States. There could not be a better one.

But, by 1932, Hoover had become the goat for the misfortunes of the American people. The Democrats capitalized on the collapse of his prophecies and Hoover was soundly defeated by Franklin D. Roosevelt. The electoral vote was 472 to 59. Beverly Smith, Jr., commented in the May 6, 1961, issue of the *Post*:

"I don't know of another President who had so abrupt a fall from universal esteem. . . . It would have broken the spirit of most men."

Herbert Hoover retired to private life, but continued public service in the Boys' Club of America, American Children's Fund and in directorship of several educational institutions. His most valuable service as ex-President, however, was his work in saving untold millions from starvation after World War II:

Hoover and Curtis, the winning team in the election of 1928.

A few weeks after succeeding to the Presidency, Truman, upon hearing the reports of approaching famine in parts of Europe, Africa, Asia and Latin

In 1928 this likeness of Hoover was pinned to many lapels.

America, called upon ex-President Herbert Hoover to make a world survey of famine conditions and to devise a plan of action. Hoover, past 70, took on the tough assignment without hesitation.

Thereafter, Herbert Hoover and Harry Truman, far apart politically, held a warm personal regard for one another. Beverly Smith, Jr., continued, "Hoover was grateful to be called back to public service on a mission of such importance; Truman appreciated the spirit and energy with which Hoover carried out his enormously difficult task." Hoover had earned his respect.

President Truman also appointed him to a commission charged with reorganizing the executive branch of government. Hoover did an outstanding job and, a few years later, President Eisenhower appointed him to a similar assignment. Smith had this to say:

> Today all students of government know the value of reports made by the two Hoover Commissions on the Organization of the Executive Branch of the Government. And scholars come from all over the world to do research among the unique source materials assembled at the Hoover Institution on War, Revolution and Peace at Stanford University. He has become "a historian's historian."

It is generally agreed among historians today that the Great Depression was not the fault of Herbert Hoover. Arthur Krock concluded in his aforementioned *Post* article: " . . . I continue to believe that a full-length study of Hoover's public career will convince history that he deserves a far higher place than contemporary judgment has granted him."

An Announcement
by Herbert Hoover

Believing as I do that the people of the United States retain their demonstrated high sense of responsibility and their broad conception of what may rightly be ex-pected of them under given circumstances, I cannot think that we need anything more than this plain and indisputable fact to go on with: There are three and a half million children in Eastern and Central Europe still dependent upon us for their lives!

This fact is the basis of what I hope may prove to be our final problem of humanitarian duty in connection with the great conflict and catastrophe through the after effects of which the world is now struggling.

Soon after the armistice, and under the generous authority of Congress, we—the American people—undertook the rescue of five million children in the territories that had been shut off from us for more than four years by the western battle front. Hundreds of thousands of these children had been orphaned by the war; other thousands were waifs astray in the general chaos, and all of them were suffering the physical consequences of a long-drawn-out period of undernourishment that in many localities approached the verge of actual starvation.

Under governmental supervision, and with a congressional appropriation to cover the necessities, we created an organization the function of which was to furnish moral support and financial backing to local branch organizations in the countries involved, to the end that these children should be fed and clothed and brought back in as large numbers as is humanly possible to a normal condition . . . .

Built in 1871 by Hoover's parents, Jesse and Hulda, the humble two-room cottage (below), where Herbert Hoover was born, is one of several buildings on Downey Street restored by the National Park Service. The Hoovers lived in the house until 1879, when Jesse Hoover sold it and moved his family into a larger dwelling farther south on Downey Street. Today, some 400,000 visitors pass through the West Branch, Iowa, home annually.

Photo by Dorothy Abner

We thought out a plan in December, 1919, and named it the American Relief Administration Warehouses . . . .

Briefly set forth, it was that we should stock warehouses in various parts of Central and Eastern Europe with food supplies and then sell Food Drafts on these warehouses to people in the United States which would call for the delivery of specific quantities of foods to designated persons . . . .

When it came to the detail of working out the form of the Food Drafts we decided upon two denominations—one for ten dollars and another for fifty. The ten-dollar Food Draft called for 24½ pounds of flour, 10 pounds of beans or rice, 8 pounds of bacon and 8 cans of milk; or a kosher package designed for Jewish consumption containing 24½ pounds of flour, 10 pounds of beans or rice, 7½ pounds of cottonseed oil and 12 cans of milk. The fifty-dollar Food Draft called for 140 pounds of flour, 50 pounds of beans or rice, 16 pounds of bacon, 15 pounds of lard, 12 pounds of corned beef and 48 cans of milk; or a kosher package containing 140 pounds of flour, 50 pounds of beans or rice, 45 pounds of cottonseed oil and 48 cans of milk . . . .

We began operations early in 1920, and on the

Originally "Boulder Dam," the name was changed to "Hoover Dam" in 1947 to honor the man who had for years sought its construction.

Fleeting Renown

Dwight D. Eisenhower told the story of how Mr. Hoover was approached by a boy for an autograph. The ex-President readily complied with the boy's wishes and was signing his name, when the boy asked for a second signature. "You see," the boy explained, much to the amusement of the ex-President, "it takes two of yours in trade to get one of Babe Ruth's."

—May 13, 1961, Post.

twenty-third day of January the first Food Draft was cold. At the end of August, 1920, our books showed a sale of 165,814 drafts for $3,738,900, and by the end of September this had increased to 177,915 drafts for $4,156,810, and more than 80,000 canceled drafts had been received in New York representing completed transactions. At the close of business on July thirty-first, which is the latest completed report we have to refer to, the public accountants who audit our books found that we were in possession of a balance of profit of $605,194.61, which was immediately divided among the various nations in proportion to the number of Food Drafts purchased for each country and made available for child feeding. It was to get at this item in some detail that I have briefly sketched the story of the Food Drafts . . . .

America's work in Europe under the American Relief Administration, European Children's Fund, has been done to a great extent by the various European peoples themselves. If this were not so it could not have been done . . . .

In the growth of our system it has developed that the local organizations secure for themselves and disburse between two and three dollars a month for the support of each child. The American assistance has amounted to about one dollar per month per child in imported supplies, which shows that we have contributed not more than a third of the funds that are required for the enterprise . . . .

HELPING HOOVER IN OUR U. S. SCHOOL GARDEN

WWI poster released by Food Administrator Hoover.

During his senior year at Stanford, Herbert Hoover met Miss Lou Henry (right), then a freshman majoring in Geology. In 1899, while working in Australia, he was offered a job in China. He proposed to Miss Henry by cable and they were married in California that same year. "He came all that distance just to get Lou," her mother wrote a friend.

America does not and never will fight children, and the children of every race and creed, of friend and former enemy alike, have been cared for on a basis of absolute equality; and it is a fact that nothing America has ever done as an act of grace has sunk so deep in the heart of the world. In the minds of millions of men and women of ten different nations there dwells a thought which supersedes all others with regard to us, and that is the thought of our solicitude for their children.

When the American Congress made its splendid charitable appropriation to meet the desperate conditions in Europe it was thought that the necessities would not extend beyond the harvest of 1919. But, as we all know now, the establishment of peace and the restoration of industry, economic stability and orderly conduct among the European peoples have proved to be tasks much more difficult of accomplishment than was expected, and a situation still exists which demands of us yet another season of humanitarian service . . . .

Typical of the general situation was the city of Warsaw in January, 1919, where there was never a child to be seen playing in the streets. If the harrowing, absolute truth must be told, the children of Warsaw were clinging to the hands and the skirts of their elders, crying for food which their elders were unable to provide. But within three months after the American Relief Administration had established its system the streets of Warsaw were filled with children, more than two hundred thousand of them, adequately fed and comfortably clothed for the first time in five years, frolicking and

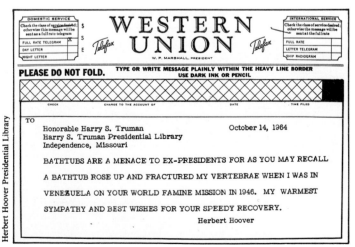

When Hoover heard in October, 1964, of his friend's fall, he sent the above telegram—his last communication before his death.

playing games. No American who saw that miracle of modern civilization could ever forget it or ever underestimate its value.

Since I am making a direct appeal—for the last time, I sincerely hope—I want every American to know just what is being done and how it is being done. My conception of this work is that every man and woman in the United States has a responsible share in it, and I wish above all things that I could induce every man and woman to acknowledge it . . . .

The twenty-three million dollars which we need—the estimate being based on a careful calculation—added to former expenditures, will make a total outlay in excess of sixty million dollars. It sounds like an important sum, but far more important than its size is the fact that it represents the saving of five million children. No one shrinks from asking for charitable support more than I do, yet my chief occupation for five awful years has been begging at the feet of the civilized world . . . .

. . . They are not my children any more than they are yours, but I know exactly what they will have to face without us, and I therefore have no hesitation in asking the readers of *The Saturday Evening Post* to consider whether they cannot now and periodically during the winter give support to the American Relief Administration agencies throughout the country or through the head office at 42 Broadway, New York.

As an item to be specially noted it should be added that any contributor who wishes to specify the country for which his money is to be expended may do so with a certainty that his instructions will be carried out.

—November 20, 1920, Post.

121

Hooverian Nights Entertainment

Editor's Note: The following is excerpted from an article by Wallace Irwin which appeared in the June 20, 1931, issue of The Saturday Evening Post. *The cartoons are by Herbert Johnson.*

HERBI HOOVEH was a Kalif
From the State where Kalifs grow—
Kalif-ornia I refer to.
Doubt this point, if you prefer to,
   Yet I'll stick to what I know.
Herbi Hooveh's Kalifate
Covered many a savage state
From Alaska's frozen spots
To Miami's vacant lots.

Dervishes who chant the glory
   Of his capital, Al Wash,
Oft regale us with a story;
   How he'd tire of *drooli bosh*,
Spouted by the Senatori.
Thus, when day was wan and hoary,
   He would yawn and say, "Oh, gosh!
Ray-el-Wilb, my Grand Vizeer,
Draw you near, fetch me here
Certain garments to disguise me
   So that Watson, Blaine, McNary
Or Joe Robinson the scary,
Always hinting hara-kari,
Will not recognize me."

One fine night El Wilb brought in
   To his master quite a make-up,
   Such as house detectives take up.
There were whiskers for the chin,
   Borrowed from the silken tassels
   Jay-ham Lewis shakes at vassals.
There were pants of rustic web,
Loaned by Norris, King of Neb.
Hooveh, falling for the drama,
   Quickly changed from robes of state,
Murmuring, "They'll think I am a
   Co-al-ition candidate."

The Story of Andi Mella and The Forty Thieves

A Treasurer named Andi Mell
Ran the King's Treasury so well
There was no chance for mouchers.
E'en when the Sultan's royal self
Desired a whack at Andi's pelf,
   He had to sign some vouchers.

One night in dreams this Andi felt
His hoarded gold begin to melt
   Like lard, or rain-soaked starches.
The Treasury Building's mighty dome
Creaked as the temples did when Rome
   Came down with fallen arches.

Now Andi woke with sudden chills,
Called his chief memlook, Oggi Mills,
   And spoke in consternation,
"What is the import of my dream?"
Sage Oggi, with a knowing gleam,
   Gave this interpretation:
"You're bound for the Isles of the
   Bugaboo
When gold starts running the wrong way
   to.
Ha! Congressman Fast and Senator Loose
Are out for the eggs of the Golden Goose.
"Dollars have wings,
   Dimes have legs.
Money that you borrow don't lay no eggs.
And you'll never get rich, whatever you
   do,
When somebody's spendin' your money
   for you."

Now, Andi was a thoughtful mage,
Keener than others of his age,
So thrice he clapped his hands and cried,
"Call my Mazoolehs to my side—
My Surgeon Gen. of Public Health,
My Watchdogs of the Hoarded Wealth,
My Secret Service call in force,
And my Disbursing Clerk, of course;
And don't forget to drop a hint
To my Director of the Mint."

"I hear," quoth Oggi, "and obey."
   So when the forces were assembled,
   Wise Andi spoke, and slightly trembled,
"Our treasure we must hide away
In some retreat both old and gray,
   So deep, deep, deep,
   So far, har, har,
That no one ever goes that way.
A Revnoo Agent did intone,
"Hail, Keeper of the Russian Loan!
   By Volstead! I have found the spot,
Beyond the dreams of Einstein's mystics,
   That unfrequented vacant lot
They call the Bureau of Statistics."
"Huzzah, huzzah!" the Faithful cried,
And filing forth on either side,
Descended to the vaults below;
   And there with ready pick and spade
They shoveled gold of ruddy glow
   Till seven thousand loads it made.

Thus, ere the dawn, these workers brave,
   Defying gunmen's wild ballistics,
Had fetched their treasure to a cave
   Beneath the Bureau of Statistics.
Upon the grimly armored door
   Sheik Andi with a solemn zeal
   Affixed the awful Customs Seal.
And then, to finish up his chore,
   He breathed a password, handed down
   By magic Postman-General Brown
   The cryptic phrase, as scribes agree,
   Was briefly, "Open Sesamee."

Short Pause for Change of Meter

When a week had gone by, Andi marked
   with a chill
An ominous silence from Capitol Hill.
And another bad symptom: The boys,
   who before
   Had often dropped in
   With a casual grin,
Requesting the loan of a million or more,
   Were not coming around.
   In terror profound
Andi sneaked out by the palest of
   moons
To look at the cave where he'd hid the
   doubloons.
   Nearing the spot
   He paused as though shot—
Looters were raging all over the lot!
The Treasurer blinked as he hid in the
   thickets,
   For there by the door stood a Finance
   Committee,
Smiling invitingly, giving out tickets
   Marked "Open Sesamee."
"This makes a Fess o' me,"
Agonized Andi, not feeling so strong
As the cash-burdened pirates, went
   struggling along

To the jolly old lilt of this bucaneer song:
"Gold, gold, ruddy red gold!
  Don't be afraid of it,
  Andi is made of it,
  Bathe in it, eat it and make lemonade
    of it!
Who cares a nickel if Andi's a scold?
  Treasury's full of a magical store of it,
  No one will ever get down to the core
    of it!
  Spend it and lend it and send for some
    more of it!
      Gold, gold, GOLD!!"

Senators, congressmen labored with
    urgency,
Led by Mad Mullahs who practice
    insurgency,
Giving small heed to funereal tones
Of Senator Watson and Senator Jones:
"Taxable incomes are down to the bones."
But Junior LaFollette, conducting the
    racket,
  Smiled, "It's our inning.
  We're only beginning
To pump the rich oil from the big Higher
  Bracket."
So they all disappeared in primordial fog
To the larruping lilt of this maniac clog:

"We're out for patronage and doles and
    subsidizing Muscle Shoals,
  Hi, diddle-diddle for the old home
    town!
We're out for public waterworks and more
  expensive postal clerks,
  Tune up the fiddle as the stocks go
    down.
Appropriate a billion for
Descendants of the Mexican War;
Parsimony we abhor
  When times are hard;
Tiddledywink, that's what we think.
  Our sinking fund will never sink
  While we are the Captains of the Old
  Home Guard."

Testily Andi repaired to his cave
And one ravished look at the ruin
  he gave.
Everything gone, he remarked
  amidst groans,
Save a tall pile of documents
  marked "Foreign Loans"—
But look! In a row of
  voluptuous curves

Stood several barrels—they got on the
  nerves
    Of hagridden Andi.
    But now they seemed handy
To foster the plot which our story
  deserves.
Each barrel had plainly inscribed on its
  staves
The horrid word "Deficit." Summoning
  slaves,
The Treasurer bade them to paint out
  the label
And change it to "Pork."

The Arabian fable relates how the
  bandits, returning next night,
Entered the cave with a guilty delight,
Thinking perhaps that in yesternight's
  play
They'd overlooked something worth
  taking away.
And thus it is written: When Andi came
  back
To study the scene of his vanishing jack,
He looked in the mouths of his magical
  kegs
And found them chock-full of
  congressional legs,

Faces 'neath wide senatorial hats,
Sterling Republicans, staunch Democrats
Gazed upon Andi with look so appealing
He had for a moment that Humanist
  feeling.
"Oh, Andi," they gubbled. "Oh, Andi,
  my duck,
Pray what is this stickum in which we
  are stuck?"
"Oh, Congress," chirped Andi, the
  shrewdest of elves,
"You ought to know what—since you
  brewed it yourselves.
  By Beelzebub's chef,
  You are stuck in the Def—
    Stuck in the Deficit up to the neck!"
Now wild was their clamor: "Oh, help!
  Help us out!"
But the merciless Treasurer turned
  roundabout
  And lightly tossed back
  This elderly crack:
"As Solomon said to the Smark-Aleck
Djinn who fell in a well,
  'You are wiser than I,
  Your ideas are swell.
  Now suppose that you try
To get out of that hole by the way you
  got in.' "

So he left them to starve. But I don't
  think they did.
  In the Beard of the Profit large losses
    are hid;
  I'm sure the Commissions
    On Housing Conditions
  Came to investigate, acted quite
    snappily—
  Tales in Arabia always end happily.

Pach Brothers

Franklin D. Roosevelt

★ ★ ★ ★ ★

32nd President of the United States

Born: January 30, 1882, Hyde Park, New York.
Occupation: Farmer, lawyer, public official.
Wife: Eleanor Roosevelt. *Children:* Five boys, one girl.
President: 1933-1945. Democratic party.
Vice-Presidents: John N. Garner, Henry A. Wallace, Harry S. Truman.
Died: April 12, 1945. *Buried:* Hyde Park, New York.

★ ★ ★ ★ ★

As a small boy, Franklin Roosevelt visited President Grover Cleveland while he was in office. President Cleveland patted him on the head and said, "My little man, I am going to make a strange wish for you: May you never be President of the United States." Destiny was to intervene otherwise, and this boy was to be the only man ever to be elected president four times. This, in spite of the fact that he had had polio when he was 39 which left his legs paralyzed. As is often true of strong presidents, he was, and still is today, a very controversial president. Some look upon him as a savior; others blame him for government interference and increased spending.

Franklin D. Roosevelt took office at the height of the "Great Depression." He was a man of action and with his "fireside chats" to the people, he was able to gain their confidence. He told the people, "The only thing we have to fear is fear itself." Times were so bad that the people were desperate and wanted their president to try new measures. More than 5,000 banks had closed, people were out of work, and many were hungry.

The new president's first action was to close the remaining banks, and Congress passed an emergency banking bill which strengthened the banks and made them sound. Congress had no policy of its own, so it was willing to go along with the new president. This administration was called the "New Deal" and bill after bill was passed.

Photo by Dorothy Abner

Though the public was uninformed, F.D.R. was constantly reminded.

The bills had long names and were soon known by their initials—CCC (Civilian Conservation Corps), NRA (National Recovery Administration), AAA (Agricultural Adjustment Act), TVA (Tennessee Valley Authority), and so on. A critic called them "alphabet soup."

Life in the Roosevelt White House was relaxed and informal. The grandchildren would visit, and a swing was put up on the White House lawn. A swimming pool was built so the President could exercise his paralyzed legs.

The public was kept in the dark about FDR's paralysis. It was believed that it was in the best interest of the nation that his physical impairment be concealed—a stand that the press of that time accepted and

upheld. Ollie Atkins, personal photographer for President Richard M. Nixon, tells in a Fall 1972, *Post* article how the media cooperated to keep Roosevelt's condition a secret:

> Everything was done in those early war years to conceal his infirmity. Today the public would know all about such a thing. But then it was not generally realized that he had to be virtually carried everywhere he went. And when we photographers finally got a chance to shoot him, it was all stage set in advance. He would be propped up in his chair at his desk, and it often looked as though his back were propped up as well. With another subject, it would have been a disaster. But FDR had that great smile and a fine head and somehow or other the pictures came off. But we had to work fast. And we were allowed only two flash bulbs apiece.

By this time the economy had improved, and more people were working, but the national debt rose higher than it ever had before. Meanwhile Hitler was on the march in Europe. World War II was looming on the horizon. On Sunday, December 7, 1941, Pearl Harbor was bombed by the Japanese, and a large part of the United States fleet was destroyed. This meant war for the United States. Roosevelt became the most traveled president in history as he met with allied leaders. He

During the Great Depression the new President's "fireside chats" (above) brought encouragement and confidence to a despairing nation. He instilled a renewed hope for the future, as was his aim at the Yalta Conference (top) on February 9, 1945. With Prime Minister Winston Churchill and Premier Joseph Stalin he worked on the structure of the postwar world.

was elected again in 1944. However, the long years of hard work and the strain of the office had taken its toll. On April 12, 1945, he died suddenly in Warm Springs, Georgia.

In This Corner

The visit of President-elect Roosevelt with President Hoover some two weeks after the election of 1932 was most interesting and unusual, the only time in my many years here when the President-elect called at the White House before March third. (The custom is for the retiring President to invite the President-elect and his wife to dinner on the night of March third.) Returning from Palo Alto, where he had gone to vote, the President, on November twelfth, had wired Mr. Roosevelt inviting

Gen. Douglas MacArthur confers with F.D.R. aboard a cruiser in Pearl Harbor—already the general was having "presidential" problems.

Harris & Gifford

126

him to come to the White House to discuss the request of the European nations for reduction of the interest on and a revision of the war debts.

The visit was looked forward to with nervousness, and this tenseness increased as the day approached. The President, as a matter of course, selected the Executive Office as the place of meeting. Two circumstances, both of which had to be pointed out to him, led him to change the scene to the Red Room. This would permit the President-elect to enter the house from the south door without climbing steps and to rise by the elevator almost to the door of the Red Room, both desirable in view of what we understood his physical condition to be. It also would save Mr. Roosevelt from running a gantlet of newspapermen.

As a further deference to the President-elect's condition, the President and Secretary Mills awaited his coming in the Red Room. The White House custom is that the President appears only after the visitor has arrived and is waiting. If it had been followed here, it probably would have necessitated Mr. Roosevelt's rising from his chair on the entrance of the President, so Mr. Hoover came first and remained standing. It was agreed that each principal be accompanied by one second, as in a boxing match. The President-elect was bringing Prof. Ray Moley; Mills was in the Hoover corner.

As his car pulled up at the south door, Mr. Roosevelt greeted those at the door jovially. He was, however, plainly nervous as he was helped out and escorted to the elevator.

Just after the President had come over from the office, word had followed him that it was reported there that Mr. Roosevelt was bringing Vice-President-elect Garner with him, as well as Mr. Moley. The President did not relish this, and showed it plainly. He ruled that if Mr. Roosevelt brought two seconds, then Secretary of State Stimson was to be summoned to even the sides. This sensitiveness to being outnumbered illustrates the nervousness which surrounded the parley. The rumor was false, and Mr. Garner did not come.

Upon being shown into the Red Room, the President-elect was announced as "The Governor of New York," with the intent of emphasizing the informality of the meeting and minimizing the recent contest. At the announcement, the President stepped forward, shook hands and said, "I am glad to see you, Governor, and thank you for coming." The President then shook hands with Professor Moley, and Mr. Roosevelt and Mr. Moley greeted Secretary Mills.

The President invited the President-elect to be seated, suggesting several chairs from which he might take his choice. A bantering conversation opened between Mr.

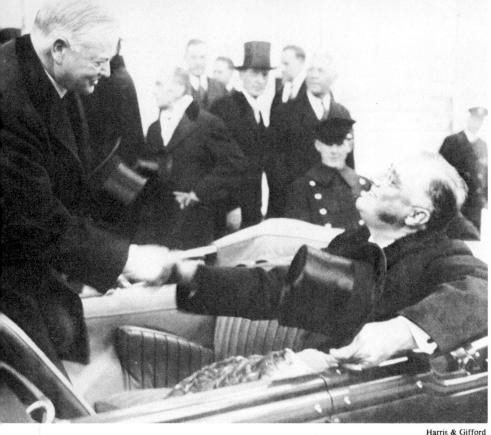

Roosevelt and Mr. Mills, old acquaintances. They spoke of their respective estates on the Hudson and jested of events in the recent campaign. Cigars and cigarettes were brought in and passed. A pitcher of orangeade and one of ice water also were put on a convenient table. It now became the duty of all outsiders to retire and close the doors.

The doors remained closed for exactly one hour, when Secretary Mills and Professor Moley walked out in the corridor. The two principals remained alone for seventeen minutes longer, at the end of which time the President rang the bell to the usher's office, the prearranged signal that the conference was over. When attendants entered the Red Room, the President already was on his feet. The President-elect was helped to his feet and, with a rather formal good-by, the President left the room first. Mr. Roosevelt followed him out. Mr. Hoover insisted that Mr. Roosevelt use the elevator first, as they would be going in opposite directions, the one down, the other up, and this was done. They both looked haggard and wan, and we had no doubt that the meeting had been an ordeal to each. It was noticed that cigars and cigarettes had been burned at a great rate, that the water pitcher was empty and the orangeade pitcher nearly so.

The President-elect went directly to his car at the south door, and with a wave of his hand and a remark more significant, probably, than he intended—"I'll be seeing you"—rolled off into the dark.

—excerpted from the Irwin H. (Ike) Hoover series in the September 29, 1934, issue of the Post.

Unlike Hoover, when Roosevelt took office in 1932 (top) he called for vast government intervention to relieve the Depression. A grateful nation reelected him for a fourth term (above) hoping he would also see them through the war. He died one month before Japan surrendered.

Can the Vice-President be Useful?

by Franklin D. Roosevelt

There is probably no better example of what might be called the industrial waste at Washington than is shown by the traditional conception of the duties of the Vice President. Here is a man supposedly fully capable in an emergency to act as President of the United States; who has been nominated and elected by exactly the same procedure as that surrounding the nomination and election of the President himself. No precaution which the framers of our Constitution could design was neglected to assure the people that their Vice President would be chosen with the same care with which the President is chosen and elected to office by the will of the majority of the citizens. Yet the only official work devised for him to do is to preside over the Senate, which is in session hardly more than half of each day and hardly more than half the days of each year, and, moreover—notably during long set speeches—is often presided over by a senator called to the chair by the Vice President. And lest even the semblance of really constructive work might be suggested by the duties of the Vice President, his task as presiding officer is carefully confined—except in the rare event of a tie, when he may vote—to interpretation of parliamentary rules of order and official announcement of how many senators voted "aye" and how many senators voted "no."

The duties of the Vice President in relation to the Senate are, in short, largely perfunctory. He has no duties in relation to either the executive or the judicial branch of the Government. There is no little truth, then, in the witticism that the Vice President constitutes a kind of fourth branch of the Government—a branch condemned by tradition to sit in lonely grandeur with remote responsibilities but very little to do. If, in fact, there ever was a waste of man power it would seem to be here.

The country simply took the Vice Presidency as a matter of course until the war shook us out of the rut and demonstrated the urgent need of general reorganization in Washington.

It is certain that no Congressional commission can succeed in reorganizing the executive departments and bureaus without the cooperation of the President and the heads of the departments and bureaus, though such a body as the Congressional Commission on Reclassification of Government Personnel, which does not disturb the various entities, might succeed in its particular task. And certainly no President can achieve reorganization of even the executive departments without such cooperation from Congress as will result in necessary legislation. It follows, in other words, that harmony is the shibboleth. And the question remains: Cannot the Vice President aid in achieving harmony?

Largely because of the very need of perfection of the governmental machinery a great deal of time is required to accomplish tasks that would seem relatively simple if direct and improved procedure

Anna Eleanor Roosevelt, T.R.'s niece, married her fifth cousin, Franklin, in 1905. Above, the young father-to-be knits as the couple await the birth of the first of six children. In 1932, Roosevelt built the modest cottage at Warm Springs, Georgia, known as the Little White House (right). His sponsorship helped to make Warm Springs famous as a polio treatment center.

When her husband was stricken with polio in 1921, Eleanor Roosevelt, to encourage him, discarded her shyness and began a remarkable 40 years of public service. As First Lady, she spoke for the President often on human rights and upon his death, she was appointed the U.S. representative to the United Nations, where she served for 16 years.

were possible, as in a private corporation.

The question, then, that occurs to one at this juncture is: Would it be possible for the Vice President, who is not tied down to a desk, to help?

In other words, the question should be asked whether the President could not profitably avail himself of a Vice President who, while informing himself of duties that he may at any time be called upon to fulfill, would execute a kind of roving commission for the Chief Executive, lending a hand wherever possible.

If the Vice President were thus able to aid the President he would bear much closer analogy to the vice president in a modern corporation, who has, however, direct executive authority such as the Vice President could not without legislation employ.

There are now many congressmen and senators who solemnly aver that the whole trouble in Washington is the fault of the management of the executive departments. Congress at present does far more administrative work, especially of an organizing kind, than it permits the White House and the executive departments to do.

It has been said very frequently, by executives in Washington that the trouble all lies with Congress.

But the broader view is that the trouble is the result of lack of plan, or, more accurately, our inability to adjust our tremendous growth to the old, existing plan: and running that idea back you soon discover that the dire need of adjustments—in other words, the dire need of reorganization—is largely due to the wide gap between the executive and the legislative families.

We return thus to our starting point—the need of utilizing every possible aid in overcoming the gap between Congress and the executive branch of the Government—and the desirability of making fuller and more satisfactory use of the Vice President in overcoming that gap.

—taken from the October 16, 1920, issue of the Post, *reported by Donald Wilhelm.*

Song and Dance

William D. Hassett tells the following story about Mrs. Roosevelt's unique brand of entertaining:

During their visit shortly before World War II, Mrs. Roosevelt served to King George VI and Queen Elizabeth hot dogs and hamburgers with mustard.

Although the manner in which the majesties gamely tackled the hot dog drew much publicity, it was upstaged by the sideshow organized by Mrs. Roosevelt—an American Indian dancer hired to demonstrate the ancient customs of the country.

He donned a magnificent war bonnet, complete with gayly colored feathers, shook a bowl full of shelled corn and proceded to dance about the terrace, singing in convincing Indian chant, the song of the corn.

All went quite well until a sudden gust of wind blew off his headdress and unveiled for all to see, his shining, *lily-white*, bald head!

—taken from a story told in the October 31, 1953, Post.

Harry S. Truman Library

Harry S. Truman

★ ★ ★ ★ ★

33rd President of the United States

Born: May 8, 1884, Lamar, Missouri.
Occupation: Farmer, businessman, public official.
Wife: Bess Wallace. *Children*: One girl.
President: 1945-1953. Democratic party.
Vice-Presidents: Edward R. Stettinius, Jr., James F.
  Byrnes, George C. Marshall, Secretaries of State;
  Joseph W. Martin*, Speaker of the House of
  Representatives; Alben W. Barkley.
Died: December 26, 1972. *Buried*: Independence,
  Missouri.

*The Succession Law of 1947 established the Speaker of the House of Representatives as first in succession.

130

Harry Truman's early years were not spectacular. He was a sickly child with very bad eyesight; thus he was forced into the world of books and music instead of sports. He wanted to go to West Point, but was turned down because of his eyes.

An active Mason and Legionnaire, Truman was 38 when he entered politics. Backed by a political boss out of Kansas City, he reached the U.S. Senate in 1935. He was an effective senator and saved the country billions of dollars by investigating war contracts. Arthur Krock of *The New York Times* wrote in a *Post* article in the September 7, 1968, issue:

> I recall admiring his objectivity at the total expense of partisanship in heading the Senate committee on the conduct of the Second World War. I had been particularly impressed with Truman's quality as a statesman in a certain exchange on the Senate floor with Arthur H. Vandenberg of Michigan.
>
> Chairman Truman had reported to the Senate a delay of 18 months in steps vital to the successful conduct of the war. Whereupon Vandenberg interrupted to inquire "at whose doorstep" the blame could be laid. "The White House," calmly replied Truman.

Truman was selected by Roosevelt to be his running mate in 1944. Three months after the inauguration, Truman found himself President of the United States, with all of its awesome responsibilities. He said that he felt as if the whole weight of the moon and the stars had fallen on him, but he was determined to do his best.

The Truman presidency faced some of the most perplexing and far-reaching problems of any administration. Everyone wondered how the "little man from Missouri" would solve them. History tends to treat him kindly because on the big decisions he was usually right. Mr. Krock asked the President if he was not troubled when he got conflicting counsel on great decisions from advisers equally able, informed, loyal and sincere? No, said the President, he came to his decisions by the best rationalization within his powers and then didn't "worry about them. There is always a new one waiting to be made." (September 7, 1968, *Post*)

His conversations were often peppery and he has been quoted as saying, "If you can't stand the heat, get out of the kitchen" and "the buck stops here." There was no doubt who was boss. One of his most difficult decisions pertained to the atomic bomb which the United States had developed. Should he order it dropped on Japan and force that country to surrender, or should he risk an invasion of its shores with a great loss of American lives? Truman elected to drop the bomb. The Second World War was over on August 14, 1945.

Thomas E. Dewey was Truman's opponent in the presidential race of 1948. The opinion polls, most of the

The Chicago Daily Tribune *learned a lesson in politics following Truman's surprise claim to 24,000,000 of the popular votes and 304 electoral votes to Thomas E. Dewey's 189 in the 1948 election.*

press and even many in his own party predicted the President would lose. He conducted a vigorous campaign, traveling throughout the country giving speeches. Much to the surprise of many, he won. *The Chicago Tribune* had been so sure Dewey would win that they put out in their early editions a headline which read "Dewey Defeats Truman." During the next four years, the Cold War with Russia began, the Korean War broke out in 1950 and Truman fired General MacArthur over insubordination.

Although Franklin Delano Roosevelt's use of the radio for his famous "fireside chats" was a first in bridging the gap between the president and the people, it was Harry Truman who made the first television broadcast from the White House in 1947; a step which brought the president, finally, in full view of the public. His most memorable program was the informal tour of the newly repaired White House in May of 1952. Author Sidney Shalett wrote of the event in the May 21, 1955, issue of the *Post*:

> . . . the President was enthusiastic about the idea for the program. Not only did Mr. Truman have a fund of historical knowledge about the White House but "he felt the taxpayers had a right to see how their money was spent."

Arrangements were made with a committee representing three networks—NBC, CBS and ABC. Cameras and lights were set up in the White House, and commentators for the participating networks—Walter Cronkite, Bryson Rash and Frank Bourgholtzer—took

turns walking with the President through the public rooms, while Mr. Truman poured out a flood of information and anecdote.

The hit of the show was Truman's piano playing. This was an impromptu coup brought off by Bourgholtzer, according to Julian Goodman, who represents NBC on the network liaison committee. "Frank was dying to get Mr. Truman to hit a note when they got to the pianos in the East Room, but everybody warned him that mentioning it in advance would cause the President to refuse," Goodman said. "So, when they get to the first piano, Frank innocently asks the President if he, Bourgholtzer, can plink it to let the people hear how it sounds. 'Why, I'll show 'em how it sounds,' says the President, and he sits down and rolls off a number of bars."

In 1953, Harry Truman retired to his home in Independence, Missouri, and set up the Harry S. Truman Library which contains his presidential papers. Beverly Smith, Jr., *Post* editor, wrote of the ex-President's retirement in the May 6, 1961, *Post* issue:

> Much of the public bases its picture of Mr. Truman on his quadrennial re-emergence as "Give-'em-hell Harry." But in between times he does a great deal of solid work which is less well known. Few think of him as a historian, as a preacher, as an educator. Yet such occupations, far more than campaigning, have been his major interests since he left the White House. He has devoted untiring personal care to the creation of the Truman Library in Independence, where the documents of his administration—of the fateful years which saw the dawn of the nuclear

Norman Rockwell captured the election excitement of "Dewey vs. Truman" on the cover of the October 30, 1948, issue of the Post.

131

age—are preserved for students and historians. He has answered invitations from one end of the country to the other to deliver lay sermons to assemblages of Protestants, Catholics and Jews—talks which combine homely humor with a moving sincerity. And he has long been working on a book soon to be published, a history of the American Presidency for high-school readers.

Harry S. Truman died at the age of 88, and is buried in the courtyard of his library.

A Former President's Busy Life

On a hillside overlooking U.S. Highway 24 in Independence, Mo., stands a 600-foot-long, boomerang-shaped limestone structure called the Harry S. Truman Library. Inside, just beyond a reproduction of the President's White House office, is a small auditorium where, not long ago, a group of Kansas City schoolboys gathered to ask questions of the brisk, white-haired man on the stage.

"Mr. President, sir," inquired one of the boys, "what was your most memorable moment in public life?"

"When I had to save the Republic of Korea," replied Harry Truman.

"Sir, how can I become a Senate page boy?" another asked.

"You've got to get hold of your senator," said Mr. Truman, "and get him to appoint you. I can't do anything about it."

One boy with a broken arm asked the President to sign his cast. This stopped Mr. Truman for a moment. Then he replied, "You'll have to come back to my office. If I start signing autographs here, I'll never get through. Every kid will want one."

Harry Truman obviously relishes his schoolmaster role, which he plays several times a week. He also enjoys escorting visitors around the library's museum, which draws about 150,000 visitors a year. Among his proudest mementos is a framed map of his whistle-stop campaign of 1948: 31,739 miles, 355 speeches.

But the old Give-'em-hell-Harry side of Truman is rarely seen in Independence. Nowadays most of Truman's acidulous observations are reserved for his early morning walks in Manhattan, when he goes to visit his daughter, Margaret Truman Daniel, her husband, Clifton, and their three sons.

There is even evidence that he is mellowing toward some old Republican antagonists. At a recent Washington dinner, for instance, Truman greeted Richard M. Nixon amicably, although he once refused to dine in the same room with him because "I just cannot sit with that fellow."

On the other hand, the Eisenhower-Truman feud, now in its 12th year, has shown few signs of thawing. At President Kennedy's funeral Mr. Truman shared General Eisenhower's car, at Ike's invitation, but the two really didn't manage to find anything to talk about. About all they appear to have in common are their presidential libraries.

The principal function of Truman's library is, of course, to safeguard the presidential papers of Harry S. Truman, of which there are about 5.5 million, plus approximately two million other related documents. About 85 percent of these papers are already available to scholars; the rest will remain locked behind steel-mesh doors until the death of those who might be embarrassed by their disclosure.

In additon to fulfilling its main purpose, and housing a museum, the library provides the former President with a suite of offices. This area is marked by fascinating confusion. A conference table is piled high with birthday presents which will be weeks in sorting. A storeroom is stacked with portraits of American Presidents, painted from photographs by a Japanese artist.

Bookcases along the corridor walls contain thousands of volumes which, unlike the 30,000 books in the library proper, have never been catalogued. If you sent a book to Mr. Truman while he was in the White House,

Photo by Leo Stashin

Mr. Truman, usually flanked by reporters during his early morning walks, pauses to shake hands with a fellow citizen in New York City.

As he enters his ninth decade, one has a feeling that the thing which keeps him in good spirits is the work that continually needs to be done at his beloved library. When asked what he does for relaxation, he replies, "I've never had a hobby in my life."

—an article by Robert Sherrod. Reprinted from the June 13, 1964, issue of The Saturday Evening Post.

Harry S. Truman Library

The portrait of Bess Truman by Greta Kempton hangs in the White House. Childhood sweethearts, the Trumans were married in 1919.

it is probably here; apparently he never threw anything away. And on a sofa in a little-used room rests a framed letter dated December 19, 1962, from one President (Herbert Hoover) to another (Harry Truman) bitterly recalling his treatment by a third (Franklin Roosevelt). Published here for the first time, it reads in part:

"Yours has been a friendship which has reached deeper into my life than you know.

"I gave up a successful profession in 1914 to enter public service. I served through the First World War and after for a total of about 18 years.

"When the attack on Pearl Harbor came, I at once supported the President and offered to serve in any useful capacity. Because of my varied experience during the First World War, I thought my services might again be useful, however there was no response. . . .When you came to the White House within a month you opened the door to me to the only profession I knew, public service, and you undid some disgraceful action that had been taken in the prior years . . . . I am deeply grateful."

Surrounded by souvenirs like these, Harry Truman is a contented man, although the week-long celebration of his birthday—May 8—obviously exhausted him. He and Mrs. Truman live in the same 14-room house they have occupied since their marriage in 1919. About 7:30 each morning Mr. Truman may be seen climbing into his green Chrysler for the five-minute drive to the office.

"Not Afraid of the Devil Himself"

At the top of the stairs we entered a bedroom dominated by a large Early American four-poster bed with canopy.

"We call this the President's Room, because Mr. Truman picked it for his bedroom during the three years he was here," said Victoria Geaney, hostess and manager of Blair House. "He loved the rare Currier and Ives prints of American presidents and he made it his daily chore to wind the old grandmother clock on the mantelpiece. Mr. Truman was taking a nap right here just after lunch on November 1, 1950, when he heard some shots in the street below. He rushed to the window, but the guards outside frantically waved him back."

In the gun battle, one White House police officer, Leslie Coffelt, was fatally shot, and another guard and a Secret Serviceman were seriously injured as they bravely kept the would-be assassins from carrying out the plot to shoot their way into Blair House, find the President and murder him. One of the Puerto Rican assassins was killed before he could reach the house. The other was halted at the Blair House steps by a bullet from the gun of the fatally wounded Coffelt.

"President Truman went right ahead with his day's schedule," Mrs. Geaney told us. "Within half an hour he was on his way to a memorial service at Arlington Cemetery. And the next morning before breakfast he took his usual brisk walk along Pennsylvania Avenue. He sure is a banty rooster," she remarked fondly. "He isn't afraid of the devil himself."

—an excerpt from a September 17, 1960, Post *article written by Robert and Patricia Cahn.*

Norman Rockwell

Dwight D. Eisenhower

★ ★ ★ ★ ★

34th President of the United States

Born: October 14, 1890, Denison, Texas.
Occupation: Army Officer.
Wife: Mary (Mamie) Geneva Doud.
Children: Two boys.
President: 1953-1961. Republican party.
Vice-President: Richard M. Nixon.
Died: March 28, 1969. *Buried:* Abilene, Kansas.

★ ★ ★ ★ ★

The West Point motto: Duty, Honor and Country, best describes Dwight D. Eisenhower's career. A graduate of West Point, he was Supreme Allied Commander to Europe during World War II, Chief of Staff of the U.S. Army, a five-star general and President of the United States for eight years.

"President Eisenhower has a cheerful approach toward the problems which confront him. He encourages a similar attitude in those around him," Beverly Smith, Jr., Washington editor for the *Post*, wrote in 1954.

"I asked one of his associates what annoys the President most. 'People who whine and have no solutions,' he said. He recalled the bleak morning of December 19, 1944. Four days earlier the Germans had smashed through at the Bulge. Now their armored spearheads were cutting deep behind our lines and there was a whiff of panic in the air as Eisenhower called the Allied generals into conference at Verdun. He opened the meeting with the following remark:

'The present situation is to be regarded as one of opportunity for us and not of disaster. There will be only cheerful faces around this table.' "

Eisenhower did not believe that a military man should be president, but the Republican party convinced him that he was needed to save the party and the two-party system of government. Republicans had not held the office for 20 years. They had a very popular candidate in General Eisenhower, and "I Like Ike" was the slogan of the day.

During the Eisenhower administration the Korean War ended, school desegregation began. "There must be no second-class citizens in this country," he said.

Hawaii and Alaska became states in 1959 and our flag now had 50 stars. During that same year the following story appeared in the *Post*:

> During a recent trip to the mainland, William F. Quinn, the dynamic and affable young governor of the Territory of Hawaii, dropped into a bank in St. Louis, identified himself and asked if he might cash a check.
>
> "Sure you can," said the teller. "What medium of exchange do you use out there?"
>
> Somewhat taken aback, the governor replied that the islanders had used United States dollars for the past 60 years.
>
> "They do!" exclaimed the banker, incredulously. "What language do the people speak?"
>
> At this point, Governor Quinn's affability wore a bit thin. He explained that the Hawaiian Islanders spoke the same tongue as Missourians—basically at least—and that Hawaii had been American since 1898, when her people voluntarily swapped their sovereignty for proffered statehood.
>
> —*May 2, 1959*, Post.

Assemble all the facts on a problem, and it often solves itself; all generalities are false, including this one; make no mistakes in a hurry, but any decision is better than none; finally, and probably the most important, always take your job seriously, never yourself.
—Dwight David Eisenhower

Eisenhower retired in 1961 to his farm in Gettysburg, Pennsylvania. He was 70 years old and the oldest man to serve as president.

Because they had always been in public service, the Eisenhowers had never had any say about the type of home they lived in. John Alexander, in the Winter '76 issue of *The Country Gentleman*, describes the type of retirement home Ike and Mamie each had wished for from the time he was Chief of Staff:

> For my part, I wanted an escape from concrete into the countryside. Mamie, who had spent a lifetime adjusting herself to other people's housing designs, or the lack of them, wanted a place that conformed to her notions of what a home should be. In the fall of 1950 . . . we saw . . . a farm of not quite 190 acres. The house, dwarfed by an immense barn, was located at the end of a private dirt lane a half mile long.
>
> "Mamie had found the place she wanted."
>
> And so, the great military student of history, the man who may well have been the most beloved President this country elected since Washington.

Col. Eisenhower, as Chief of Staff of the 9th Army Corps, discusses procedure with Commander Harry Butcher, Navy Aide to the Chief, as they take a break in the European theatre of operations. Below, Norman Rockwell's painting of Mamie Eisenhower done shortly after the GOP nominating convention in 1952. "Always Mamie seemed close at hand in his [Ike's] thinking," Rockwell observed, "a present source of inspiration."

The Bettmann Archive, Inc.

After almost half a century of public life, they got their wish, the Eisenhowers could "go home." Mamie loved it so that she stayed on even after Ike's death in 1969.

John F. Kennedy, the youngest man ever to be president, took over where the oldest man ever to hold office had left off.

A Day in the Life of the President

Shortly before sunrise, these wintry mornings, the dusky, stocky, cheerful figure of John (lately Sergeant) Moaney tiptoes through a short passageway on the second floor of the White House. Pausing at the door of the large bedroom, he says softly, "Mr. Pres'dent, it's seven o'clock."

For breakfast he usually has fruit juice or half a grapefruit, one or two eggs—occasionally with bacon or sausage—toast and coffee. He prefers his eggs boiled or fried. Like many another veteran, he still has a prejudice against scrambled eggs, dating from the scrambled-dried-eggs concoction of the wartime overseas ration. He polishes off the meal quickly and with good appetite, and then, sipping his coffee, skims through some of the newspapers. These include the *Washington Post* and the *Times Herald*, *The New York Times*, *Herald Tribune* and *Daily News*, and the *Baltimore Sun*.

By about 7:30 he is ready to shave, bathe and dress. The speed of this combined operation has always been a matter of wonder among his old friends. In less than 20 minutes he is neatly dressed, brushed and ready to go. Those who travel with him have learned to get up a quarter of an hour ahead of him so they won't be left behind in the rush. He prefers a shower to a tub bath. He shaves with a standard make of safety razor, hoeing away so briskly that his friends are afraid he will gash himself. His dressing speed is helped by the fact that Moaney has everything laid out just so, including his clothes for the day.

By 7:45 his Military Aide, Lt. Col. Robert L. Schulz,

is at the door, ready to walk with the President to his offices in the West Wing. They go down to the ground floor; then walk westward out-of-doors under the portico to the executive offices. It is a peculiarity of White House architecture that there is no enclosed passageway to the West Wing; on blustery days the President gets a dash of rain or snow in his face on this brief walk.

One constant problem is how much time shall be

The famous Eisenhower grin was as quickly summoned on the golf courses of Palm Springs, as it was in the halls of Congress (left). He "may well have been the most beloved President this country elected since Washington."

THE WHITE HOUSE

WASHINGTON

Dear Homer:

The sixth of June is a significant day for you and for me.

In my memory, I think of it as the Normandy D-Day. To me it stands for the courage and ability of a great liberating force united in the attainment of a most difficult objective. The members of this force took severe casualties but they pushed forward to victory.

The birth of a man, I believe, is a kind of D-Day. Life is a continual battle with great objectives along the way. Against these you have steadily advanced over the years. Your courage and ability inspire the respect of us all. On your birthday I am delighted to send my congratulations and best wishes.

With warm regard,

Sincerely,

Dwight Eisenhower

The Honorable Homer E. Capehart
United States Senate
Washington, D. C.

White Church in the Country, *painted by Eisenhower in 1961, appeared on the Winter '76 cover of* The Country Gentleman. *Right, Lt. Eisenhower and his bride, the former Mamie Doud, in 1916. After nearly 50 years of public service, the Eisenhowers went "home" to the country.*

given to the leaders of religious, civic, charitable, fraternal and other voluntary groups. By old tradition such organizations—a bevy of churchmen, or Boy Scouts, or Red Cross volunteers, or 4-H champions—convening in Washington, expect to be greeted by the President. Some thinkers argue that these formalities, pleasant enough in the leisurely old days, have become an inexcusable burden now that the fate of the whole world rests so heavily on the man in the White House. Eisenhower doesn't seem to see it that way. He does about as much of this ceremonial work as his predecessors. By such meetings, he recently told a friend, he draws strength from the emotions, the heart, of the American people.

One o'clock is lunchtime. Even if no guests are scheduled, the President does not like to have the meal served at his desk, but hustles back to the residential quarters to have lunch with Mrs. Eisenhower. But on most days there are guests—frequently many guests.

After lunch the President returns immediately to his office to resume the round of appointments. Doctor Snyder has suggested that he might enjoy a brief nap, like many of his predecessors, at this hour of the day. Eisenhower has so far resisted the idea. He has never been in the habit of taking naps, and he figures that it would just make him that much later in getting away from the office at the day's end.

Tom Stephens, Eisenhower's Appointment Secretary, tries to wind up the official appointments by mid-afternoon, so that the President can tackle the mass of paperwork which some 20 members of his staff have been digesting and preparing for him. In spite of the efforts of his staff to reduce the number of routine signatures required of the President, he still must sign an average of about 200 documents a day, and he must know just what he is signing; each signature carries its burden of responsibility.

Following his late-afternoon exercise (golf is his favorite), the President showers, changes and joins Mrs. Eisenhower in the living room upstairs. Now this man and his wife can really relax, and talk a little foolishness maybe, and swap a bit of family gossip—just like the old days. Relax anyway until eight o'clock, when the President and the First Lady may be expected in the State Dining Room downstairs to preside at a dinner.

Mr. and Mrs. Eisenhower are as hospitable and as sociable as the next couple. But they treasure most those evenings when there are no guests at all. Then they can have their dinner served to them on a tray in their room upstairs. They can turn in early, perhaps as soon as nine, and comfortably read in bed.

All too soon the hours of sleep will pass, and the gentle voice of Sergeant Moaney will again awaken Dwight Eisenhower to the toughest job in this careening world.

—taken from the January 30, 1954, issue of The Saturday Evening Post.

137

John F. Kennedy

★ ★ ★ ★ ★

35th President of the United States

Born: May 29, 1917, Brookline, Massachusetts.
Occupation: Author, naval officer, public official.
Wife: Jacqueline Bouvier. *Children:* Two boys, two girls.
President: 1961-1963. Democratic party.
Vice-President: Lyndon B. Johnson.
Died: November 22, 1963. *Buried:* Arlington
   National Cemetery.

★ ★ ★ ★ ★

John F. Kennedy was the youngest man, the wealthiest and the first Catholic ever elected president. He was a PT boat commander in World War II, and had his boat cut in two by a Japanese destroyer. Although wounded himself, he towed one man to safety and saved his crew of 10.

Arthur M. Schlesinger, Jr., a close friend and associate of Kennedy's, wrote in an article published in the *Post* on December 18, 1963, that "the hard experience of war deepened and toughened him. He was, of course, an authentic hero, a man of valor and hope. As a young skipper on a PT boat, he displayed his capacity for command, which always meant for him, not the compulsion to bark orders, but the capacity to enlist confidence and assume responsibility. After the war, he was broken in health but lively in spirit."

In 1961, after a hard-fought presidential campaign, Kennedy said in his inaugural speech, ". . .ask not what your country can do for you—ask what you can do for your country."

"There used to be a fashion of criticizing John Kennedy for being ambitious," Schlesinger writes, "as if anyone ever became President of the United States who had not schemed and labored to that end. Of course he wanted to be President. But he wanted to be President not because he wanted power for its own sake: He wanted to be President because he wanted to use power to advance the purpose of the nation."

The country looked forward to his administration with great expectation because he was a young, vigorous man with a great deal of poise and confidence. As President he broke new paths in a dozen sectors of national policy—in civil rights, in economic policy, in the reorientation of military strategy, in the reconstruction of foreign aid, in the exploration of space, in the encouragement of the arts. And, Mr. Schlesinger adds, "He was the most civilized President we have had since Jefferson, and his wife made the White House the most civilized house in America. Statecraft was for him not an end in itself; it was a means of moving forward toward a spacious and splendid America."

On November 22, 1963, President Kennedy was shot while riding in a motorcade in Dallas,

Lt. Kennedy was decorated for courage and leadership in the South Pacific in 1943.

Texas. Stunned with disbelief that this handsome young man had been assassinated, dignitaries from around the world came to his funeral. The American people, in deepest grief, buried their young president in Arlington National Cemetery.

And so a crazed political fanatic shot him down. With this act of violence, and with the violence that followed, the idea of America as a civilized nation—the idea which John F. Kennedy so supremely embodied—suffered a grievous blow.

—December 18, 1963, *Post.*

That Wit in the White House

Stripped of its glamour, the White House is a forbidding place, and the Presidency is a lonely and austere responsibility.

At the height of the Civil War, when his country stood on the edge of disaster, and brother slew brother, Abraham Lincoln said, "If I did not laugh I should die."

Lincoln knew that without the leavening effect of humor his dreadful responsibility would be too great even for his shoulders to bear.

Today as another President confronts another crisis of immeasurable dimension and uncertain future, the therapeutic value of humor softens the harsh edges of thought and performance. For John F. Kennedy also belongs to the political breed, whose essential companion is humor. For him it is a saving grace, a bright beam in the dark corners of hard decision.

It is so today and it has always been so in the life of John Kennedy. But nowhere does the Kennedy humor display itself in such generous proportions as it does in his pursuit of the political trade. In Boston, the land of the Sullivans and the O'Neills, the way to the voter's heart is as straight as the spire on the Old North Church.

A family that has known triumph and tragedy, the Kennedy's in 1934—four of the children were to meet with violent death. Standing, from left: Joseph Jr., John, Mrs. Joseph Kennedy, Jean, Patricia. Seated, from left: Robert, Edward, Joseph Kennedy, Eunice, Rosemary, Kathleen.

"And now, friendly sons of St. Patrick, it is my great honor to introduce to you the main speaker of the evening, your candidate, a servant of the Peepul, a great American and"—here the voice reaches a crescendo and the words are pounded for emphasis—"A MAN WHO CAME UP THE HARD WAY...."

Waiting to make one of his first big speeches at a political picnic in 1946 as a candidate for Congress from the tough Eleventh Congressional District in Boston, youthful Jack Kennedy heard one Democrat after another who preceded him to the rostrum introduced with the highest accolade—"a man who came up the hard way."

When Kennedy's turn came, the key phrase was never uttered. He stepped up and grinned at the sweaty, shirt-sleeved crowd. "I'm the one who didn't come up the hard way," he said and heard a roar of delight from the audience.

In a curious way this small story tells a lot about the highly individual way the new President of the United States mixes humor with politics. Long ago Kennedy discovered what Lincoln knew—that the way to kill off an apparent political liability is not to ignore it, but to kid the devil out of it.

When Kennedy decided to run for the Presidency, his opponents encouraged the suspicion that his family's money was being used by the cartload to "buy" political position and votes. Stories to that effect were making the rounds in 1958, when Senator Kennedy spoke at the Gridiron Dinner in Washington. He brought down the house when he fished out a "telegram" from his father, ostensibly sent from the Riviera, where Mr. Kennedy was taking the sun, and said, "I have just received the following wire from my generous daddy. It says, 'Dear Jack, don't buy a single vote more than is necessary. I'll be damned if I'm going to pay for a landslide.'"

A classic example of Kennedy poking fun at his own exposed positions came early this year, when the President made an informal talk at the Alfalfa Club dinner in Washington. The Alfalfa is an aggregation of politicians and local bigwigs who find pleasure in cudgeling one another—orally of course.

There had been a good deal of criticism at that time about the President's nomination of his brother Robert as Attorney General. The charge was that Bobby was deficient in legal experience, having never hung out a shingle of his own.

The President's take-off at the dinner was roughly as follows: "I must say that I am somewhat surprised at the criticism about my appointing my brother to be Attorney General. I don't see what's wrong with giving Bobby a little experience before he starts to practice law."

The situation early last year, when Kennedy went to California to speak at a dinner in honor of Gov. Edmund (Pat) Brown, was made to order for a Kennedy special. Brown, a Catholic, was widely regarded as a receptive Democratic Vice Presidential candidate and Kennedy, a contender for the Presidential nomination, had to take note of it. The trouble was both were Catholics, and no Catholic had ever been elected Presi-

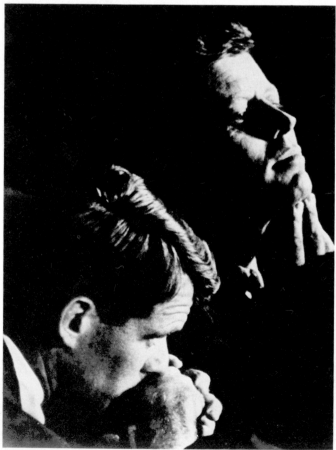

Politics acquired a new image when Jack and brother Bobby (left) waged and won the battle for the presidency in 1960. Above, Pierre Salinger and Dave Powers with the candidate in the family-owned campaign plane.

Rockwell, who met Kennedy during the 1960 campaign (above), seized a serious mood of the President for the April 6, 1963, Post cover (right).

dent or Vice President in history.

"I know there has been talk out here about a Kennedy-Brown ticket," Kennedy started, "and I sincerely wish that we could arrange that. Unfortunately I come from Massachusetts and the governor comes from California, and I don't believe the country is ready yet for a ticket that stretches from the Atlantic to the Pacific."

The crowd loved it. Every politician there knew that an East-West ticket would be a campaign manager's dream. They also knew that what the country really wasn't ready for was two Catholics on the same ticket.

President Kennedy would have trouble keeping his humorous turn of mind under cover if he tried. It crops out whatever he may be doing, wherever he may be doing it. When he accidentally dropped the medal of spaceman Alan Shepard, he picked it up and handed it over with the remark that it came "from the ground up"; addressing the assembly in the ornate *Hotel de Ville* in Paris, he said that Congress had paid only $3000 to Pierre l'Enfant, designer of the City of Washington, instead of the $90,000 he tried to collect "and some have been unkind enough to suggest that the dress designers of Paris have been collecting his bill ever since."

At a Paris luncheon for the press the President started off, "I do not think it altogether inappropriate to introduce myself to this audience. I am the man who accompanied Jacqueline Kennedy to Paris, and I have enjoyed it."

Whatever our own politics, and whatever Kennedy's other attributes, we citizens may rejoice that the President possesses the genius of humor. In that place which he occupies, in these times of high danger and awful responsibilities, humor is indeed the saving grace.

—excerpted from a September 2, 1961,
Post article written
by Rowland Evans, Jr.

Take the Academies Out of Politics
by John F. Kennedy

Gen. George C. Marshall never went to West Point because his family and their congressman were on different sides of the political fence.

Ulysses S. Grant almost lost his chance at the academy because his father and congressman did not see eye to eye politically.

Today, as hundreds of service-academy openings go begging, potential George Marshalls and Ulysses Grants all over the country are devoting their talents to other fields less vital to our national security and less challenging to their ability—all because they feel they don't stand a chance to enter West Point or Annapolis under the ancient congressional appointment system. Members of Congress, by default or indifference, are failing to fill vacancies at the two service academies that are worth thousands of dollars, and, more important, are costing the nation vitally needed leaders for the atomic future.

Eight out of every ten West Pointers and six out of every ten midshipmen owe their appointments to their congressmen. The responsibility for defects in the appointment system is largely ours.

Favoritism, unfairness and unsoundness in the selection of future officer material are not even avoided by those congressmen who exclude politics in their appointments by relying exclusively on the results of the competitive examinations offered. The highest grades in these examinations are quite likely to be received by those from relatively well-to-do families who can afford private tutoring.

Moreover, such a system places too much emphasis on mere "grades" to the exclusion of other factors essential for future military leadership. Good grades are not enough. Native intelligence, aptitude, character and desire are just as essential, if not more essential.

In short, as the result of the present outmoded congressional appointment system at two of the finest institutions this country possesses, from one third to nearly one half of the possible appointments are never filled; about a third of those nominated never finish; at least one out of seven graduates gives up his military career before completing ten years' service; and unknown quantities of men—superior to those who do reach the battlefield—are engaged in other occupations less satisfying to them and less essential to our nation.

When I came to Congress nine years ago, I conducted a study of this entire question. As a result of this study, I initiated a "pilot" selection system for my academy appointments which I have used continuously since that time. It may not be the system for every congressman. But it represents, I believe, one method of eliminating the abuses that have afflicted congressional appointments.

Each year I publicly announce that examinations, open to all, will be held for the appointments I am entitled to make to the academies. Newspapers, radio and television media throughout the state cooperate as a public service in carrying these announcements. In addition, the headmaster or dean of every school and college in Massachusetts is informed of the competition and is asked to encourage all interested candidates to apply.

The first step for each boy is to undergo an examina-

After the unsuccessful Bay of Pigs action in Cuba and the sighting of Soviet missiles based there in 1962, most Americans wanted action.

"IN THE MIDDLE OF THE STREAM"

Courtesy of the Estate of Homer E. Capehart

The striking beauty of Jackie Kennedy in the portrait (left) by Aaron Shikler in 1970, can be matched only by the unwavering strength she portrayed following the assassination. The family stands in silent mourning (above) and John-John salutes as his father's casket passes by.

tion to make certain he is physically qualified for entrance. This is essential, for between 15 and 20 percent of all congressional appointees fail to meet the physical requirements at the service academies each year.

Candidates found physically acceptable are then given aptitude and achievement tests, specially tailored by the Test Development Section of the United States Civil Service Commission. Scholastic records in high school, prep school or college are carefully compiled and evaluated. At that point, every boy's file is processed and screened, and the entire list of candidates is given a competitive ranking.

This is merely the beginning. Objective questionnaires devised to bring out data on the candidate's character and personality are sent to former teachers, employers and others closely acquainted with him. The questionnaries are deliberately and scientifically fashioned to make it almost impossible to give any candidates perfect marks. We want something more useful than a polite letter of recommendation.

With these facts at hand, a special selection board, serving without pay, takes over. This year, for example, my selection board consisted of the headmaster of a preparatory school who is himself a West Point graduate; a clergyman who was formerly an Army chaplain in the combat zone; and a physician with extensive Navy and educational experience.

Perhaps my proudest recollection came when I found my system gave the son of a Chinese laundryman the same chance to go to Annapolis as the son of a prominent ex-mayor in my district.

Self-reform by Congress itself is long overdue. Let us send to our academies young men who are more than good students, able athletes or militarily poised robots. By using available modern selective methods, we in Congress can get the type of boys we need to become the guardians of our future security.

*—excerpted from the June 2, 1956,
issue of* The Saturday Evening Post.

Lyndon B. Johnson

★ ★ ★ ★ ★

36th President of the United States

Born: August 27, 1908, near Stonewall, Texas.
Occupation: Teacher, navy commander, public official.
Wife: Claudia Taylor (Lady Bird). *Children*: Two girls.
President: 1963-1969. Democratic party.
Vice-President: John William McCormack, Speaker of the House of Representatives; Hubert Humphrey.
Died: January 22, 1973. *Buried*: L.B.J. Ranch, Texas.

★ ★ ★ ★ ★

Lyndon Baines Johnson was born near Stonewall, Texas, the first-born of "Little Sam" and Rebekah Johnson. When he was five, they moved to Johnson City where his mother, one of the few college-educated women in the county, imparted to him, his brother and three sisters her belief in the necessity and value of education as well as an inherent compassion for human needs.

Ambitious and restless, his father, State Legislator Sam Johnson, taught his son the facts of political life and leadership in the tradition of agrarian liberalism. The home echoed the political and moral sentiments of self-reliance and social consciousness which would surface time and time again as the basis for Lyndon's political thinking.

Lyndon graduated from high school at 15 and, after working and saving his money, entered Southwest Teachers' College. He later taught history in Houston.

He then met Claudia Taylor and married her after a two-month courtship. Her father, who had money and a real liking for Lyndon, loaned him enough money for a congressional campaign. He was subsequently elected to Congress and spent most of the rest of his life in public office.

In 1948 he was elected to the U.S. Senate, where he served until 1961 when he became vice-president. The last five years in the Senate he had been Majority Leader. The assassination of President John F. Kennedy on November 22, 1963, brought him unexpectedly to the presidency.

Lyndon B. Johnson took the oath of office in the same plane which carried the body of the slain president back to Washington. Beside him stood his wife, Lady Bird, and the widow, Mrs. Kennedy.

Johnson continued the policies of Kennedy, actually getting more bills through Congress than his predecessor. He called his plan for America "The Great Society," and pushed through much social reform.

As he stated in an article in the October 31, 1964, *Post*:

> The challenge of the next half century is whether we have the wisdom to use our wealth to enrich and elevate our national life, and to advance the quality of our American civilization.
>
> Imagination, initiative and indignation will determine whether we build a society where progress is the servant of our needs—or a society where old values and new visions are buried under unbridled growth. We have the opportunity to move, not only toward the rich society and the powerful society, but upward to the Great Society.

Lyndon Baines Johnson was, doubtless, the last president whose roots and early experiences would bridge the gap between the old America of local frontiers, crossroads and close neighbors, and the new America of world power, big cities and unknown neighbors. His deepest motivation as a public figure was to make people neighbors again.

The Johnson Touch

From dusty El Paso to the cloud-hung Northwest, from palm-shaded Sacramento to a New England aflame with the colors of fall, the pattern was always the same. Hours before the President's blue-and-silver jet was scheduled to arrive, the crowds began to gather at the windswept airports, pressing hard against the improvised barricades of rope or wire or portable snow fence. Bass horns grunted like beasts in pain, and piccolos rippled their bird notes as the bandsmen, gaudy as hussars in their bright uniforms, ran through the unfamiliar music of *Hail to the Chief*.

Cub Scouts and Brownies and Scouts of both sexes, sharp in their clean uniforms, nervously waited to dip their banners and snap a sharp salute as the Great Man passed. Massed in clusters, jabbering and elbowing each other, were the squealers and jumpers, a phenomenon in both camps during this campaign—the teen-agers who, in the absence of the Beatles, have turned their hysterical hero worship upon the candidates. Behind these early rail birds stood yet other thousands with hand-lettered signs, exercising their freedom of choice.

"Lyndon Johnson's advance men tell the local politicians not to send the people out with a lot of commercially printed signs and banners," an old reporter said. "They think that it looks too organized. This hand-lettered stuff seems more spontaneous. Also, what they write on their signs sometimes tells the President what's on their mind."

At airport after airport, the bands strike up, the steps roll out, the door opens. The tall man who suddenly appears there makes no dramatic gesture in answer to the crowd's roaring welcome, and to the blare and thump of the bands. Instead, he gives a curious flapping wave—"L.B.J.'s fishtail flutter," the reporters call it—and smiles a small smile which is almost shy.

The birthplace (upper right) of Lyndon Baines Johnson, built in 1889, stands today as a guesthouse. In 1951, Senator Lyndon Johnson and his wife bought and renovated the "big house" (below), referred to as the Texas White House while he was President. A frontier heritage, important to the Johnson family, shaped Lyndon's life and character (lower right).

Lyndon Johnson is sworn in on the plane as 36th President of the United States shortly after the tragic death of John F. Kennedy. His wife and Mrs. Kennedy are at his side.

The crowds in this campaign have seen two Lyndon Johnsons. One is the President of the United States, the tall man on the platform, with the flag and seal of his high office around him, invoking in slow and solemn tones the image of a powerful, prosperous and progressive America—with himself as the calm, wise leader, the President of all the people. His formal speeches touch only obliquely on partisan politics. He stresses instead the national issues—jobs and opportunity for all, regardless of race or color; the safety of the nation, maintained by strength of arms and will; his dream of peace for the world, brought about not by threats and ultimatums but by slow persuasion. He speaks of unity and responsibility, of a nation utilizing the newest ideas, the best brains both parties can provide to keep America moving forward toward his vision of the Great Society.

The man the crowds will remember is the earthy Texan, campaigning in the streets like any crossroads candidate for Congress, kissing small children, reaching out scratched and swollen hands to any hand that reaches out to him, rasping hoarsely through a bullhorn from the backseat of an open car.

"The one thing Lyndon enjoys more than being President is running for President," an observer said. "Getting mauled by a mob does for him what golf did for Ike. It's a kind of therapy for him. He comes out of it feeling exhilarated."

The greeting of the dignitaries never takes long, and Johnson, lifting both hands to smooth back the graying hair that is growing a little thin on top, always heads directly for the yelling crowd that surges against the fence with hands outstretched. Photographers, walking backward in front of him as he moves, trip over each other and go down in a clatter of cameras. Johnson, sidling swiftly, shaking with both hands, does not notice.

"He winks so much I thought at first he had a tic," a reporter said. "It took me a week to figure out it was just part of his technique, his way of getting through to those he can't reach out and touch."

"Thirteen times in seven miles he's stopped already," another reporter says, shaking his head. "Call it corn he's giving them, call it schmaltz, call it what you like. Whatever it is, they like it."

But many of the reporters following Johnson today were with President Kennedy at Dallas and the memory of that horror is still fresh in their minds. Like the Secret Service men who move in concentric circles around the President, they know the normal pattern of a jostling mob, and any sudden flurry near him sends the quick thought racing through their minds that some lunatic is trying to get at him with a knife or gun or bomb.

Making his stop-and-start way from airport to town, Johnson keeps his euphoric mood until he finally reaches the rostrum where he is to deliver his formal

---

I Beg Your Pardon

In one of his frequent contributions to the *Post* during the 50s and 60s, Don Oberdorfer tells one of President Johnson's favorite stories. It concerns L.B.J. and his young assistant, Bill D. Moyers:

Moyers was asked to say grace before the meal at a private gathering in the family quarters of the White House. He began praying softly, when the President interrupted him with "Speak up, Bill! Speak up!"

Moyers, a former Baptist minister from east Texas, stopped in mid-sentence, raised his bowed head and replied steadily, "I wasn't addressing you, Mr. President."

—October 23, 1965, Post.

speech. Then, suddenly, a change seems to come over him. "Ladies and Gentlemen, The President of the United States." He rises slowly, moves to the rostrum, and stands motionless, smiling faintly while the crowd, rising, sends up a great cheer. He lets it go on for a long minute, and then, with a motion of the hand, asks for silence. As the cheers continue, he leans toward the microphone. "Did you come to hear me, or did I come to hear you?" he drawls.

His salutation, after many years in the Senate where such things are important, is graceful. All governors are "distinguished," all senators, whether Democrat or Republican, are "my beloved colleagues." In the West, his greeting always ended, "my fellow Westerners," for in Montana his sensitive political antennae picked up the fact that the citizens of that state attributed certain virtues to his opponent because of his birth in Arizona.

His introductory remarks are humorous, or sentimental, as befits his mood. He remembers to praise those outstanding men and women, both Democrat and Republican, whom each state has sent to Washington.

Sometimes he uses local lore to convey him smoothly into the main theme of his speech. In Montana he said, "When Captain Lewis first saw the Great Falls of Montana, he reported that in a few days he was attacked by a grizzly bear, a mountain lion, three buffalo bulls, and he woke up the next morning staring at a rattlesnake. Those were truly impressive dangers, but today the people of Montana and the people of the world face far more towering threats in an age of nuclear power and defense."

With this he made a swift transition, reminding Montanans that, since the nuclear missiles buried beneath Montana's prairies would be the first to fire against an adversary, Montana in turn would be a primary target. The implication was clear. Montana would be unwise to vote for a man who might recklessly goad an enemy to attack.

"There's no doubt about it," a veteran reporter said. "He's determined not only to be a good President. He wants the name of Lyndon Johnson to be listed among the great ones. That's egotism, sure. But what higher ambition could you ask of him? And I'd be the last to bet that he won't make it." Only history can venture to say whether he made it or not.

—excerpted from an article in the October 31, 1964, issue of The Saturday Evening Post, by Harold H. Martin.

Lady Bird Johnson (right) was a very political First Lady. Often compared to Eleanor Roosevelt, she worked primarily for her husband, but also sponsored some programs of her own. His 12 years in the House, 12 years in the Senate and three years in the vice-presidency gave her more experience in politics than any First Lady before her.

Encyclopedia of Political Buttons, Bk. I, by Ted Hake

Johnson (left) campaigning in 1964. "Getting mauled by a mob," a reporter once said, "does for Lyndon Johnson what golf did for Ike. It's a kind of therapy for him." Above, campaign buttons and mention of Hubert Humphrey, Johnson's running mate in that election. Humphrey later ran for the presidency himself in the 1968 campaign, but lost to Richard M. Nixon.

Richard M. Nixon

★ ★ ★ ★ ★

37th President of the United States

Born: January 9, 1913, Yorba Linda, California.
Occupation: Lawyer, public official.
Wife: Thelma "Pat" Ryan. *Children:* Two girls.
President: 1968-1974. Republican party.
Vice-Presidents: Spiro T. Agnew, Gerald R. Ford.

★ ★ ★ ★ ★

Richard Nixon was born of poor hard-working, Quaker parents. *Post* editor Stewart Alsop interviewed Nixon prior to his bid for the 1960 Republican presidential nomination. In "The Mystery of Richard Nixon" (July 12, 1958, *Post*) Alsop wrote:

> His Quaker background is very much part of him. His

great-grandmother and his great-great-grandmother on his mother's side were well-known itinerant Quaker lady preachers. His mother, a strongly religious and personally charming lady . . . hoped Richard would become a preacher, too, but she soon learned that he had his heart set on being a lawyer. She remembers when little Richard was sprawled in front of the fire, reading in the papers about the Teapot Dome scandal. He turned to her and said: "I know what I want to be when I grow up—an honest lawyer who doesn't cheat people but helps them."

Nixon graduated from Whittier College, where he was second in his class, president of the student body and a champion debater. His scholarship to Duke University Law School in North Carolina was not, however, for football, as Alsop related:

> "He was a lousy player, but he sure had guts," recalls a football star of his day. Once in a long while, Nixon would be permitted to play in the last few minutes of a game. When that happened, a classmate who was then football linesman recalls: "I always got out the five-yard-penalty marker. Dick was so eager I knew he'd be offside just about every play."
>
> In college, Nixon was a model boy. He neither drank nor smoked—although he took an occasional beer in law school—and he went to church four times on Sunday. The only youthful escapade any of his contemporaries can recall involved his crawling over the transom to get into the dean's office, in law school. But his purpose was not to booby-trap the dean's desk or some such shenanigans. It was to discover, from the dean's records, where he stood scholastically.

After law school, Nixon became a junior partner in an old family friend's law business. He was president of the Twenty-Thirty Club, and active in Kiwanis and in the Whittier Little Theater movement. There he met Thelma Ryan—"Pat"—a high school teacher and occasional Hollywood bit player. He married her in 1940.

After serving in the Navy, where it is told that Nixon became a "brilliant poker player," he entered politics and was a member of both houses of Congress. Alsop continued:

> In 1946, Nixon, still in uniform, accepted an invitation from another family friend, a Whittier banker, to appear before a local Republican group which was looking for a Republican hopeful to oppose Representative Jerry Voorhis, a high-minded, well-entrenched Democrat. Nixon was chosen, and beat Voorhis in what he has called a "fighting, rocking, rolling campaign." He was elected easily again in 1948, and in his second term he won a national reputation when he was given a large share of the credit—which he deserved—for bringing Alger Hiss to justice. In 1950, he beat Helen Gahagan Douglas in a race for the Senate—another "rocking, rolling" campaign.

Mr. Eisenhower chose him as his running mate in 1952. Alsop wrote of Nixon's eight years as Vice-President:

He instantly recognized and publicly acknowledged the real meaning of the first Soviet satellite, when other Administration spokesmen were smugly attempting to laugh it off with weak jokes. He was the first to recognize that the recession was a serious matter, demanding a serious Government policy to deal with it. And it has been difficult for even the most cynical of the anti-Nixonites to detect a political motivation in some of the positions Nixon has taken, like his strong advocacy of the politically unpopular foreign-aid program.

Since 1836, when Martin Van Buren inherited the role from Andrew Jackson, no Vice-President had been nominated as his party's Presidential candidate.

He not only won the nomination in 1968, but was elected president by the American people. During his first term, he made trips to Communist China and to the Soviet Union. In 1972, he was reelected by a wide margin.

In June, 1972, an incident occurred which was to change the course of events. The Democratic National Committee headquarters, located in a building named Watergate, was broken into. A Senate investigation was made and a special prosecutor appointed. Top aides to the President resigned. Tapes implicating the President were found, and on August 9, 1974, President Nixon resigned. He admitted no wrongdoing, but felt that it was best for the country not to be involved in a long impeachment trial. He retired to his home in San Clemente, California.

In the Fall 1972 issue of the *Post*, the President wrote:

When historians study all the records of the Nixon years, I hope they will conclude that these were good years, years in which we ended a difficult war, achieved significant arms control agreements and made peaceful negotiation the way of life among nations. I hope, too, that this Administration will be remembered as one which reordered an economy which had grown dependent on wartime spending, decentralized and revitalized a Federal bureaucracy which had grown rigid and unresponsive, and helped a divided Nation substitute the rule of reason for confrontation and disorder.

Richard Nixon

President of the United States

L.B.J. Should Debate on TV
by Richard M. Nixon

"Could you tell us," the reporter asked, "to clear the air on this, whether, if you are a candidate in 1964, you

At a banquet during the summit in China, President Nixon listens to the words of Premier Chou En-lai while attempting to partake of an Eastern delicacy carefully balanced on chopsticks.

President Nixon and trusted advisor Dr. Henry Kissinger hold a hurried discussion during a walk down a street in the Kremlin.

Photo by Ollie Atkins

Photo by Ollie Atkins

would agree to debate with your opponent?"

The President replied, "I would, sir."

On two other occasions before his death, President Kennedy stated unequivocally in press conferences that he would participate in television debates with his Republican opponent.

A recent Gallup poll shows that 71 percent of Americans want to see the 1964 candidates debate on television. The networks have offered free time, and Congress has removed the last legal obstacle by waiving the equal-time requirement. But at this writing it appears that there will be no debates, because President Johnson has repeatedly refused to participate in them.

I suppose I should be the last person to advocate television debates, in view of what happened in 1960. Most observers agree with Earl Mazo of *The New York Times*, who wrote, "If there had been no debates on

---

Where Is Your Leader?

In May of 1958, Vice-President Richard Nixon and his wife, Pat, returned from a South American "goodwill" tour. The American envoy had not been at all well received by our southern American neighbors.

Stewart Alsop asked Nixon, in a *Post* article which appeared in the July 12, 1958, issue, how he felt in Peru and Venezuela, when he realized he was in physical danger from the Communist-led mobs. Was he scared?

"How did I feel? Well, that's hard to describe. Generally speaking, my reaction . . . to stress, a challenge, some great difficulty—it is sort of chemically delayed. While it is going on, I feel cold, matter-of-fact, analytical. At Lima, for example, when I saw the mob before the university, I made the decision to get out of the car and walk up to the mob on foot. I tried to analyze each face, to separate the Communists from the neutrals or the friendly ones. And I kept asking, 'Where is your leader?' It was deliberately calculated to put the Communists on the spot. Then when I saw the soft answer would not work, that they wouldn't let me speak, I allowed myself the luxury of showing my temper and called them cowards. It was deliberate, letting my temper show—not that I didn't really feel it; it was a terrible thing the Communists were doing, using these poor, often ignorant people in that way. Then after a crisis like that is over, I feel this tremendous letdown, a fatigue, as though I'd been in battle."

---

television, Nixon would have been elected President." As the late Claude Robinson, who did the polling for our campaign, pointed out in a confidential memorandum to me, "Kennedy started the campaign as the less well-known candidate. By participating in debates with him, Nixon gave him the opportunity to remove that liability and to fight the campaign out on even terms."

President Johnson faces the same problem I did. He is better-known than any one of the potential Republican nominees. He will be urged, as I was, not to give up this advantage by participating in television debates.

But the issue of debates this year, as in 1960, is much bigger than whether they will help the Democratic or the Republican nominee. Television debates were not designed to serve a candidate for office; they were designed to serve the public.

It has been estimated that over one hundred million people saw at least part of the Kennedy-Nixon debates. Interest in the campaign, according to polls, rose 12 percent from the time of the first debate on September 26 until the last one on October 21, compared to a one percent increase in interest during the same period in the campaign of 1956. Almost seven million more people voted in 1960 than in 1956, whereas less than half a million more voted in 1956 than in 1952. This spectacular increase in the number of voters, according to most observers, was due in large part to the interest created by the television debates.

Moreover, millions of Americans who would never go out to hear a political speech, or even listen to one on television, tuned in to the debates to see a fight and stayed to learn about the issues. As a result, the electorate in 1960 was probably the best-informed in the nation's history.

Some people object that a meeting of candidates on television puts too much emphasis on debating skill. Perhaps it does. But a President today must be quick on his feet, must be able to respond to questions under pressure, must be articulate. It may not have been necessary in the world of 50 or 100 years ago, but it is today. Voters want to see the way a man handles himself under fire. A confrontation on television is an excellent test of a candidate. The TV camera shows the man, and the people sense his qualities, not the synthetic product of public-relations experts.

I believe there could be some improvements in the format for the television debates in 1964. For example:

There should be at least one debate between the two candidates for Vice-President. President Eisenhower's three serious illnesses, together with President Kennedy's assassination, have brought home to the American people with shattering impact the immense importance of the Vice-Presidency. This year, more than any other time in American history, the voters will be giving the qualifications of the vice-presidential candidates the same thoughtful study that they give those of the presidential candidates.

Four years ago the United States took a bold new step forward in political campaigning. Lincoln and Douglas were running for the Senate: 1960 marked the first debate between American presidential candidates.

America has given the world a new and exciting technique in democracy, and we should not allow it now to be discarded in our own country.

—*excerpted from the June 27-July 4, 1964, issue of* The Saturday Evening Post.

Photo by Ollie Atkins

Rare, stolen moments of time for the man within the President. Alongside the man, the woman who for 40 years "has acted as a sort of extra backbone for a man whose backbone already had great tensile strength." Presidential photographer Ollie Atkins captures the President and First Lady Pat in a relaxing moment at San Clemente. They smile, perhaps remembering the quiet times of reading to their children, Tricia and Julie, and the carefree times of a romp with King Timahoe, the big red setter, under the Florida sun. Both of the girls grew up to be married in the White House, Julie to the grandson of another president, Dwight David Eisenhower. In 1973-74 Julie was employed by The Curtis Publishing Company. Although the children's stories for The Saturday Evening Post were her greatest "love," she contributed in many facets.

Photo by Ollie Atkins

Gerald R. Ford

★ ★ ★ ★ ★

38th President of the United States

Born: July 14, 1913, Omaha, Nebraska.
Occupation: Lawyer, public official.
Wife: Elizabeth Bloomer. *Children:* Three boys, one girl.
President: 1974-1977. Republican party.
Vice-President: Nelson Rockefeller.

★ ★ ★ ★ ★

Gerald Ford is the only man in our history who has held the office of president and vice-president without being elected to either office by the American people. He began his career as a lawyer from Grand Rapids, Michigan. He had been elected to the House of Representatives 13 times, and had also served as House minority leader. He had a reputation as a hard worker, a loyal Republican and an honest and dependable man.

When Vice-President Agnew was forced to resign, President Nixon chose Gerald Ford to be his vice-president. He was able to do this under the 25th Amendment which permits a president to appoint a new vice-president, with the approval of Congress, when the office is vacant.

After Nixon's resignation, Ford became president. He attempted to restore the American people's faith in their government by bringing honesty, openness and warmth to the White House.

In the September '76 issue of the *Post,* his wife, Betty, speaks of their evenings in the White House:

"We've been married 28 years now and I can always sense his attitude and whether he's had a good day or bad. I certainly don't bring up any problems. I make a point not to, and I don't go into matters like how his schedule might be conflicting with mine. Or even on something like we're getting our Virginia house painted, and that there are problems with it. I think it is a sensitivity thing between two people who have lived together for a certain period of time. He wouldn't bring up anything to distress me either.

"He particularly enjoys music at dinner. One of his favorites is *Oklahoma!,* though I get a little tired of it. He likes musicals, but on the light side. He doesn't carry his troubles with him. He leaves the office behind.

"He loves to eat. I feel sorry for him because he really loves food, and he has to hold back. I tend to kid him facetiously about that. He likes butter-pecan ice cream every night, though he sometimes eats other desserts.

"At dinner, we talk mostly about the children. His interest lies where they are and what they are doing. It's a family hour. Susan and Jack are often there for dinner, too. That pleases him more than anything else.

"After dinner, my husband and I usually go to what we call 'our' room. We just moved everything from the room where we kept all our junk in our Arlington home to a room here. It has his old leather chair, his footstool and the pipe rack. We kept all the pictures taken of the children over the years which he kept on the mantel. He was so fond of that. We have Susan from yea-high to where she is now, and that's tall.

"We often watch television, some sort of detective story. We like Angie Dickinson ('Police Woman') and Bill Conrad ('Cannon'). I call it 'escape hour,' situations where he can escape. He does some work while he's watching, but it doesn't require concentration. He signs photographs and letters and so forth. If there's a basketball game, he'll watch the whole thing. And he'll watch the eleven o'clock news."

In 1976, when Gerald Ford ran for president, there

was an energy crisis on and inflation and unemployment were high. Sentiments of the American people toward Republicans (due to the Watergate trials of the Nixon period) were, despite Ford's efforts to prove otherwise, still distrustful. Ford fought a hard campaign, but was narrowly defeated by Jimmy Carter, a Democrat from Georgia.

A Bicentennial Message

by Gerald Ford

This Bicentennial celebration of the birth of the United States of America is more than a parade of our national past. It is a preview of our future.

Whenever I am reminded of one of the great events or outstanding accomplishments of our history, and as I travel around this great country today, I ask myself: if we have come so far in 200 years, how much more can we achieve for our posterity?

If we can only discern clearly the secret of our unique success as a nation, if we can identify and perpetuate the fundamental force that has powered our progress, surely there are no limits to how much further we can go.

History, which is mostly written by the learned about the victors, leads us to ascribe the success of our revolution to the founding fathers with their wisdom and foresight and to the iron determination and leadership of George Washington. We cannot honor them enough, but it is important to remember that the final success in that struggle, and in the many struggles that have followed throughout these 200 years, was due to the strength and support of ordinary men and women who were motivated by three powerful impulses—personal freedom, self-government and national unity.

The development of these ideas on the virgin American continent has been characterized as the greatest political experiment in all history, but it was more than that; it involved a social and economic revolution far more profound than the differences between the British parliamentary government and our original federal system.

The American assertion that "all men are created equal" was a daring one in 1776, but it had ancient

A casual collar projects Ford's "one of the people" image as he beams down at the cheering crowds from the sun-roof of a moving car during the 1976 presidential race. Betty, whose candid remarks to the press on several occasions helped create the limelight they now share, is her usual gracious self.

Photo by David Hume Kennerly

153

antecedents even as it has modern distortions. Far more revolutionary was the notion that men and women, despite their disparate interests and individual selfish motives, are nevertheless capable in a free society of uniting and governing themselves for the common good.

As far back as 1619 colonists challenged the dictates of a distant regime that sought to impose government without the consent of the governed. Those colonists envisioned a new way of life strikingly different from the lives of common people in the Europe of that day. At Jamestown and at Plymouth were sowed the seeds of an idea that would make Americans to this day strive for control over their own lives.

That idea was of individual independence.

Alexis de Tocqueville, the French historian, wrote of our beginnings: "In that land, the great experiment was to be made, by civilized men, of the attempt to construct society on a new basis."

Over the decades the great experiment has continued, enduring many severe tests. Could a society endure half-slave and half-free? Could a vast mixture of nationalities and religions and colors and culture become one nation? Could it escape being consumed by the materialism of its own natural riches?

The United States of America has survived, but the great experiment has not finally succeeded. It is still going on. Challenge and adversity have given us confidence and experience. From every testing we have emerged a stronger and, I believe, a better nation.

During our first century of independence, we pushed westward from the Atlantic seaboard with relentless energy to the Pacific and the Arctic seas. We did not create colonies, but into these areas transplanted our peculiar political institutions; the sovereign people; representative government at all levels; tripartite government with separate executive, legislative and judicial branches; fundamental rights and liberties guaranteed by state as well as national constitutions.

In turn the new territories became states, their frontier spirit changing and broadening our original political institutions. Inevitably, the moral defect of the Constitution was rectified by a tragic fraternal war, and a more perfect union of free citizens became basic law.

Those first hundred years might be called the century of political independence—the development of free institutions responsible to the people and the participation of more and more citizens in the process of self-government.

Our second century of independence, some of which we have lived for ourselves, was preeminently a century of unprecedented economic and technological growth.

The explosion of productivity and knowledge that

Candid Comments

Betty Ford is certainly the most celebrated First Lady since Eleanor Roosevelt. Even those who don't like her views or her casual manner join the majority of Americans who agree that she has captivated the public in a most astonishing manner.

The quick explanation for all this fascination and popularity is that Mrs. Ford spoke her mind with startling frankness on the CBS-TV "Sixty Minutes" program. She said that she "wouldn't be surprised" if her eighteen-year-old daughter, Susan, decided to have an affair, allowed that premarital sex with the right partner might lower the divorce rate and remarked that she assumed all her children had tried marijuana (they hadn't).

Never had a First Lady been so outspoken, and seldom was there such a reaction to an interview with a famous person in the White House.

After her experience with "Sixty Minutes," she was quick to point out that she considered herself a responsible, loving parent, who wanted her children to discuss their difficulties with the people in the world who cared the most—their mother and father. And she added: "My husband and I have lived twenty-eight years of faithfulness in marriage. I do not believe in premarital relations. But I realize many in today's generation do not share my views."

She had also made it clear that she supported the 1973 Supreme Court ruling for liberalized abortion, saying that she was glad to see abortion "brought out of the backwoods and put in the hospitals where it belongs." She was and is a firm supporter of the Equal Rights Amendment.

She was just as lively when talking about her breast operation. "For those who have gone through it," she said, "I don't see anything so great about it. All you need is a little foam rubber."

—an excerpt from a September '76 Post article written by Nick Thimmesch.

began with the industrial revolution and the harnessing of new kinds of energy has been felt worldwide, but it was the United States of America that set the pace. Not only did our factories and farms surpass all others, but the wealth they created was more equitably shared than in any economic order.

Both these achievements of our second century were

Photo by David Hume Kennerly

Below (lower) Gerald R. Ford is inaugurated 38th President of the United States in 1974 following Nixon's unprecedented exit from the White House and (upper), Ford calls on past college football days as he sprints past reporters and their questions. At left is Betty's official White House portrait. The entourage of reporters, the portraits of Presidents and their First Ladies, the sassy slogans of campaign buttons (center)—all are by-products of a successful political career that spanned 27 years, progressed to the office of Chief Executive.

UPI

Political Buttons,
Book II, by Theodore Hake

BETTY'S HUSBAND FOR PRESIDENT IN '76
GOP FEMINIST CAUCUS - MINNESOTA

Brown Brothers

possible because of the persistence of the original and uniquely American idea of self-reliance and individual initiative. So our second 100 years as a nation can be called our century of economic independence, giving us the highest material level of well-being in the world.

What will our third century of independence bring? We cannot know the answer, any more than the legendary Betsy Ross could know that the flag, with 50 stars, would one day be implanted on the moon. But I would like to think of it as the century of individual independence.

In the course of making vast advances in our political and economic institutions, we have lost some of our most precious resource, the identity and individuality of each American. We must reassert our inalienable right to do our own thing, with all respect for the same rights of others. We must resist the pressures of conformity whether they come from massive government, massive business, massive labor, massive education or massive communication.

The independence for which every American yearns—to be dealt with and to deal with others in the spirit of equal rights and equal responsibilities—is the unfinished business of our Bicentennial. It is a goal worthy of our great past, and a guidepost to an even more glorious future.

—*July/August '76 Post.*

James E. Carter

★ ★ ★ ★ ★

39th President of the United States

Born: October 1, 1924, Plains, Georgia.
Occupation: Farmer, engineer, scientist, businessman.
Wife: Rosalynn Smith. *Children:* Three boys, one girl.
President: 1977-   . Democratic party.
Vice-President: Walter F. Mondale.

★ ★ ★ ★ ★

Jimmy Carter, as he is known, is the first governor elected president since Franklin D. Roosevelt. He is also the first man to be elected president from the "Deep South" in the 20th century. He grew up in Plains, Georgia, and graduated from the United States Naval Academy in 1947.

While in the Navy he supervised the construction of nuclear submarines. His teachers at Union College in Schenectady, New York, where he studied the characteristics of nuclear power for the Navy, remember him as an exceptionally bright student. The 1947 *Lucky Bag*, the Naval Academy's yearbook, read, "Studies never bothered Jimmy; in fact the only time he opened his books was when his classmates desired help on problems." An Annapolis classmate and shipmate says:

> Carter was quiet, purposeful, sincere. He was a lot more intellectual than he ever let you know but he wasn't afraid to do the dirty work, the nuts-and-bolts stuff down in the engine room.
>
> He was the kind of guy who could work all night and appear completely unruffled in the morning. He was really interested in the enlisted men and if they had problems he was the one they went to.
>
> —*taken from the Summer, 1976, issue
> of* The Country Gentleman, *in an
> article by F.X. O'Connor, Jr.*

When his father died in 1953, he returned to Georgia to help out in the family business—peanut farming. He was an active church member in the Plains Baptist Church and became interested in politics. He was governor of Georgia from 1971-1975. Then he started campaigning for the Democratic presidential nomination.

F.X. O'Connor, Jr. continued in the above-mentioned article:

> "My religion means more to me than anything else in the world," Carter says. A Baptist, he teaches Sunday school, and before he started running for the presidency he toured New England states with his church group. But he was willing to defy the entire congregation of the Baptist church in Plains when he voted to admit black members. He describes himself as "a born-again Christian." His supporters have always tried to push this image of rebirth, too, assuring listeners that Carter was instrumental in bringing Georgia and the South into modern times from the dark and lingering maladies of the Civil War. Campaign rhetoric perhaps, but the Carter approach is one of the few that promises an administration based on knowledge of rural life and the difficulties farmers face.

Carter worried in 1942 that his dream of attending the Naval Academy might not come true due to the malocclusion of his teeth and flat feet. Above, his wife and mother, Miss Lillian, attend his Annapolis graduation in 1947.

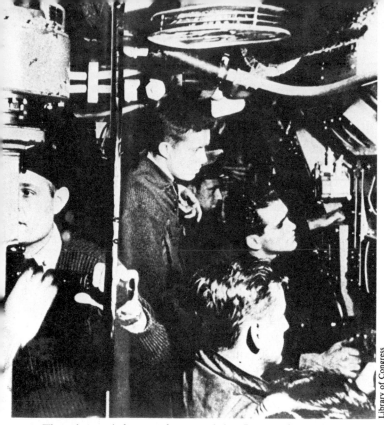

The isolation of submarine duty appealed to Carter as he could solve scientific problems without distraction. But the diversity of his background led some to believe that he "floated" on the issues, depending on his audience.

"Jimmy who?" was the noted phrase in 1976 but he conducted a vigorous campaign and won the election, promising a better economy and a more responsive government. In 1978 he was praised for his part in the Middle East Peace Treaty, but by 1980 the rate of inflation had risen to 80 percent, the price of gold to over $700 per ounce, the price of a gallon of gasoline to over $1.00, and even the farmers were demonstrating in Washington, D.C.

Peanut Farmer from Plains

Georgia planted 520,000 acres in peanuts last year, about a third of the nation's total, to produce 1,726,400 pounds of the nitrogen-generating legume. Half of the crop went into peanut butter and the second largest use was for confectionery—salted nuts or candy, and the Carters of Plains, a town of 683 in the Georgia Piedmont, are a typical family of farmers who have moved into the business end of the profitable "goober."

The Carters have about 1,500 acres of their own land, and they buy peanuts from farmers around Sumter County to store in their warehouses where the shelling

Carter Versus the Backstroke Bunny

It was the *President—1*, and the *bunny rabbit—0*, after their encounter at a Webster County, Georgia, fishing pond.

The bunny, obviously fleeing from some predator, jumped into the pond and began swimming toward the President's boat.

"It was a fairly robust-looking rabbit who was swimming, apparently with no difficulty," the President told reporters. As the bunny neared, hoping for rescue aboard the boat, the President chased it off with a canoe paddle.

"I determined this would be an unpleasant situation for me and the rabbit," the President said.

The President was not injured, although the reports were unclear about what happened to the bunny.

No news photographers were present but it was said that a White House photographer took a picture of the "attack," which the President had developed and enlarged to prove to doubting staff members that the incident had occurred.

Rosalynn, probably the best informed of all the First Ladies, regularly attends high-level government meetings and discussions.

157

and processing of the peanuts [averaging around $370-per-ton] goes on all winter.

This Scotch-Irish family settled here in the 1830s and became part of the fiercely independent yeomen who disdained the rich coastal areas of the Carolinas and Georgia and Alabama, where plantations amounting almost to city-states flourished, for the hard life of the foothills. The soil was thin, but the air was free. Slavery was anathema to most of these Georgians and many supported the union in the 1860s.

"I'm basically a redneck," Jimmy Carter tells people, grinning widely, but he believes that the sincerity of the land, the assets of rural virtue and the basic values of farm life ought to be a ruling factor in Washington.

When his father, James Earl Carter, Sr., a farmer and small businessman, died in 1953, Jimmy gave up a promising career in the Navy—he had been handpicked by Admiral Rickover for duty in the new nuclear submarine force. "I felt the work my father did in the community was important," he says. Rosalynn, Jimmy's wife, didn't want to go back. In the Fifties, life on a farm seemed a dead end. They quarreled, but Jimmy won, "as usual," says his mother, and the young Carters took on the farm and the town.

He bought a peanut sheller—"He remembered what

picking those things by hand was like," says a fellow Plainsman—and then he and his brother built a warehouse for processing other people's peanuts. The business prospered and the Carter warehouses became part of the landscape of Plains with its two filling stations, two grocery stores, Seaboard Coast Line tracks and hardware store. Small-town life put Carter in the governor's mansion in Georgia, too, when he ran in 1970, and in 1976, it put him in the White House.

The income from the peanut business gave the Carters about $80,000 last year, and it has helped Jimmy establish a fortune of nearly half a million—not bad, he says, for the first person in his family on his father's side to finish high school.

Although Carter's image of a small-town farmer may hurt him in the area of foreign policy, his quip that "if the experts have got the country into this mess, maybe we ought to try a nonexpert" makes some sense.

Carter is not naive enough to suppose that Plains or even Georgia is the same as Washington and the nation and the world. But he does believe the way he grew up is good for people. "He gets up early, and he works late," says his neighbors. "We didn't have electricity then, the bathroom was outside, the only way to pick peanuts was by hand," says a friend from Americus,

Courtesy, Georgia Department of Archives and History

Library of Congress

The picturesque, small-town railroad depot at left is actually the Southern Coast Line Railroad Depot of Plains, Georgia, which housed Carter's presidential campaign activities in 1976. Above, Carter executes a tried and true rule of campaigning: establish eye contact.

It was Carter who broke the silence of the 28-minute network audio blackout during the first of the '76 debates. As he sat back on his stool and folded his arms, cheers rang out in the studio audience. Ford also folded his arms in a patient gesture, but remained standing.

the county seat for the proud community of Plains.

Now combines harvest the peanuts and more is known about the calcium requirements of this South American legume that along with cotton, rice, tobacco, corn and wheat was one of the six basic commodities determined in the Roosevelt years for parity. Four of these basic commodities grow in the South, and it was this agrarian leg-up that allowed the South, coupled with the seniority system, to wield some power in the Congress though its population and economic wealth were small compared to the North or West.

The Carters don't live on a farm anymore; their expansive ranch-style house in town is evidence of their success and hard work, but their house and their loyalties lie close to the land; there always is a garden getting started or finishing up at their place, and of course his business depends on farming. In an era of neglect for farmers and farms, paradoxically at a time when America's most successful export is agriculture, it is reassuring to see a farmer being listened to by the national ear.

Political Buttons, Book II, by Theodore Hake

Carter's appeal to the young lies perhaps as much in the land itself as in the things he has to say. Carter made the choice to return to the land long before it was a popular thing to do. Carter and his wife spent the first year after their return to farm life in a public housing project, but he believes in free enterprise because he himself survived that way.

Much has changed in the South agriculturally. Cotton is no longer king and the peanut, which in many countries is still grown mainly for its oil, has changed too. Where once it was used as feed for livestock, only the tops now go for hay. The politicians have changed too. The white-suited, string-tied, Panama-hatted stentorian orator of yesterday has vanished, and people like Carter are taking his place, businessmen essentially, but not believing in any exceptions to moral rules in the name of commerce, and with a strong back and background tied to the land.

—*excerpted from an article in the Summer, 1976, issue of* The Country Gentleman, *by F.X. O'Connor, Jr.*

159

Acknowledgments

Text Credits

Special acknowledgment goes to:

"The Hayes Administration and the Woman Question" by Dr. Beverly Beeton, from *Hayes Historical Journal*, Spring 1978, copyright 1978 by The Hayes Historical Society.

Berkeley Plantation
Rt. 2, Box 79
Charles City, Virginia

The following *Post* series:
Henry Watterson (1919).
Irwin H. (Ike) Hoover (1934).
Arthur Krock (1968).

The following *Post* editors:
Samuel G. Blythe (1908-23).
Beverly Smith, Jr. (1946-60).
Stewart Alsop (1961-68).

★

Photo Credits

Special acknowledgment goes to:
Mr. Ted Hake
Americana & Collectibles Press
P.O. Box 1444
York, Pennsylvania 17405

Mrs. Jeannette Robinson, Indianapolis, In.

Mrs. Ollie Atkins, Washington, D.C.

Caroline M. Capehart and Dorothy Abner, of Indianapolis, for photos provided.

Theodore Roosevelt's Letters to His Children, edited by Joseph Bucklin Bishop. © 1919 Charles Scribner's Sons; renewal © 1947 Edith K. Carow Roosevelt.

★

We wish to acknowledge the following individuals and organizations who have supplied us with the art used throughout the book:

United States Department of the Interior National Park Service:

Grant A. Petersen, Superintendent
Herbert Hoover National Historic Site
P.O. Box 607
West Branch, Iowa

Hugh A. Lawing, Park Historian
Andrew Johnson National Historic Site
Greeneville, Tennessee

Roy F. Beasley, Jr., Superintendent
Sagamore Hill National Historic Site
Cove Neck Road, Box 304
Oyster Bay, New York

William N. Jackson, Historian
Martin Van Buren National Historic Site
P.O. Box 545
Kinderhook, New York

★

General Services Administration
National Archives and Records Service:

Thomas T. Thalken, Director
J. Patrick Wildenberg, Archivist
Herbert Hoover Presidential Library
West Branch, Iowa

John F. Kennedy Library
380 Trapelo Road
Waltham, Massachusetts

William R. Emerson, Director
Franklin D. Roosevelt Library
Hyde Park, New York

★

Department of Conservation:

Thomas A. Campbell, Jr., Superintendent
Grant Home State Historic Site
509 Bouthillier Street
Galena, Illinois

★

Carolyn C. Holmes, Curator
Ash Lawn
Home of President James Monroe
Charlottesville, Virginia

Malcolm Jameson, Owner/Operator
Berkeley Plantation
Rt. 2, Box 79
Charles City, Virginia

Wilma C. Bertling
Buffalo and Erie County Historical Society
25 Nottingham Court
Buffalo, New York

George Dow, Photographer
Marshfield, Massachusetts

Virginia Vezolles
Benjamin Harrison Memorial Home
1230 North Delaware
Indianapolis, Indiana

Watt P. Marchman, Director
The Rutherford B. Hayes Library
1337 Hayes Avenue
Fremont, Ohio

Elizabeth Smith, Secretary
Thomas Jefferson Memorial Foundation
P.O. Box 316
Charlottesville, Virginia

Stark County Historical Center
Canton, Ohio

Mrs. Robert W. Sturdivant, Regent
The Ladies' Hermitage Assocation
Hermitage, Tennessee

Stuart Downs, Director
James Madison Museum
129 Caroline Street
Orange, Virginia

National Portrait Gallery
Smithsonian Institution
F Street at Eighth, N.W.
Washington, D.C.

National Trust for Historic Preservation
Robert Mawson, Asst. Administrator
The Woodrow Wilson House
2340 S. Street, N.W.
Washington, D.C.

Francis Rainey
James K. Polk Ancestral Home
Box 741
Columbia, Tennessee

Pat Thompson, Manager
Sherwood Forest Plantation
Home of President John Tyler
Charles City County, Virginia

Eleanor M. Richardson, Librarian
South Caroliniana Library
University of South Carolina
Columbia, South Carolina

Fran Schell, Librarian
Tennessee State Library
403 7th Avenue N
Nashville, Tennessee

George H. Curtis, Asst. Director
Harry S. Truman Library
Independence, Missouri

Thomas H. Hartig, Ph.D., Exec. Director
Woodrow Wilson Birthplace Foundation
P.O. Box 24
Staunton, Virginia

★

Illustrations and text not otherwise credited are from the pages of *The Saturday Evening Post* or *The Country Gentleman* and are the copyrighted property of The Curtis Publishing Company or The Saturday Evening Post Company.

An effort has been made to trace the ownership of all text and photographs included. Any errors or omissions will be corrected in subsequent editions, provided the publisher is notified.

★ ★ ★ ★ ★

Special
Ronald Reagan
Supplement

★ ★ ★ ★ ★

Ronald Reagan

★ ★ ★ ★ ★

40th President of the United States

Born: February 6, 1911, Tampico, Illinois.
Occupation: Actor, public official.
Wives: Jane Wyman, Nancy Davis. *Children:*
Two boys, two girls.
President: 1981-   . Republican party.
Vice-President: George Bush.

★ ★ ★ ★ ★

Ronald Reagan was born above a store on Main Street, Tampico, Illinois, the son of a shoe salesman. It was in this small-town atmosphere that his mother introduced him to the world of reading through the Bible and where he formulated the values to which he would always adhere.

In high school, he was a star in the junior class play and on the football team, talents he was able to combine successfully at the height of his acting career.

By working as a lifeguard, swimming coach, dishwasher and busboy, he managed to earn enough money to enter Eureka College in Peoria, Illinois in 1928. There he had his first taste of political activism, when, as a freshman, he was elected leader of the student body to protest a cutback in programs that threatened to prevent the graduation of upperclassmen.

There too, along with pursuing his passion for the stage, he became fascinated with the role radio played in politics, which led him to embark on a radio broadcasting career.

Several years later, in 1937, a Hollywood screen test landed him a $200-a-week contract with Warner Brothers. Thus began his respectable, though not spectacular, movie career. "Knute Rockne—All American" in which he played Notre Dame football hero, George Gipp, and the highly dramatic "Kings Row" were among his most popular films. These were followed by several World War II films, after which Reagan found himself gradually being replaced by younger actors.

In an effort to right this injustice, he turned to the Screen Actors Guild, where he was elected president six times during the 1940s and '50s—his first real political leadership role. His involvement with the SAG contributed to the dissolution of his eight-year marriage to actress Jane Wyman and, ironically, introduced him to a young actress named Nancy Davis, whom he later married.

By this time, Reagan had become more familiar to the television audience than to the movie audience, serving as the host of "General Electric Theater" and "Death Valley Days." With the change in his career came also a change in party politics—one which had been evolving for years. He had always been a Democrat, but in 1952 and 1956, he supported GOP candidate Dwight Eisenhower.

By 1964 he was recognized as a solid Republican and was appointed state co-chairman of Citizens for Goldwater-Miller. His refusal to concede defeat in the waning days of that campaign brought him to the attention of his Republican colleagues, who approached him to run for governor of California in 1966.

He did so and overwhelmingly defeated incumbent Edmund G. (Pat) Brown, and was resoundingly re-elected four years later. His first act as governor was to impose a hiring freeze, but his prize accomplishment was passage of the 1971 Welfare Reform Act which significantly narrowed the eligibility rules for welfare recipients while increasing the benefits and cost-of-living allotments available to those who still remained eligible.

1980 campaign buttons support a 1968 prophecy made by the National Review: *Ronald Reagan "may become a part of American History."*

support; the leading spokesman for the Middle America which feels itself abandoned, a spokesman—Reagan says —"for which it urgently yearns."

Reagan's call for tax reduction, for national security and national strength; his ability to articulate what others feel—"Government doesn't cure inflation, government causes inflation. . . .If we can get the federal government out of our nation's schools, maybe we can get God back in. . . .I don't care if we're liked around the world. I just want us to be respected"—have stirred a large part of an electorate tired of being bullied by officials who ignore the very constituents they purport they are serving.

Asked to profile varied issues and personalities, Reagan responded as follows:

• Inflation. "We have to reduce the cost of the federal government, cut down its influence and size. We have to restore productivity. We have to renew incentive. We can lessen federal spending by returning functions to state and local governments."

• National defense. "Never have we been weaker abroad. If we are to command respect overseas we must have a military which *deserves* respect. We have to increase the pay scale in all our armed services so that military service becomes a profession young people can afford to enter."

• Energy. "Conservation is fine—we're all for it—but you can't conserve when there's nothing to save. Instead, we have to get the federal government out of the energy business—and we have to let private enterprise produce the domestic reserves that will end once and for all our crippling dependence on foreign oil."

• Busing and quotas. "Busing has been a colossal failure. It does nothing except inflame racial tensions and make teaching our children even more difficult. And what of quotas? They are nothing more than a new form of discrimination—reverse discrimination."

• The Shah of Iran. "He has been viciously maligned. For years he was a friend of ours. And how did we treat him? We stabbed him in the back. Two years ago I was in Iran; I saw what the Shah was trying to do. He was striving to ensure freedom of worship, to guarantee that women's rights were upheld in a country where they had been denied. He was pushing land reform, low-cost housing, increased education for the young. Our betrayal of him is a sin we will not soon forget."

• Richard Nixon. "His problems arose from an unwise attempt to protect others under him in his administration. But he was—and is—a brilliant man. I have met with many heads of state around the world and almost invariably they praise the Nixon foreign policy as perhaps the most visionary we will see in our lifetimes. He, quite simply, understood the world as it was—not as he wished it were."

• Jimmy Carter. "All he really had was a compulsion to be president. He had no program, no ideas, no vision of what he would do when he became president. And because of that, the entire nation has been afflicted."

• Nancy Reagan. "She has been," he says, "the most important influence on my life."

"The old ways *can* be best," he is fond of saying. Reagan celebrates traditional values—"The Republican message shouldn't consist of big economic theories or complicated details," he once claimed in a 1978 speech. "Instead, it should consist of five words: family, work, neighborhood, freedom, peace."

If Reagan's vision is derided in Georgetown, Manhattan and Harvard Yard, it is applauded in Albuquerque, Peoria and the farmlands of Ohio. What he offers is a philosophy for the future—a philosophy, he believes, whose time has come.

—*excerpted from a November '80*
Post *article written by Curt Smith.*

The Candid Camera

Since he began his political career, Ronald Reagan has endured an onslaught of adverse comments concerning his former profession as an actor. His response to the accusation that his ability to "act" on television enhanced his political image was, "Let me reveal something known to all actors—you can't lie to the camera. When it rolls in for that bigger-than-life close-up, you'd better mean what you say, for insincerity will show up like a putty nose."

He was lured to Washington, however, and after fighting Richard Nixon in 1968 and Gerald Ford in 1976, Reagan attained the GOP nomination in 1980. Advocating a "return to the values of neighborhood, peace, family and work," Reagan took his campaign to the blue-collar American. He described his followers in the November '80 *Post* as:

> . . .people who get up every day and go to work, look after their children, support their churches, and schools, believe in standards of right and wrong and ask nothing more of government than simply to be kept safe in their homes.

In that same month he swept the country off its feet, amazing pollsters and voters alike with 489 electoral votes to President Jimmy Carter's 49.

Ronald Reagan's Greatest Role

For more than two decades Ronald Reagan has been the conservative's conservative—preaching to the choir, seeking new converts to the cause, spreading the gospel of self-reliance at home and military strength abroad. Reagan still delights in light-hearted self-deprecation, still retains the polish and urgency which have always marked his platform presence; his public appearances are as adroit and smooth as ever.

If Reagan has not changed, though, the nation surely has. After nearly five decades of liberal Democratic rule, a time in which Republicans have controlled Congress for only four of 50 years, America's voting pulse has veered sharply to the right. Today apostles of the ultra-left no longer speak for the genuine values and concerns of America; nearly twice as many citizens labeled themselves "conservative" as "liberal" in several 1979 Harris and Gallup polls. "To many people, conservative used to be a dirty word," Reagan reminisces, "but liberal mistakes—and people realizing that government cannot solve all our problems—have helped to purify it."

Because his is a centrist conservatism, one that incessantly speaks of economic productivity and spiritual rebirth, Reagan emerged in 1980 as the man who did best in either party's primaries among voters who were paid by the hour, a key characteristic of working-class members; the man who startled reporters with his ability to attract traditionally Democratic blue-collar

The first boy in the second row from the bottom grew up and became famous. The name is Ronald Reagan, man of many careers. "Knute Rockne—All American" (far right) and "Kings Row" (bottom) were highlights of his movie career. Pictured below is his wife Nancy, who Reagan says, "made up her own mind that marriage was a career in itself."